THE
EVERYTHING®
LARGE-PRINT BIBLE
WORD SEARCH BOOK

Dear Reader,

The words in the Bible have inspired billions of people and profoundly impacted the course of history. My hope is that the puzzles in this book will be a fun and engaging way for you to interact with these powerful words. As you circle the words hidden in the grids, you will also be reviewing Bible topics and verses. I think this can be a great way to exercise the brain and nourish the spirit.

One of the joys of creating this book was choosing the Bible verses that are featured in many of the puzzles. Taken from all parts of the Bible, a lot of the verses are well-known and all of them are thought-provoking. I wanted these puzzles to be printed with large letters to make solving them less tedious. Your word-finding abilities will be tested, not your vision.

May you find these puzzles both entertaining and enlightening!

Charles Timmerman

Welcome to the EVERYTHING® Series!

These handy, accessible books give you all you need to tackle a difficult project, gain a new hobby, comprehend a fascinating topic, prepare for an exam, or even brush up on something you learned back in school but have since forgotten.

You can choose to read an Everything® book from cover to cover or just pick out the information you want from our four useful boxes: e-questions, e-facts, e-alerts, and e-ssentials. We give you everything you need to know on the subject, but throw in a lot of fun stuff along the way, too.

We now have more than 400 Everything® books in print, spanning such wide-ranging categories as weddings, pregnancy, cooking, music instruction, foreign language, crafts, pets, New Age, and so much more. When you're done reading them all, you can finally say you know Everything®!

PUBLISHER Karen Cooper

DIRECTOR OF ACQUISITIONS AND INNOVATION Paula Munier

MANAGING EDITOR, EVERYTHING® SERIES Lisa Laing

COPY CHIEF Casey Ebert

ACQUISITIONS EDITOR Lisa Laing

EDITORIAL ASSISTANT Ross Weisman

EVERYTHING® SERIES COVER DESIGNER Erin Alexander

LAYOUT DESIGNERS Colleen Cunningham, Elisabeth Lariviere, Ashley Vierra, Denise Wallace

Visit the entire Everything® series at *www.everything.com*

THE
EVERYTHING
LARGE-PRINT
BIBLE
WORD SEARCH
BOOK

150 inspirational puzzles—now in large print!

Charles Timmerman
Founder of Funster.com

Adams Media
New York London Toronto Sydney New Delhi

Aadamsmedia

Adams Media
An Imprint of Simon & Schuster, Inc.
57 Littlefield Street
Avon, Massachusetts 02322

An Everything® Series Book.
Everything® and everything.com® are registered trademarks of Simon & Schuster, Inc.

ADAMS MEDIA and colophon are trademarks of Simon and Schuster.

For information about special discounts for bulk purchases, please contact Simon & Schuster Special Sales at 1-866-506-1949 or business@simonandschuster.com.

The Simon & Schuster Speakers Bureau can bring authors to your live event. For more information or to book an event contact the Simon & Schuster Speakers Bureau at 1-866-248-3049 or visit our website at www.simonspeakers.com.

Manufactured in the United States of America

17 2020

ISBN 978-1-4405-3071-5

In memory of my mom; she loved the
Bible and word search puzzles.

Contents

Acknowledgments

I would like to thank each and every one of the more than half a million people who have visited my website, *www.funster.com*, to play word games and puzzles. You have shown me how much fun puzzles can be and how addictive they can become!

It is a pleasure to acknowledge the folks at Adams Media who made this book possible. I particularly want to thank my editor, Lisa Laing, for so skillfully managing the many projects we have worked on together.

Introduction

The puzzles in this book are in the traditional word-search format. The words you will be searching for will either be in a list or underlined in a Bible verse. Words are hidden in the grid in any direction: up, down, forward, backward, or diagonal. The words are always found in a straight line and letters are never skipped. Words can overlap. For example, the letters at the end of the word "mast" could be used as the start of the word "stern." Only uppercased letters are used, and any spaces in an entry are removed. For example, "Song of Solomon" would be found in the grid as "SONGOFSOLOMON." Apostrophes and hyphens are also omitted in the grids. Draw a circle around each word you find in the grid. Then cross the word off the list (or the verse) so you will always know which words remain to be found.

A favorite strategy is to look for the first letter in a word, then to see if the second letter is in any of the neighboring letters, and so on until the word is found. Or instead of searching for the first letter in a word, it is sometimes easier to look for letters that stand out, like Q, U, X, and Z. Double letters in a word will also stand out and be easier to find in the grid. Another strategy is to simply scan each row, column, and diagonal looking for any words.

Puzzles

Holy Bible

ANIMALS

ASHAMED

BANISHED

BIBLE

CAIN

CHILDREN

CREATION

DEVIL

DUST

EDEN

FALL

FIG LEAVES

FIRST MAN

FORBIDDEN

FRUIT

GARDEN

GENESIS

GOOD

HEAVEN

INNOCENCE

KNOWLEDGE

LIFE

LOVE

LUST

MARRIAGE

NAKEDNESS

PARADISE

PUNISHMENT

RIBS

SATAN

SERPENT

SIN

TREE

WOMAN

Adam and Eve

```
R F O D Q M Z E Q T E G R D
W N F K G T S U D S R D Z N
S N E I N N O C E N C E E O
A E A R R P J T M N R D E O
T D V M D S F N A A E D P W
A D L A O L T E H K A N A G
N I C R E W I M S E T E R K
S B I R G L W H A D I V A Q
F R T I D I G S C N O A D X
F O S A E F A I I E N E I M
L F U G L E R N F S H H S E
T R L E W J D U I S E L E D
S U L U O K E P I M O N D O
N I A C N W N N G V A K E O
S T F Z K M A D E V I L A G
U E L B I B T N E P R E S W
```

Solution on Page 304

ACCOUNT	LOVE
ACTS	LUKE
ANCIENT	MARY
APOSTLES	MATTHEW
BAPTISM	MESSAGE
BIBLE	MIRACLES
BOOKS	NAZARETH
CHRISTIAN	PARABLES
CHURCH	PAUL
CROSS	PREACH
EPISTLES	PSALMS
FAITH	RELIGION
FATHER	SALVATION
GENESIS	SERMON
HEALING	SIN
HOLY	STORIES
JESUS	TEACHINGS
JOHN	TESTAMENT
LATIN	TRUTH
LIFE	VERSES

Y L F M F S M L A S P A U L
H N N A A A V E R S E S G T
M C I H T R E L I G I O N S
Z T R T O H Y C R M E E I S
H T H U A J E H I N M E L O
R E S R H L A R O A P V A R
W A J T O C A I T I R O E C
R C E K C C T S S L E L H D
B H S O L A E T H I A M S E
A I U E V T L I T F C E E N
P N S L R E E A E E H S I E
T G A V S M Y N R L O S R Q
I S E L T S O P A B L A O V
S I S E N E G N Z I Y G T L
M L U K E P A R A B L E S K
B O O K S B G T N E I C N A

Solution on Page 304

ANIMALS

ARARAT

BELIEF

BIBLE

BOAT

BUILDING

COVENANT

CUBITS

DOVE

EARTH

FAITH

FAMILY

FLOOD

FORTY DAYS

GENESIS

GOD

MAN

MOUNTAINS

NOAH

OLIVE LEAF

PAIRS

RAINBOW

RAVEN

RELIGION

REPOPULATE

RIGHTEOUS

SHEM

SHIP

SIN

SONS

STORY

TRUST

TWO

VESSEL

WATER

WIND

WOOD

```
V S Q G L S A N I M A L S G
R N O Q I G N I D L I U B R
V E C N R E L I G I O N P Q
I P I H S I S E N E G A D M
N D E V T R U S T M I O F Z
H E O S E M S H E R W B Y R
D C V O N S G H S T O R Y E
X D U A L I S Y L I M A F P
J D T B R F A E L E V I L O
B Q A Q I D D T L D Q W W P
N Z R H Y T N A N E V O C U
O T A T D N S I F U B O E L
M A R R O D W M A N O D U A
H O A A G B E L I E F M L T
F B H E V O D A T B I B L E
O U W A T E R C H Z K A W O
```

Solution on Page 304

AARON	LORD
ADULTERY	LOVE
ARK	MORALITY
BIBLE	MOSES
BLASPHEMY	MOUNTAIN
COVENANT	MURDER
COVETING	NEIGHBOR
DECALOGUE	PARENTS
EXODUS	RELIGIOUS
GOD	REVELATION
HOLY	SABBATH
HONOR	SINAI
IDOLS	STEALING
IMAGES	STONE
ISRAELITES	TABLETS
JEWS	TEN
JUDAISM	THEFT
KILLING	VAIN
LAWS	WORSHIP
LIE	

Solution on Page 304

The Ten Commandments

```
E T H E F T D L T U Q D L G
X A A R O N I M A G E S N M
O B I B L E S N C C I I S Y
D L C C O V E N A N T I S P
U E S S J I S L A E A F U R
S T U E G O O I V D Y L O H
T S W H T G M O U N T A I N
N S B E U I C J N I A V G S
E O R E V E L A T I O N I A
R O N O H Y M E H P S A L B
A Y R E T L U D A R K U E B
P I E E Y T I L A R O M R A
S T D G N I L A E T S N E T
W D R O L M G N I L L I K H
A S U D L W O R S H I P Y A
L D M J S S T O N E V O L R
```

Solution on Page 304

ADMISSION	IMMERSION
BABY	INFANTS
BAPTIST	JOHN
BELIEVER	ORDINANCE
BIBLE	POOL
BLESSING	PRAYER
BLOOD	PRIEST
BORN AGAIN	PURIFIED
CATHOLIC	REBIRTH
CEREMONY	RELIGION
CHRISTIAN	RITUAL
CHURCH	RIVER
CLEANSING	SACRAMENT
EVENT	SALVATION
FAITH	SINS
FAMILY	SON
FATHER	SPIRIT
FIRE	WASHING
FONT	
GODPARENTS	

Solution on Page 304

```
H S H T I A F D O O L B N W
C A T H O L I C R E V I R A
R F P N I A G A N R O B B S
U O C L E A N S I N G L A H
H N O I S R E M M I E E P I
C T R R Y Y A R F S A T T N
Y C E E D N L P S A N K I G
B H L B V I O I D E T N S N
A R I I V E N M M O F H T F
B I G R R G I A E A G O E I
T S I T W S R L N R F J L R
N T O H S C O T E C E N A E
E I N I A O S A I B E C U Y
V A O S P U R I F I E D T A
E N O I T A V L A S Q S I R
S N I S P I R I T S E I R P
```

Solution on Page 305

ANGEL	JOACHIM
BABY	JOSEPH
BELIEFS	LUKE
BIBLE	MADONNA
BIRTH	MANGER
BLESSED	MATTHEW
CATHOLIC	MIRACLE
CHOSEN	MOTHER
CHURCH	NATIVITY
DEVOTION	NAZARETH
DIVINE	PRAYER
GABRIEL	PREGNANT
GALILEE	PURE
GOSPEL	QUEEN
GRACE	ROSARY
HAIL	STAR
HOLY	VIRGIN
INN	WIFE
JESUS	WOMAN
JEWISH	WORSHIP

Solution on Page 305

Mother Mary

L U K E U H C R U H C A R V
H O L Y T H A H E S U S E J
S H H R P T T P O G Z T H W
I C I E S J G B R S N W T I
W B S M A D O N N A E A O F
E O M L Y G R A N L Y N M E
J C R G O T F O C I L E G V
H Q I S H E I A S H E K R I
A U P L H T R V E A I D A R
I E S H O I E U I L R M C G
L E F V M H P R P T B Y E I
A N E W E H T T A M A I W N
N D I A J Y B A B Z G N B N
G A L I L E E U C N A M O W
E E E X M P R E G N A N T R
L Z B L E S S E D I V I N E

Solution on Page 305

ANGEL	LOVE
ARMY	MARRIAGE
BEES	MESSENGER
BIBLICAL	OATH
BLINDED	PHILISTINE
DAGON	PILLARS
DELILAH	RELIGIOUS
EGO	RIDDLE
EYES	ROPE
GATE	SHAVE
GAZA	SIN
GOD	SLAY
HAIR	SON
HEBREW	STORY
HEROIC	STRENGTH
HONEY	STRONG
JAWBONE	SUN
JEWISH	TEMPLE
JUDGES	TRIBE
LION	WRESTLING

Solutions Page 305

R W A D M E B G A T E A V F
Z E A E Y L S O R E Y Z D Y
J R Q D P D T D M N H A I M
L B T N S D O A Y O A G L E
X E L I T I R G O B L N G S
O H J L R R Y N P W I O K P
K T U B I B L I C A L R R H
T G D A B P L L H J E T O I
M N G E E L E T O G D S P L
E E E A A G E S N B H J E I
Y R S R N M C E E H T E V S
E T S A P I S R Y N A W O T
S S J L O S S W O N O I L I
O E E R E L I G I O U S R N
N U E M E V A H S C J H U E
D H E B M D R V T A X S Y N

Solution on Page 305

ABIGAIL

ABITAL

BATHSHEBA

DEBORAH

DELILAH

DINAH

DORCAS

ELISABETH

ELISHEBA

ESTHER

EUNICE

EVE

GOMER

HAGAR

HANNAH

JEMIMA

JEZEBEL

JOANNA

JUDITH

LEAH

LILITH

LOIS

LYDIA

MARTHA

MIRIAM

NAOMI

ORPAH

PHOEBE

PRISCILLA

RACHEL

RAHAB

REBEKAH

RUTH

SALOME

SARAH

TABITHA

TAMAR

ZIPPORAH

Women in the Bible

```
L Y D I A H T R A M Q M R C
M I R I A M T A M A R L J R
D H A N I D A M I M E J S J
B O N K F I B H R E M O G S
H A R O P P I Z A E A O L A
H A T C F B T E N L H O I L
T A G H A L H L L I I T H O
I E R A S S A I P S V L S M
L W U A R H C S B H B E E E
I M U N S S E A A E O B R D
L I A G I B A B H B F E G E
H T U R P C I E A A B Z B V
O R P A H M E T R E K E L E
P D E B O R A H K G I J E F
L Y W A B I T A L E H C A R
A N N A O J H T I D U J H H
```

Solution on Page 305

ABLE

ARAMAIC

BEGINNING

BIBLE

BOOKS

CANON

CHRISTIAN

CHURCH

COVENANT

DANIEL

DAVID

EGYPT

ESTHER

EVE

EXODUS

GENESIS

GOD

HEBREW

HISTORY

ISAIAH

ISRAEL

JESUS

JEWISH

JONAH

JOSHUA

JUDAISM

JUDGES

KINGS

LAWS

LEVITICUS

NUMBERS

PROPHETS

PROVERBS

PSALMS

RELIGION

RUTH

SAMUEL

SOLOMON

TEMPLE

TORAH

Solution on Page 305

```
V L E X O D U S N O N A C R
C E E Y H A R O T R S Y S U
H I V L R E M B E K E A J T
U N A E B O S H O S M U J H
R A S M L I T O I U D U K D
C D U O A S B S E A D O G A
H N S T E R E L I G I O N V
E S E B N N A S E H A A I I
B M J G E A M S F B I A N D
R L G G Y V N W L T H U N K
E A T E M P L E S C B H I K
W S S U C I T I V E L S G I
S P R O V E R B S O A O E N
W P R O P H E T S I C J B G
A S U Z C G L E A R S I J S
L H E J O N A H S I W E J U
```

Solution on Page 306

ACTS	LITERATURE
APOCALYPSE	LITURGY
APOSTLES	LUKE
BAPTISM	MARY
BIBLE	MATTHEW
BOOKS	MESSIAH
CHURCH	MIRACLES
DISCIPLES	PARABLES
EASTER	PAUL
EPHESIANS	PETER
EPISTLES	RELIGION
GALATIANS	REVELATION
GOSPELS	SALVATION
GREEK	SCRIPTURE
HEBREWS	THEOLOGY
JESUS	TIMOTHY
JOHN	
JOSEPH	
LATIN	
LETTERS	

The New Testament

```
L S N A I T A L A G B S J A
A N H P A R A B L E S Z O P
T H E O L O G Y B O O K S M
I O B C S N A I S E H P E A
N J R A P O A G R E E K P T
T Y E L B I B U D R U O H T
D Y W Y Y T T G S U S E J H
I G S P S A L V A T I O N E
S R R S R L N L L P A U L W
C U E E B E R E L I G I O N
I T T K A V S H C R U H C D
P I T U P E S E L C A R I M
L L E L T R P G O S P E L S
E U L T I M O T H Y S T C A
S E L T S I P E A S T E R S
Y Y R A M E S S I A H P P V
```

Solution on Page 306

AUTHOR	POWER
BABY	PROPHETS
BATHSHEBA	PROVERBS
BIBLE	PSALMS
BOOK	RICH
BUILDER	RULER
CHRONICLES	SEAL
CONCUBINES	SINS
CROWN	SONS
ENEMIES	TALMUD
GOLD	TEMPLE
HEBREW	THRONE
IDOLATRY	WEALTHY
ISRAEL	WISDOM
JERUSALEM	
JEWISH	
JUDGMENT	
KING DAVID	
KINGDOM	
MANY WIVES	

Solomon

```
E L B I B M P S G G Z Z D N
S R U O Q K Y W E A L T H Y
J E I S R K N H S I W E J E
U W L P K I N G D O M G H L
D O D C O N C U B I N E S P
G P E K I N G D A V I D N M
M S R M A N Y W I V E S W E
E E A J B I O R I C H T O T
N A L J E H S R T Y U E R Z
T L U A H B E R H A Y H C H
H D J T S P A B A C L P J R
R O P A H U S B R E V O R P
O E D L T O R A Y E L R D S
N V L M A A R E L V W P I I
E D O U B O O K J M S N O S
O J G D R T M K W I S D O M
```

Solution on Page 306

APOSTLES	LOVE
BAPTISM	MANGER
BETHLEHEM	MARY
BIBLE	MESSIAH
CHRISTMAS	MIRACLES
CHURCH	NATIVITY
CROSS	NAZARETH
DEATH	PARABLES
EASTER	PRAYER
FAITH	PROPHET
GALILEE	RELIGION
GOSPELS	ROBE
HEALING	SACRIFICE
HEAVEN	SAVIOR
HOLY	SERMON
JEWISH	SINS
JOSEPH	TEACHER
KINGDOM	TOMB
LEADER	TRINITY
LORD	WINE

```
S E L A C R O S S Y L O H F
F N B P H S L E P S O G P R
D A I O U S E R M O N A E H
L R I S R R O M M I R L S T
E O O T C P M S L A I I O A
A O V L H E I A B G W L J E
D M B E S T E L I E L E X D
E L T S P H E O J M N E M Y
R G I A M S N A Z A R E T H
E A B M A E K Y T I N I R T
H B E T H L E H E M V X E R
C I A S A C R I F I C E G E
A B S I M A R Y T O M B N Y
E L T R F R S A V I O R A A
T E E H W I N E V A E H M R
E D R C A M O D G N I K B P
```

Solution on Page 306

ACADEMIC

ANGELS

ARAMAIC

BIBLE

CATHOLIC

CHAPTER

CHURCHES

COLLEGE

CREATION

DIVINE

EXEGESIS

FAITH

GOSPELS

GREEK

HEAVEN

HEBREW

HISTORY

HOLY

JESUS

JEWISH

JUDAISM

LANGUAGE

LATIN

LEARNING

MARK

ORTHODOX

PRAYER

PRIESTS

READING

REFLECT

SCHOLAR

SEMINARY

SIN

STUDY

TEXTS

THEOLOGY

TORAH

VERSES

Solution on Page 305

```
J  S  E  S  R  E  V  J  E  W  I  S  H  K
U  V  E  G  O  S  P  E  L  S  T  X  E  T
D  N  G  Y  J  C  C  X  G  H  O  E  B  R
A  C  A  D  E  M  I  C  O  E  R  B  R  A
I  A  U  U  S  V  Y  L  L  G  L  S  E  L
S  Q  G  T  U  L  Y  R  O  A  E  L  W  O
M  F  N  S  S  X  O  D  O  H  T  R  O  H
A  R  A  M  A  I  C  C  C  T  T  I  E  C
N  E  L  I  A  N  S  R  H  O  S  A  N  S
G  A  R  G  T  R  U  E  R  A  V  I  C  T
E  D  E  E  R  H  K  A  G  E  P  N  H  S
L  I  F  M  C  D  H  T  N  E  Y  T  G  E
S  N  L  E  A  R  N  I  N  G  X  A  E  I
I  G  E  Y  G  O  L  O  E  H  T  E  R  R
N  D  C  B  Y  R  A  N  I  M  E  S  G  P
E  A  T  B  I  B  L  E  N  I  V  I  D  E
```

Solution on Page 307

ACACIA	GARLIC
ALMOND	HEMLOCK
ALOE	HENNA
ANISE	HYSSOP
APPLE	LENTIL
BARLEY	LILY
BEANS	MINT
BRAMBLE	MUSTARD
CANE	MYRRH
CAPER	OAK
CAROB	OLIVE
CEDAR	ONION
CITRON	PINE
COCKLE	ROSE
COTTON	SAGE
CUMIN	THORNS
CYPRESS	TREES
DILL	WALNUT
FIG	WHEAT
FLAX	WILLOW

Solution: Page 307

```
R B R A M B L E G N K S N W
J Y H O N O I N O A A S O L
O R E P A C I T O G R L R E
W Y W L L I T N E L L L T N
Y E G K R O N S F I E Z I A
R B A I C A C A W S U X C C
M S P R F O B D I L L Y O D
I U P A W A L N U T P R C T
N Y L D B M A M I R B Y K W
T R E E S T U K E N A A L P
A H R C P O S S Y H I L E I
E C R A S N S N T H X M O N
H P Y R R F L U A A E O U E
W R O O Y O L I V E R N V C
R S H B I M R A L U B D N R
E T I Y X V T H X Y I Q U A
```

Solution on Page 307

ACTS

ANDREW

BAPTISM

BIBLE

CHOSEN

CHRIST

CHURCH

CREED

DISCIPLES

FISHERMEN

FOLLOWERS

GALILEE

GENTILES

GOSPELS

JAMES

JESUS

JOHN

JUDE

LUKE

MARK

MATTHEW

MESSENGER

MIRACLES

PARABLES

PAUL

PENTECOST

PETER

PHILIP

PREACH

PROPHET

RELIGION

SAINT

SIMON

STUDENT

TESTAMENT

THADDEUS

THOMAS

TWELVE

WITNESS

Solution on Page 307

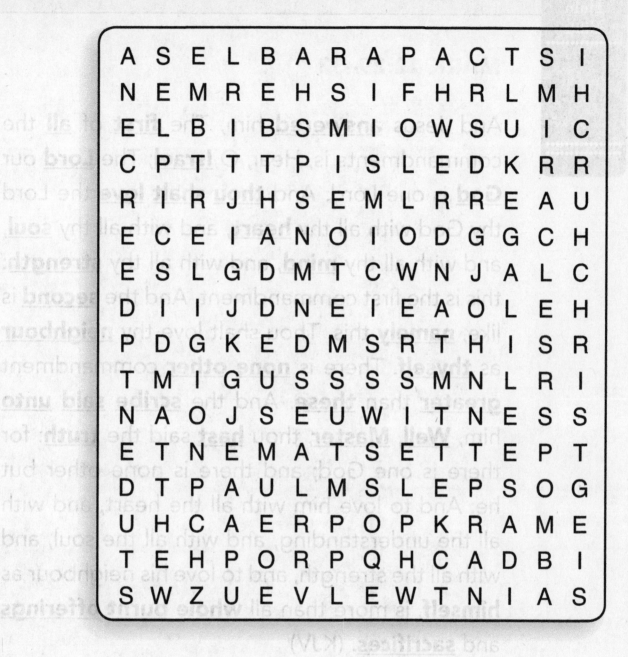

```
A S E L B A R A P A C T S I
N E M R E H S I F H R L M H
E L B I B S M I O W S U I C
C P T T T P I S L E D K R R
R I R J H S E M L R R E A U
E C E I A N O I O D G G C H
E S L G D M T C W N J A L C
D I I J D N E I E A O L E H
P D G K E D M S R T H I S R
T M I G U S S S S M N L R I
N A O J S E U W I T N E S S
E T N E M A T S E T T E P T
D T P A U L M S L E P S O G
U H C A E R P O P K R A M E
T E H P O R P Q H C A D B I
S W Z U E V L E W T N I A S
```

MARK 12:29–33

And Jesus **answered** him, The **first** of **all** the commandments is, Hear, O **Israel**; The **Lord** our **God** is one Lord: And **thou** **shalt** **love** the Lord thy God with all thy **heart**, and with all thy **soul**, and with all thy **mind**, and with all thy **strength**: this is the first commandment. And the **second** is like, **namely** this, Thou shalt love thy **neighbour** as **thyself**. There is **none** **other** commandment **greater** than **these**. And the **scribe** **said** **unto** him, **Well**, **Master**, thou **hast** said the **truth**: for there is one God; and there is none other but he: And to love him with all the heart, and with all the understanding, and with all the soul, and with all the strength, and to love his neighbour as **himself**, is more than all **whole** **burnt** **offerings** and **sacrifices**. (KJV)

Solution on Page 307

The First Commandment

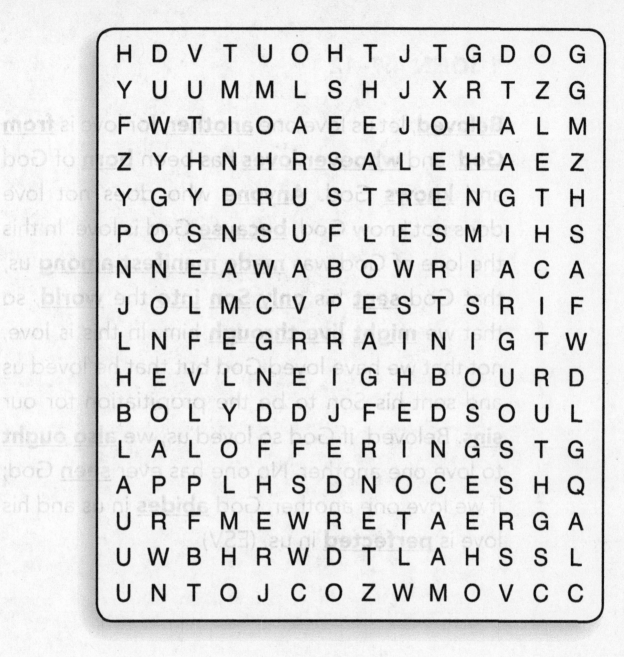

```
H D V T U O H T J T G D O G
Y U U M M L S H J X R T Z G
F W T I O A E E J O H A L M
Z Y H N H R S A L E H A E Z
Y G Y D R U S T R E N G T H
P O S N S U F L E S M I H S
N N E A W A B O W R I A C A
J O L M C V P E S T S R I F
L N F E G R R A I N I G T W
H E V L N E I G H B O U R D
B O L Y D D J F E D S O U L
L A L O F F E R I N G S T G
A P P L H S D N O C E S H Q
U R F M E W R E T A E R G A
U W B H R W D T L A H S S L
U N T O J C O Z W M O V C C
```

Solution on Page 308

1 JOHN 4:7–12

Beloved, let us love one **another**, for love is **from God**, and **whoever loves** has been **born** of God and **knows** God. **Anyone** who does not love does not know God, **because** God is love. In this the love of God was **made manifest among** us, that God **sent** his **only Son into** the **world**, so that we **might live through** him. In this is love, not that we have loved God but that he loved us and sent his Son to be the propitiation for our **sins**. Beloved, if God so loved us, we **also ought** to love one another. No one has ever **seen** God; if we love one another, God **abides** in us and his love is **perfected** in us. (ESV)

Solution on Page 303

God Is Love

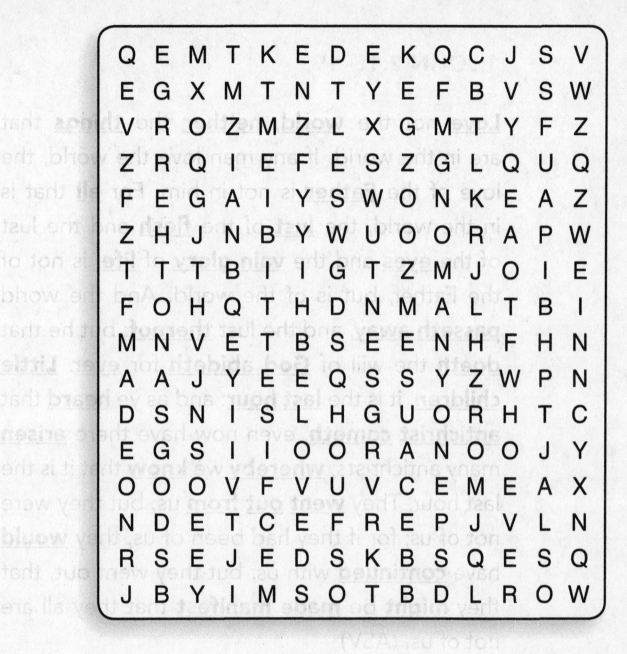

```
Q E M T K E D E K Q C J S V
E G X M T N T Y E F B V S W
V R O Z M Z L X G M T Y F Z
Z R Q I E F E S Z G L Q U Q
F E G A I Y S W O N K E A Z
Z H J N B Y W U O O R A P W
T T T B I I G T Z M J O I E
F O H Q T H D N M A L T B I
M N V E T B S E E N H F H N
A A J Y E E Q S S Y Z W P N
D S N I S L H G U O R H T C
E G S I I O O R A N O O J Y
O O O V F V U V C E M E A X
N D E T C E F R E P J V L N
R S E J E D S K B S Q E S Q
J B Y I M S O T B D L R O W
```

Solution on Page 308

1 JOHN 2:15–19

Love not the **world**, **neither** the **things** that are in the world. If any man love the world, the love of the **Father** is not in him. For **all** that is in the world, the **lust** of the **flesh** and the lust of the **eyes** and the **vain glory** of **life**, is not of the Father, but is of the world. And the world **passeth away**, and the lust **thereof**: but he that **doeth** the will of **God abideth** for **ever**. **Little children**, it is the **last hour**: and as ye **heard** that **antichrist cometh**, even now have there **arisen** many antichrists; **whereby** we **know** that it is the last hour. They **went out from** us, but they were not of us; for if they had been of us, they **would** have **continued** with us: but they went out, that they **might** be **made manifest** that they all are not of us. (ASV)

Solution on Page 308

Do Not Love the World

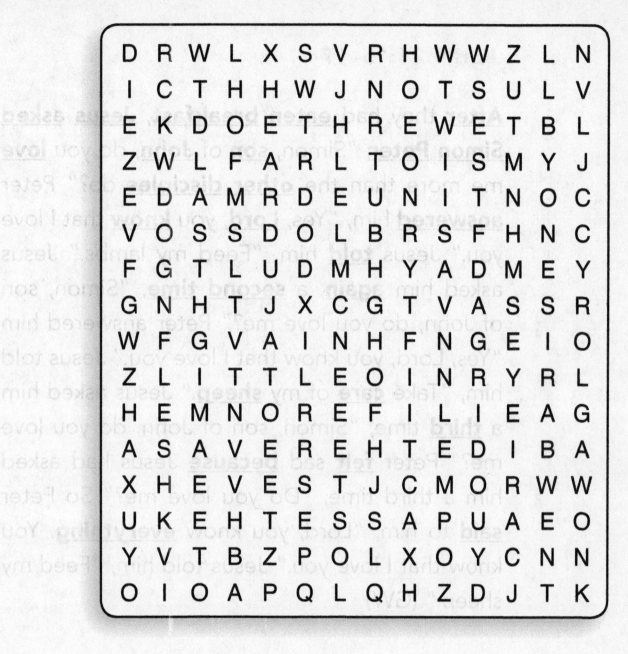

```
D R W L X S V R H W W Z L N
I C T H H W J N O T S U L V
E K D O E T H R E W E T B L
Z W L F A R L T O I S M Y J
E D A M R D E U N I T N O C
V O S S D O L B R S F H N C
F G T L U D M H Y A D M E Y
G N H T J X C G T V A S S R
W F G V A I N H F N G E I O
Z L I T T L E O I N R Y R L
H E M N O R E F I L I E A G
A S A V E R E H T E D I B A
X H E V E S T J C M O R W W
U K E H T E S S A P U A E O
Y V T B Z P O L X O Y C N N
O I O A P Q L Q H Z D J T K
```

Solution on Page 308

JOHN 21:15–17

After they had **eaten breakfast**, **Jesus asked Simon Peter**, "Simon, **son** of **John**, do you **love** me more than the **other disciples** do?" Peter **answered** him, "Yes, **Lord**, you **know** that I love you." Jesus **told** him, "Feed my lambs." Jesus asked him **again**, a **second time**, "Simon, son of John, do you love me?" Peter answered him "Yes, Lord, you know that I love you." Jesus told him, "Take **care** of my **sheep**." Jesus asked him a **third** time, "Simon, son of John, do you love me?" Peter **felt** sad **because** Jesus had asked him a third time, "Do you love me?" So Peter **said** to him, "Lord, you know **everything**. You know that I love you." Jesus told him, "Feed my sheep." (GW)

```
A F T E R H E I J P S U M G
S V P L V F E O T L E F J H
K C O Y L E D B X J L T F L
E R P V E F R L E N P O E C
D C O Z W E H Y O O I S V R
A R A T I M S S T T C I C E
S H O S F E A B A E H S M U E
T B O H F H U D A E I O G I
S I N G T S C B F R D N P P
M U M P E M H S K S E I G S
Q X S K W R E E A E R A C I
G T N E S U A C E B E G B S
Y G Z G J O P O R P W A T U
T W V N J O H N B W S A I D
E W V Z X G F D W O N K M C
N A X Q I O C N E T A E E E
```

Solution on Page 308

1 JOHN 4:17–21

And as we **live** in **God**, our love **grows** more **perfect**. So we will not be **afraid** on the **day** of **judgment**, but we can **face** him with **confidence** **because** we live like **Jesus** **here** in this **world**. **Such** love has no **fear**, because perfect love **expels** all fear. If we are afraid, it is for fear of **punishment**, and this **shows** that we have not **fully** experienced his perfect love. We love **each** other because he **loved** us **first**. If **someone** **says**, "I love God," but **hates** a **Christian** brother or sister, that **person** is a **liar**; for if we don't love **people** we can **see**, how can we love God, **whom** we **cannot** see? And he has **given** us this **command**: **Those** who love God **must** **also** love **their** Christian **brothers** and **sisters**. (NLT)

Perfect Love

E S O H T A A U B X P H S S
D R T H E I R W H U M U W N
G E C N E D I F N O C O O J
W H O M E V E I B H H S R P
G T C H A M S V P S R A L Z
C O F O P H G Q O E I M D T
S R J U M E C D P L S Z S E
S B I E L M R A U L T R S O
X W N P E L A F E J I U D S
N T O K J S Y N E F A T I L
F E A R C O L R D C N S A A
P W V J G A E E E A T U R F
T J Y I E H N B P E Y M F A
N S M V G S D N R X M I A C
V P I O X S U S O M E O N E
B L D U S A Y S E T A H M X

Solution on Page 309

PSALM 118:1–9

Oh **give** **thanks** to the **LORD**, for he is **good**; for his **steadfast** **love** **endures** **forever**! Let **Israel** **say**, "His steadfast love endures forever." Let the **house** of **Aaron** say, "His steadfast love endures forever." Let **those** who **fear** the LORD say, "His steadfast love endures forever." **Out** of my **distress** I **called** on the LORD; the LORD **answered** me and **set** me **free**. The LORD is on my **side**; I will not fear. **What** can **man** do to me? The LORD is on my side as my **helper**; I **shall** **look** in **triumph** on those who **hate** me. It is **better** to **take** **refuge** in the LORD than to **trust** in man. It is better to take refuge in the LORD than to trust in **princes**. (ESV)

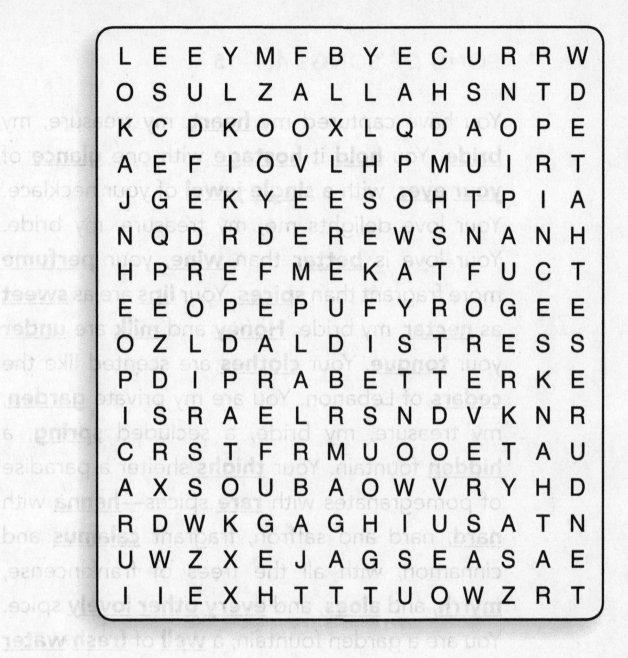

```
L E E Y M F B Y E C U R R W
O S U L Z A L L A H S N T D
K C D K O O X L Q D A O P E
A E F I O V L H P M U I R T
J G E K Y E E S O H T P I A
N Q D R D E R E W S N A N H
H P R E F M E K A T F U C T
E E O P E P U F Y R O G E E
O Z L D A L D I S T R E S S
P D I P R A B E T T E R K E
I S R A E L R S N D V K N R
C R S T F R M U O O E T A U
A X S O U B A O W V R Y H D
R D W K G A G H I U S A T N
U W Z X E J A G S E A S A E
I I E X H T T T U O W Z R T
```

Solution on Page 309

SONG OF SONGS 4:9–15

You have captured my **heart**, my treasure, my **bride**. You **hold** it **hostage** with one **glance** of **your** **eyes**, with a **single** **jewel** of your necklace. Your love delights me, my treasure, my bride. Your love is **better** than **wine**, your **perfume** more fragrant than **spices**. Your **lips** are as **sweet** as **nectar**, my bride. **Honey** and **milk** are **under** your **tongue**. Your **clothes** are scented like the **cedars** of Lebanon. You are my private **garden**, my treasure, my bride, a secluded **spring**, a **hidden** fountain. Your **thighs** shelter a paradise of pomegranates with **rare** spices—**henna** with **nard**, nard and saffron, fragrant **calamus** and cinnamon, with all the trees of frankincense, **myrrh**, and **aloes**, and **every** **other** **lovely** spice. You are a garden fountain, a **well** of **fresh** **water** streaming **down** **from** Lebanon's mountains. (NLT)

Solution on Page 309

Better than Wine

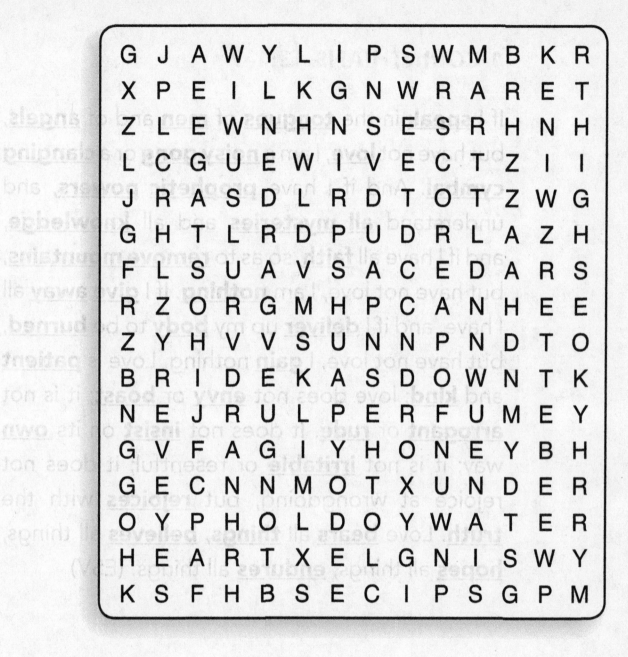

```
G J A W Y L I P S W M B K R
X P E I L K G N W R A R E T
Z L E W N H N S E S R H N H
L C G U E W I V E C T Z I I
J R A S D L R D T O T Z W G
G H T L R D P U D R L A Z H
F L S U A V S A C E D A R S
R Z O R G M H P C A N H E E
Z Y H V V S U N N P N D T O
B R I D E K A S D O W N T K
N E J R U L P E R F U M E Y
G V F A G I Y H O N E Y B H
G E C N N M O T X U N D E R
O Y P H O L D O Y W A T E R
H E A R T X E L G N I S W Y
K S F H B S E C I P S G P M
```

Solution on Page 309

1 CORINTHIANS 13:1–7

If I **speak** in the **tongues** of **men** and of **angels**, but have not **love**, I am a **noisy gong** or a **clanging cymbal**. And if I have **prophetic powers**, and understand **all mysteries** and all **knowledge**, and if I have all **faith**, so as to **remove mountains**, but have not love, I am **nothing**. If I **give away** all I have, and if I **deliver** up my **body** to be **burned**, but have not love, I **gain** nothing. Love is **patient** and **kind**; love does not **envy** or **boast**; it is not **arrogant** or **rude**. It does not **insist** on its **own** way; it is not **irritable** or resentful; it does not rejoice at wrongdoing, but **rejoices** with the **truth**. Love **bears** all **things**, **believes** all things, **hopes** all things, **endures** all things. (ESV)

Solution on Page 309

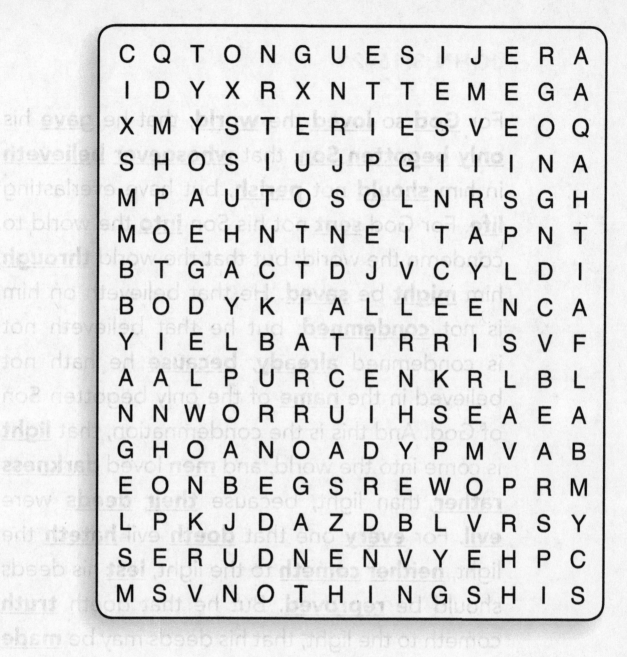

```
C Q T O N G U E S I J E R A
I D Y X R X N T T E M E G A
X M Y S T E R I E S V E O Q
S H O S I U J P G I I I N A
M P A U T O S O L N R S G H
M O E H N T N E I T A P N T
B T G A C T D J V C Y L D I
B O D Y K I A L L E E N C A
Y I E L B A T I R R I S V F
A A L P U R C E N K R L B L
N N W O R R U I H S E A E A
G H O A N O A D Y P M V A B
E O N B E G S R E W O P R M
L P K J D A Z D B L V R S Y
S E R U D N E N V Y E H P C
M S V N O T H I N G S H I S
```

Solution on Page 309

JOHN 3:16–21

For **God** so **loved** the **world**, that he **gave** his **only** **begotten** **Son**, that **whosoever** **believeth** in him **should** not **perish**, but have everlasting **life**. For God **sent** not his Son **into** the world to condemn the world; but that the world **through** him **might** be **saved**. He that believeth on him is not **condemned**: but he that believeth not is condemned **already**, **because** he hath not believed in the **name** of the only begotten Son of God. And this is the condemnation, that **light** is come into the world, and **men** loved **darkness** **rather** than light, because **their** **deeds** were **evil**. For **every** one that **doeth** evil **hateth** the light, **neither** **cometh** to the light, **lest** his deeds should be **reproved**. But he that doeth **truth** cometh to the light, that his deeds may be **made** **manifest**, that they are **wrought** in God. (KJV)

Solution on Page 309

God Loves the World

```
F M M W P L E Y R E V E I L
T E T O I M G T I A B N K S
I N H F A R H M N D T T A U
S S E N K R A D O O H H L R
W I I S O N Y E Z G T J E V
P N R U I P T N I E M L S R
T B G F E H B M V G C T T C
R H E R R E V E O S O H W S
U S I C F A I D G B M G W H
T S D X A L Q N N O E I Y O
H E L E E U P O H B T L D U
G Y R B E D S C E D H T A L
U L O V E D R E P R O V E D
O N W V V V N E I T H E R N
R O A R A M I M A D E Q L H
W S K T G N Q L H T E T A H
```

Solution on Page 310

JOHN 15:12–17

This is my commandment, that you love one **another** as I have **loved** you. **Greater** love has no one than this, that **someone lay down** his **life** for his **friends**. You are my friends if you do what I **command** you. No **longer** do I call you **servants**, for the servant does not know what his **master** is **doing**; but I have **called** you friends, for all that I have **heard from** my **Father** I have **made known** to you. You **did** not **choose** me, but I chose you and **appointed** you that you **should** go and **bear fruit** and that **your** fruit should **abide**, so that **whatever** you **ask** the Father in my **name**, he may **give** it to you. **These things** I command you, so that you will love one another. (ESV)

Love as I Have Loved

```
A A P C C R D F R H T Q S T
C P N H U W M S H O U L D C
Y A P O W H A T E V E R Z V
N Q Y O T N D N A M M O C E
P E K S I H E A S K S Y A L
Y O N E R N E V O D F W L L
F G R O F E T R N I I D L G
L N G R E A T E R D E O E V
G I F R O M I S D E V Y D T
L O N G E R O F A E H F E I
T D F V F E J S D M Y T M U
J R D K E C G D E D I B A R
R A A S K N O W N V L B N F
P E E E I F Y W F D I Q T M
L H B H B Q O S R Y F G K Y
T R T G D D V F L A E N M Z
```

Solution on Page 310

LUKE 6:27–33

But I say **unto** you that **hear, Love your enemies**, do good to them that **hate** you, **bless** them that **curse** you, **pray** for them that despitefully **use** you. To him that **smiteth thee** on the **one cheek offer also** the **other**; and **from** him that **taketh away** thy **cloak withhold** not thy **coat** also. **Give** to **every** one that **asketh** thee; and of him that taketh away thy **goods** ask them not **again**. And as ye **would** that **men should** do to you, do ye also to them **likewise**. And if ye love them that love you, **what thank** have ye? For even **sinners** love **those** that love them. And if ye do good to them that do good to you, what thank have ye? for even sinners do the **same**. (ASV)

Solution on Page 310

Love Your Enemies

```
R N I Z C E D R U O Y H E W
O V L R L O S C A U N S A T
D T Q O S L A E W E T A N W
F F V B D W C T M H H J I K
W E P L O L V H D Y A W A X
O T N U O O T H E R N T G N
G Y L A G P V H T E K S A U
O D K O P W G H T E K A T G
Z H E N E M I E S E S O H T
J S C E M P D T C S T W S C
U O C J D L U O H S E I H M
F R F U V B E T A H N L M U
U U L F R O M V L N O S B S
M G I V E S I W E K I L H K
N B H V V R E R D R B Z D C
T H E E M A S R B E Y A R P
```

Solution on Page 310

ROMANS 8:28–33

We **know** that all **things** **work** **together** for the **good** of **those** who **love** God—those **whom** he has **called** **according** to his **plan**. This is true **because** he **already** **knew** his **people** and had already **appointed** them to have the **same** **form** as the **image** of his **Son**. Therefore, his Son is the **firstborn** **among** **many** **children**. He **also** called those whom he had already appointed. He **approved** of those whom he had called, and he **gave** **glory** to those whom he had approved of. **What** can we say **about** all of this? If God is for us, who can be **against** us? God didn't **spare** his **own** Son but **handed** him **over** to **death** for all of us. So he will also **give** us everything **along** with him. Who will **accuse** those whom God has **chosen**? God has approved of them. (GW)

Those Who Love God

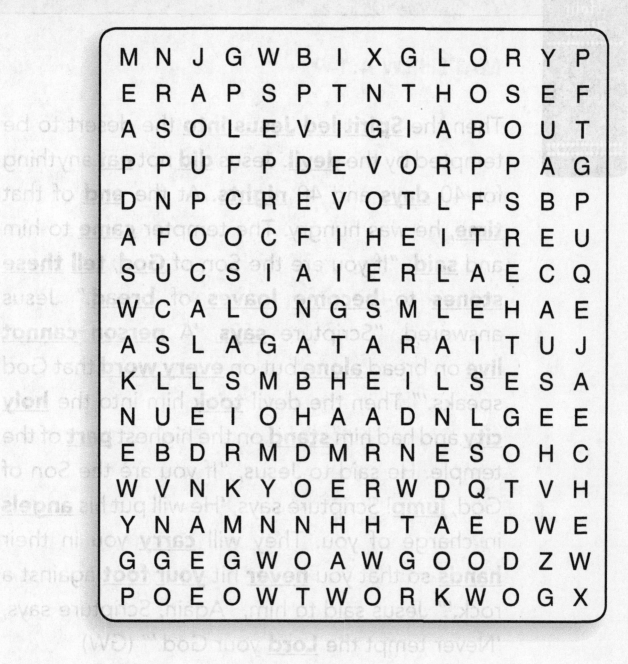

```
M N J G W B I X G L O R Y P
E R A P S P T N T H O S E F
A S O L E V I G I A B O U T
P P U F P D E V O R P P A G
D N P C R E V O T L F S B P
A F O O C F I H E I T R E U
S U C S I A I E R L A E C Q
W C A L O N G S M L E H A E
A S L A G A T A R A I T U J
K L L S M B H E I L S E S A
N U E I O H A A D N L G E E
E B D R M D M R N E S O H C
W V N K Y O E R W D Q T V H
Y N A M N N H H T A E D W E
G G E G W O A W G O O D Z W
P O E O W T W O R K W O G X
```

Solution on Page 310

Holy
Bible

MATTHEW 4:1–7

Then the **Spirit led Jesus into** the desert to be tempted by the **devil**. Jesus **did** not **eat** anything for 40 **days** and 40 **nights**. At the **end** of that **time**, he was hungry. The tempter **came** to him and **said**, "If you are the Son of **God**, **tell these stones** to **become loaves** of **bread**." Jesus answered, "Scripture **says**, 'A **person cannot live** on bread **alone** but on **every word** that God speaks.'" Then the devil **took** him into the **holy city** and had him **stand** on the highest **part** of the temple. He said to Jesus, "If you are the Son of God, **jump**! Scripture says, 'He will put his **angels** in charge of you. They will **carry** you in their **hands** so that you **never** hit **your foot** against a rock.'" Jesus said to him, "Again, Scripture says, 'Never tempt the **Lord** your God.'" (GW)

Solution on Page 310

Puzzles

```
W L E C A C F D D R O W Q P
H D I A S E I G Y T K O J F
Y F A N T H M T N R R X N Z
B P H N H M Y I Y L I G I B
W W A O G B E R T C O Z O J
E H N T I E L I S D A R U X
E Y D W N C L P U P E M D T
A L S E N O T S S V P D E C
K L V F K M M D E V I L S C
O N O S R E P N J V L T E F
O O T N R U O Y R R A C H N
T F B R E A D R F N H O T U
S P A N A A I E D B O S L X
A R D R B P D V V A L A E M
Q V J S H T B E H I Y Y D K
V I Q N Z M S R M H L S M A
```

Solution on Page 311

MATTHEW 27:3–8

When **Judas**, who had betrayed him, **realized** that **Jesus** had been condemned to die, he was **filled** with **remorse**. So he **took** the **thirty pieces** of **silver** **back** to the **leading priests** and the **elders**. "I have sinned," he **declared**, "for I have betrayed an innocent man." "What do we care?" they retorted. "That's **your** problem." Then Judas **threw** the silver **coins down** in the **Temple** and **went out** and **hanged himself**. The leading priests **picked** up the coins. "It wouldn't be **right** to put this **money** in the Temple treasury," they **said**, "since it was **payment** for murder." **After some** discussion they **finally decided** to **buy** the potter's **field**, and they **made** it **into** a **cemetery** for foreigners. That is why the field is **still called** the Field of **Blood**. (NLT)

The Betrayer

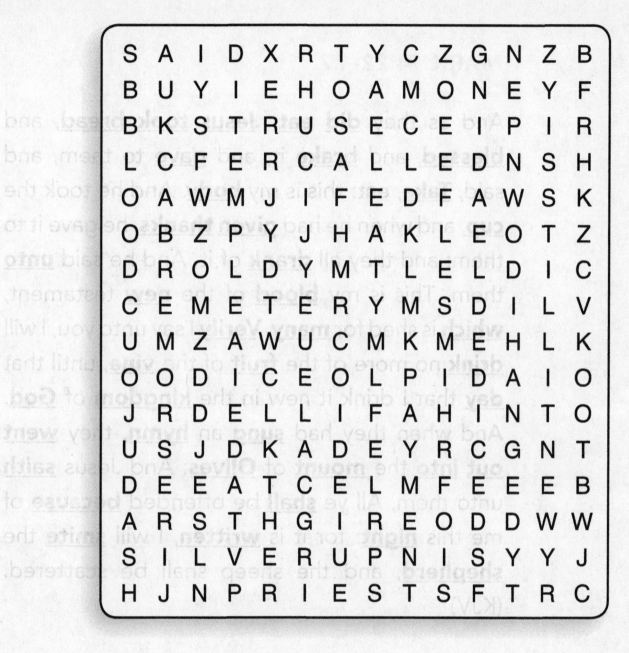

```
S A I D X R T Y C Z G N Z B
B U Y I E H O A M O N E Y F
B K S T R U S E C E I P I R
L C F E R C A L L E D N S H
O A W M J I F E D F A W S K
O B Z P Y J H A K L E O T Z
D R O L D Y M T L E L D I C
C E M E T E R Y M S D I L V
U M Z A W U C M K M E H L K
O O D I C E O L P I D A I O
J R D E L L I F A H I N T O
U S J D K A D E Y R C G N T
D E E A T C E L M F E E E B
A R S T H G I R E O D D W W
S I L V E R U P N I S Y Y J
H J N P R I E S T S F T R C
```

Solution on Page 311

MARK 14:22–27

And as they **did** **eat**, **Jesus** **took** **bread**, and **blessed**, and **brake** it, and **gave** to them, and said, **Take**, eat: this is my **body**. And he took the **cup**, and when he had **given** **thanks**, he gave it to them: and they all **drank** of it. And he said **unto** them, This is my **blood** of the **new** testament, **which** is shed for **many**. **Verily** I say unto you, I will **drink** no more of the **fruit** of the **vine**, until that **day** that I drink it new in the **kingdom** of **God**. And when they had **sung** an **hymn**, they **went** **out** **into** the **mount** of **Olives**. And Jesus **saith** unto them, All ye **shall** be offended **because** of me this **night**: for it is **written**, I will **smite** the **shepherd**, and the sheep shall be scattered. (KJV)

Solution on Page 311

The Lord's Supper

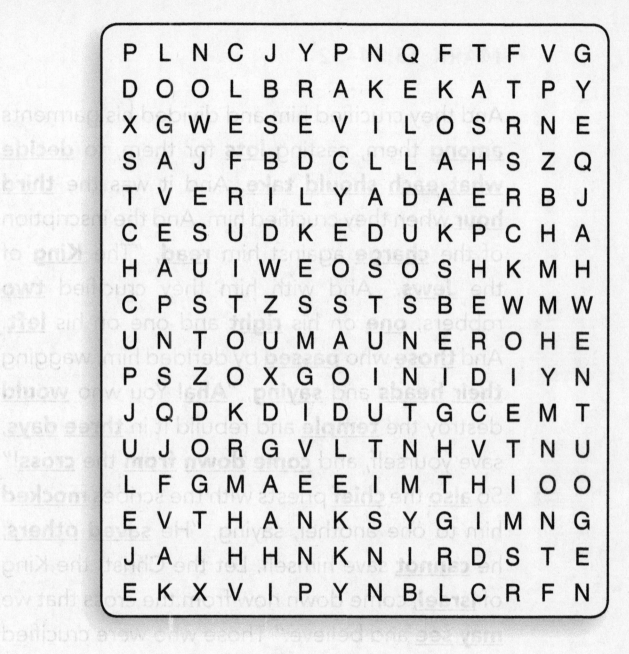

```
P L N C J Y P N Q F T F V G
D O O L B R A K E K A T P Y
X G W E S E V I L O S R N E
S A J F B D C L L A H S Z Q
T V E R I L Y A D A E R B J
C E S U D K E D U K P C H A
H A U I W E O S O S H K M H
C P S T Z S S T S B E W M W
U N T O U M A U N E R O H E
P S Z O X G O I N I D I Y N
J Q D K D I D U T G C E M T
U J O R G V L T N H V T N U
L F G M A E E I M T H I O O
E V T H A N K S Y G I M N G
J A I H H N K N I R D S T E
E K X V I P Y N B L C R F N
```

Solution on Page 311

MARK 15:24–32

And they crucified him and divided his garments **among** them, casting **lots** for them, to **decide what each should take**. And it was the **third hour** when they crucified him. And the inscription of the **charge** against him **read**, "The **King** of the **Jews**." And with him they crucified **two** robbers, **one** on his **right** and one on his **left**. And **those** who **passed** by derided him, wagging **their heads** and **saying**, "**Aha**! You who **would** destroy the **temple** and rebuild it in **three days**, save yourself, and **come down from** the **cross**!" So **also** the **chief** priests with the scribes **mocked** him to one another, saying, "He **saved others**; he **cannot** save himself. Let the Christ, the King of **Israel**, come down now from the cross that we **may see** and believe." Those who were crucified with him also reviled him. (ESV)

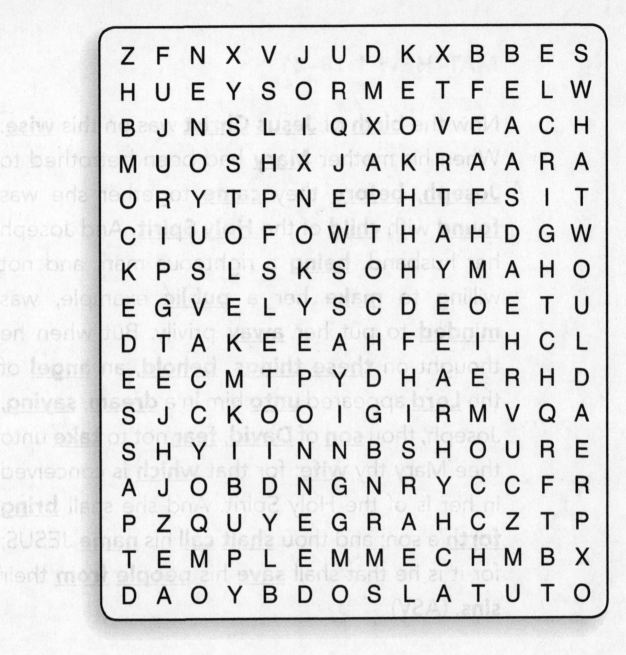

```
Z F N X V J U D K X B B E S
H U E Y S O R M E T F E L W
B J N S L I Q X O V E A C H
M U O S H X J A K R A A R A
O R Y T P N E P H T F S I T
C I U O F O W T H A H D G W
K P S L S K S O H Y M A H O
E G V E L Y S C D E O E T U
D T A K E E A H F E I H C L
E E C M T P Y D H A E R H D
S J C K O O I G I R M V Q A
S H Y I I N N B S H O U R E
A J O B D N G N R Y C C F R
P Z Q U Y E G R A H C Z T P
T E M P L E M M E C H M B X
D A O Y B D O S L A T U T O
```

Solution on Page 311

MATTHEW 1:18–21

Now the **birth** of **Jesus Christ** was on this **wise**: When his mother **Mary** had been betrothed to **Joseph**, **before** they **came** together she was **found** with **child** of the **Holy Spirit**. And Joseph her husband, **being** a righteous man, and not willing to **make** her a **public** example, was **minded** to put her **away** privily. But when he thought on **these things**, **behold**, an **angel** of the **Lord** appeared **unto** him in a **dream**, **saying**, Joseph, thou **son** of **David**, **fear** not to **take** unto thee Mary thy **wife**: for that **which** is conceived in her is of the Holy Spirit. And she shall **bring forth** a son; and thou **shalt call** his **name** JESUS; for it is he that shall **save** his **people from** their **sins**. (ASV)

The Birth of Jesus

```
R R E F S K J W Y F L C O N
E Z T M A K E A K E R T Y N
H Y T L A H S S V J M L N D
D E G V C C U A E L O R D L
A F E I J A S N D H Y D M J
S I H S K P L A R D T A H B
G W G N I R B L E D R T H Q
N N M R U W A W A Y N T A R
I O I I P W U V M E R U A A
H T D Y N E I Z P I K N O E
T N F L A D O C B M G A T F
R U S J O S E P H E C M T R
O T S I R H C D L I I E S O
F B E F O R E A P E L N E M
S L H W C I L B U P I D G L
T V A H I F N S T S O N H X
```

Solution on Page 312

JOHN 6:52–58

The **Jews** then **disputed** **among** **themselves**, **saying**, "How can this **man** **give** us his **flesh** to **eat**?" So **Jesus** **said** to them, "**Truly**, truly, I say to you, **unless** you eat the flesh of the **Son** of Man and drink his **blood**, you have no **life** in you. **Whoever** **feeds** on my flesh and **drinks** my blood has **eternal** life, and I will **raise** him up on the **last** **day**. For my flesh is true **food**, and my blood is true drink. Whoever feeds on my flesh and drinks my blood **abides** in me, and I in him. As the **living** Father **sent** me, and I live **because** of the Father, so whoever feeds on me, he **also** will live because of me. This is the **bread** that **came** **down** **from** **heaven**, not like the bread the **fathers** **ate** and **died**. Whoever feeds on this bread will live **forever**." (ESV)

Solution on Page 312

The Bread of Life

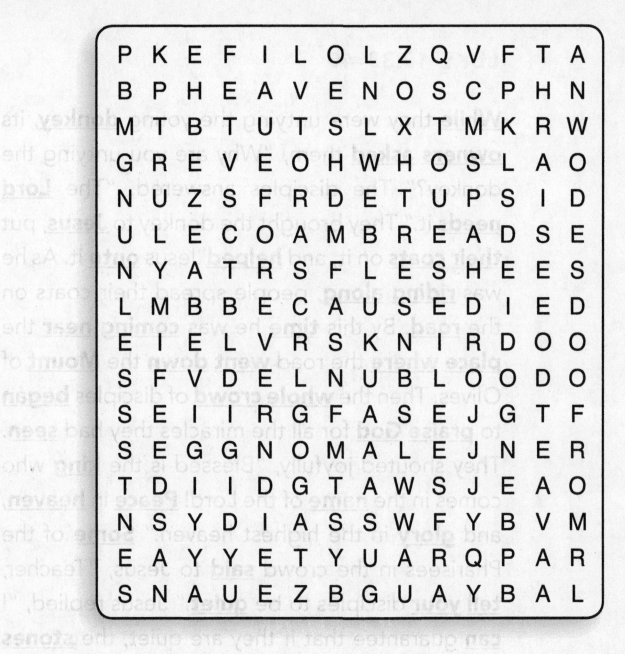

```
P K E F I L O L Z Q V F T A
B P H E A V E N O S C P H N
M T B T U T S L X T M K R W
G R E V E O H W H O S L A O
N U Z S F R D E T U P S I D
U L E C O A M B R E A D S E
N Y A T R S F L E S H E E S
L M B B E C A U S E D I E D
E I E L V R S K N I R D O O
S F V D E L N U B L O O D O
S E I I R G F A S E J G T F
S E G G N O M A L E J N E R
T D I I D G T A W S J E A O
N S Y D I A S S W F Y B V M
E A Y Y E T Y U A R Q P A R
S N A U E Z B G U A Y B A L
```

Solution on Page 312

LUKE 19:33–40

While they were untying the young **donkey**, its **owners asked** them, "Why are you untying the donkey?" The disciples answered, "The **Lord needs** it." They brought the donkey to **Jesus**, put **their coats** on it, and **helped** Jesus **onto** it. As he was **riding along**, people spread their coats on the **road**. By this **time** he was **coming near** the **place where** the road **went down** the **Mount** of Olives. Then the **whole crowd** of disciples **began** to **praise God** for all the miracles they had **seen**. They shouted joyfully, "Blessed is the **king** who comes in the **name** of the Lord! **Peace** in **heaven**, and **glory** in the highest heaven." **Some** of the Pharisees in the crowd **said** to Jesus, "Teacher, **tell your** disciples to be **quiet**." Jesus replied, "I **can** guarantee that if they are quiet, the **stones** will cry out." (GW)

Solution on Page 312

Donkey Ride

```
H S D U K K T H E I R U O Y
L G G A M O T E I U Q D C E
H O R J O E L L X G J D P
F D I E U R O P H I D R O L
C I D S N A G E B W H O L E
W A I U T V A D F S Y W W V
C S N S O V M K E M T B P N
S K G E E T P E N G T T S O
Y E K N O D N A L K N D Q L
H D D O I X C O G I E I L G
W P B T F M R N U E W P K K
F L E S E Y O W N E R S T E
E D O M C L W C C A T E G W
I M N E A R D A I A L K H R
E I I P L N E S O L J L R W
A T G T P P E C U Z G W A V
```

Solution on Page 312

JOHN 13:3–8

The **Father** had put **everything** in **Jesus'** **control**. Jesus **knew** that. He **also** knew that he had **come** **from** God and was **going** **back** to God. So he got up from the **table**, **removed** his **outer** **clothes**, **took** a **towel**, and **tied** it **around** his **waist**. Then he **poured** **water** **into** a **basin** and **began** to **wash** the disciples' **feet** and **dry** them with the towel that he had tied around his waist. When Jesus **came** to **Simon** **Peter**, Peter **asked** him, "Lord, are you going to wash my feet?" Jesus **answered** Peter, "You don't **know** now **what** I'm **doing**. You will **understand** later." Peter **told** Jesus, "You will **never** wash my feet." Jesus **replied** to Peter, "If I don't wash you, you don't **belong** to me." (GW)

```
A Z A Q R L D R Y J G E M K
N Q A C G F S E O O D P O L
V E V E R Y T H I N G O N C
P D E R E W S N A L T U E W
I C E N V A G T C L P R V T
R V O L W D S U S E J E E S
Y F O M B R E T A W W D R I
N C A M E A H V A O C E N A
N K T D J L T R O T A T S W
A O N B E L O N G M O K K N
N U M O K U L R N R E T U O
B A S I N K C E T D F R O M
D L G D S N Z H K N O W K Q
A L P E T E R T J M O I Q S
T N O I B W B A C K C C N W
W H A T T E E F E P G N B G
```

Solution on Page 312

JOHN 11:49–54

Caiaphas, who was **high priest** at that **time**, **said**, "You don't **know what** you're **talking about**! You don't **realize** that it's **better** for you that one **man should** die for the **people** than for the **whole nation** to be destroyed." He did not say this on his **own**; as high priest at that time he was led to prophesy that **Jesus would** die for the **entire** nation. And not **only** for that nation, but to **bring** together and **unite all** the children of **God** scattered **around** the **world**. So **from** that time on, the **Jewish** leaders **began** to **plot** Jesus' **death**. As a **result**, Jesus stopped his **public** ministry **among** the people and **left** Jerusalem. He **went** to a **place near** the wilderness, to the village of Ephraim, and **stayed there** with his disciples. (NLT)

```
N V Y F Q A D P Q L B Y V M
H B R V T O L P R I E S T M
Y T E Q S A U L G A N I F A
I L A G C D O G B I T F E L
G S N E A B W O H S I W E J
Z V W O D N U O R A R A E N
S F P H I T B E T T E R E W
T N E W O T A L K I N G N H
Y C O O C L A Z X U D Y S A
Y N P J I R E N M E R E H T
K D L Z L U D S Y A G J G B
B L E S B L O A M O N G A U
T R E S U L T I U N I T E H
K O O O P S L D D F R O M I
H W H I G H E M I T B J D S
N S Q N C O X J S H A S Z C
```

Solution on Page 313

JOHN 2:13–19

The **Jewish** Passover was **near**, so **Jesus went** to Jerusalem. He **found those** who were **selling cattle**, **sheep**, and **pigeons** in the **temple** courtyard. He **also** found moneychangers **sitting there**. He **made** a **whip from small ropes** and **threw** everyone with their sheep and cattle **out** of the temple courtyard. He **dumped** the moneychangers' **coins** and knocked over their **tables**. He **told** those who **sold** pigeons, "Pick up this **stuff**, and get it out of here! **Stop making** my Father's **house** a marketplace!" His disciples remembered that Scripture **said**, "Devotion for **your** house will consume me." The Jews **reacted** by **asking** Jesus, "**What** miracle can you **show** us to **justify** what you're doing?" Jesus **replied**, "Tear **down** this temple, and I'll **rebuild** it in three days." (GW)

Moneychangers Thrown Out

```
P H C Y G D T H O S E X I E
V L O A O G E J E S U S V U
N U I W T I M N E A R G E U
R Q N Q F T P D R W V T S I
E O S R E P L I E D I O U X
V U O G H O E E A N G S O O
G M M N S T K P C U N L H U
M A G I E R E H T O I A T K
E D I K Y U F M E F L O S I
J E U A P F R G D S L T H B
Z S P M U O I T I D E A O T
Y M H T P P T T A R S B W S
S A S E I E T S S K P L E I
T L S H E I D L I U B E R N
Q L W F N P T N E W J S H E
E Y T G Q X G G T W H A T P
```

Solution on Page 313

That **evening**, **Jesus** **said** to his **disciples**, "Let's cross to the **other** side." **Leaving** the **crowd**, they **took** Jesus **along** in a boat **just** as he was. Other **boats** were with him. A **violent** windstorm came up. The **waves** were **breaking** **into** the boat so that it was **quickly** **filling** up. But he was **sleeping** on a **cushion** in the **back** of the boat. So they **woke** him up and said to him, "Teacher, don't you **care** that we're **going** to die?" Then he got up, **ordered** the wind to stop, and said to the **sea**, "Be **still**, absolutely still!" The wind **stopped** **blowing**, and the sea **became** **very** **calm**. He **asked** them, "Why are you **such** **cowards**? Don't you have any **faith** yet?" They were **overcome** with **fear** and asked **each** other, "Who is this **man**? Even the wind and the sea **obey** him!" (GW)

```
N W C S L E E P I N G Y R W
U A U B L O K A K N O B E Y
Z C M B O R G N I W O L B L
H Z L E J O K K A A W D S E
A K A E I F A I T H C T V A
K C C N M E M S G B O Y I V
H O G R R A M O N P L T O I
C X O B O V C O P K P S L N
L L I T S W I E C V D U E G
S B I R H H D I B R S J N N
J E S U S E U E A I E I T I
H S X U K Q R W R R N V H L
O B C S G N O L A E C T O L
F E A R F C A C V V D K O I
D I S C I P L E S V E R Y F
D H W O K E O Q S O S S O N
```

Solution on Page 313

MATTHEW 28:5–10

And the **angel** **answered** and **said** **unto** the **women**, **Fear** not ye: for I **know** that ye **seek** **Jesus**, **which** was crucified. He is not here: for he is **risen**, as he said. **Come**, see the **place** **where** the **Lord** **lay**. And go **quickly**, and **tell** his disciples that he is risen **from** the **dead**; and, **behold**, he **goeth** **before** you **into** **Galilee**; **there** **shall** ye see him: lo, I have **told** you. And they departed quickly from the sepulchre with fear and **great** **joy**; and did **run** to **bring** his disciples word. And as they **went** to tell his disciples, behold, Jesus **met** them, **saying**, All **hail**. And they **came** and **held** him by the **feet**, and worshipped him. Then said Jesus unto them, Be not **afraid**: go tell my brethren that they go into Galilee, and there shall they see me. (KJV)

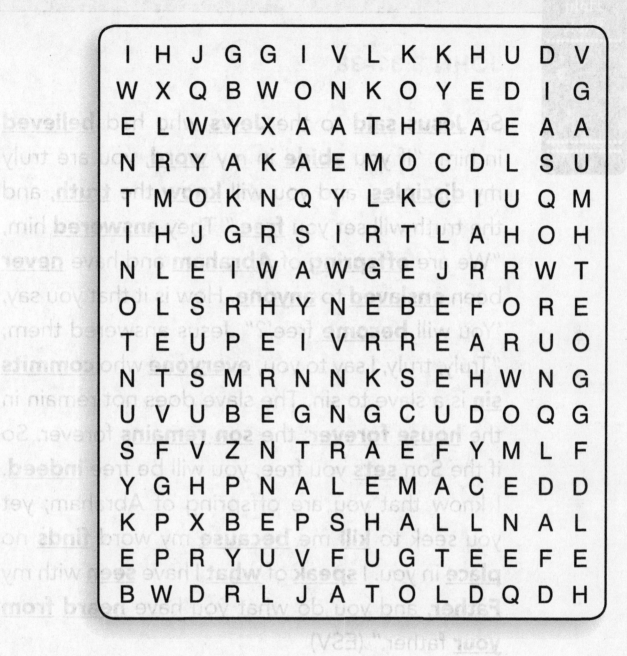

```
I H J G G I V L K K H U D V
W X Q B W O N K O Y E D I G
E L W Y X A A T H R A E A A
N R Y A K A E M O C D L S U
T M O K N Q Y L K C I U Q M
I H J G R S I R T L A H O H
N L E I W A W G E J R R W T
O L S R H Y N E B E F O R E
T E U P E I V R R E A R U O
N T S M R N N K S E H W N G
U V U B E G N G C U D O Q G
S F V Z N T R A E F Y M L F
Y G H P N A L E M A C E D D
K P X B E P S H A L L N A L
E P R Y U V F U G T E E F E
B W D R L J A T O L D Q D H
```

Solution on Page 313

Holy
Bible

JOHN 8:31–38

So **Jesus** **said** to the **Jews** who had **believed** in him, "If you **abide** in my **word**, you are truly my **disciples**, and you will **know** the **truth**, and the truth will set you **free**." They **answered** him, "We are **offspring** of **Abraham** and have **never** been **enslaved** to **anyone**. How is it that you say, 'You will **become** free'?" Jesus answered them, "Truly, truly, I say to you, **everyone** who **commits** **sin** is a slave to sin. The slave does not remain in the **house** **forever**; the **son** **remains** forever. So if the Son **sets** you free, you will be free **indeed**. I know that you are offspring of Abraham; yet you seek to **kill** me **because** my word **finds** no **place** in you. I **speak** of **what** I have **seen** with my **Father**, and you do what you have **heard** **from** **your** father." (ESV)

Solution on Page 313

The Truth Will Set You Free

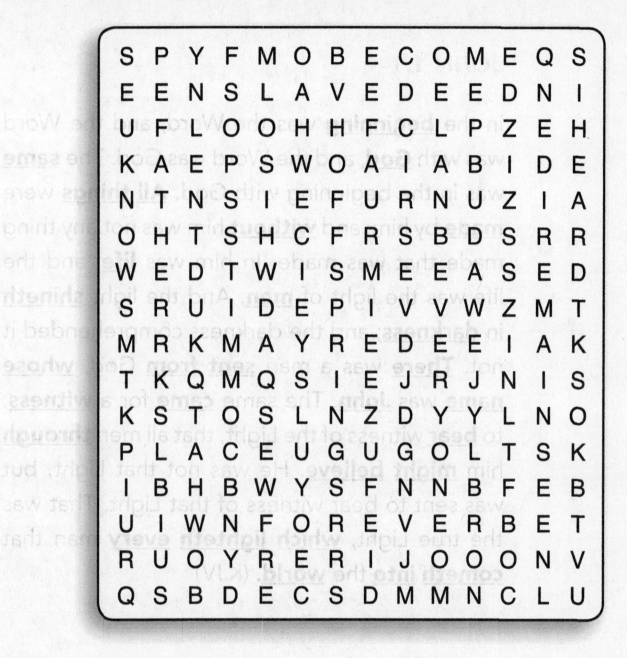

```
S P Y F M O B E C O M E Q S
E E N S L A V E D E E D N I
U F L O O H H F C L P Z E H
K A E P S W O A I A B I D E
N T N S I E F U R N U Z I A
O H T S H C F R S B D S R R
W E D T W I S M E A S E D R
S R U I D E P I V V W Z M T
M R K M A Y R E D E E I A K
T K Q M Q S I E J R J N I S
K S T O S L N Z D Y Y L N O
P L A C E U G U G O L T S K
I B H B W Y S F N N B F E B
U I W N F O R E V E R B E T
R U O Y R E R I J O O O N V
Q S B D E C S D M M N C L U
```

Solution on Page 314

JOHN 1:1–9

In the **beginning** was the Word, and the Word was with **God**, and the Word was God. The **same** was in the beginning with God. **All** **things** were **made** by him; and **without** him was not any thing made that was made. In him was **life**; and the life was the light of **men**. And the light **shineth** in **darkness**; and the darkness comprehended it not. **There** was a man **sent** **from** God, **whose** **name** was **John**. The same **came** for a **witness**, to **bear** witness of the Light, that all men **through** him **might** **believe**. He was not that Light, but was sent to bear witness of that Light. That was the true Light, **which** **lighteth** **every** man that **cometh** **into** the **world**. (KJV)

The Word Was God

```
Z H T U H G D O G N A U E V
T H F N T J A I D J G G M Y
O N L A E J R Y E A U Z U E
O S Z V N S K A X F E W V D
J B E G I N N I N G I E B A
B R E L H T E T H G I L E M
Y C A A S H S R H L S S R F
F X L D R R S A E I O T K N
P L W L B O N B M H N H M K
K L O I Z U Q V W E T G K C
V K X G T G W O R L D I S J
V M S A C H T E M O C M Z R
J H O C I Z O O K O A G E U
S O K C W Y R U G T M O H N
H F H Z A F W I T N E S S V
E M A N C F H N F I V J D V
```

Solution on Page 314

DEUTERONOMY 28:1–6

And it shall come to **pass**, if **thou shalt hearken diligently unto** the **voice** of the **LORD** thy God, to **observe** and to do **all** his commandments **which** I **command** thee this **day**, that the LORD thy God will **set** thee on **high above** all **nations** of the **earth**: And all **these blessings** shall come on thee, and **overtake** thee, if thou shalt hearken unto the voice of the LORD thy God. Blessed shalt thou be in the **city**, and blessed shalt thou be in the **field**. Blessed shall be the **fruit** of thy **body**, and the fruit of thy **ground**, and the fruit of thy **cattle**, the **increase** of thy **kine**, and the **flocks** of thy **sheep**. Blessed shall be thy **basket** and thy **store**. Blessed shalt thou be when thou **comest** in, and blessed shalt thou be when thou **goest out**. (KJV)

Solution on Page 314

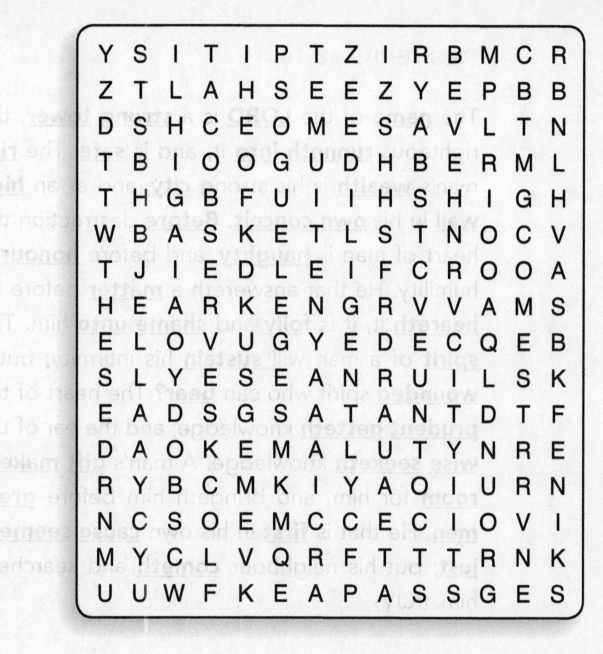

```
Y S I T I P T Z I R B M C R
Z T L A H S E E Z Y E P B B
D S H C E O M E S A V L T N
T B I O O G U D H B E R M L
T H G B F U I I H S H I G H
W B A S K E T L S T N O C V
T J I E D L E I F C R O O A
H E A R K E N G R V V A M S
E L O V U G Y E D E C Q E B
S L Y E S E A N R U I L S K
E A D S G S A T A N T D T F
D A O K E M A L U T Y N R E
R Y B C M K I Y A O I U R N
N C S O E M C C E C I O V I
M Y C L V Q R F T T T R N K
U U W F K E A P A S S G E S
```

Solution on Page 314

PROVERBS 18:10–17

The **name** of the **LORD** is a **strong** **tower**: the righteous **runneth** **into** it, and is **safe**. The **rich** man's **wealth** is his strong **city**, and as an **high** **wall** in his **own** **conceit**. **Before** destruction the heart of man is **haughty**, and before **honour** is humility. He that answereth a **matter** before he **heareth** it, it is **folly** and **shame** **unto** him. The **spirit** of a man will **sustain** his infirmity; but a **wounded** spirit who can **bear**? The heart of the **prudent** **getteth** knowledge; and the ear of the **wise** **seeketh** knowledge. A man's **gift** **maketh** **room** for him, and bringeth him before **great** **men**. He that is **first** in his own **cause** **seemeth** **just**; but his neighbour **cometh** and searcheth him. (KJV)

Solution on Page 314

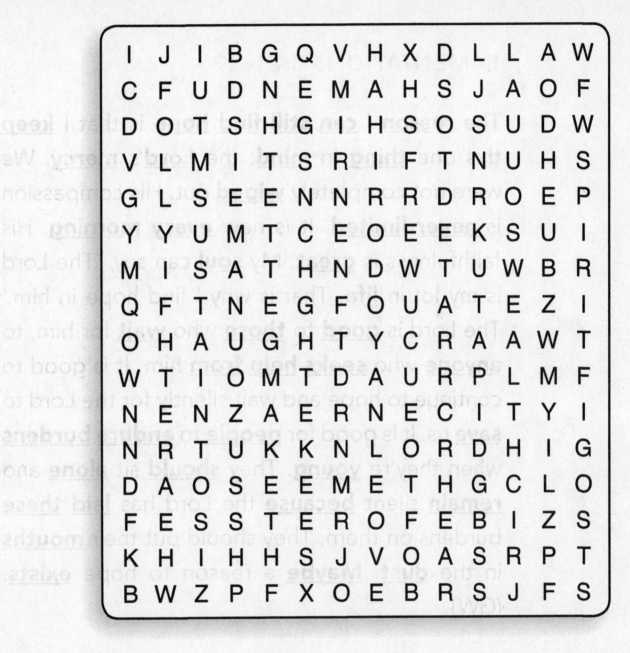

```
I J I B G Q V H X D L L A W
C F U D N E M A H S J A O F
D O T S H G I H S O S U D W
V L M I T S R I F T N U H S
G L S E E N N R R D R O E P
Y Y U M T C E O E E K S U I
M I S A T H N D W T U W B R
Q F T N E G F O U A T E Z I
O H A U G H T Y C R A A W T
W T I O M T D A U R P L M F
N E N Z A E R N E C I T Y I
N R T U K K N L O R D H I G
D A O S E E M E T H G C L O
F E S S T E R O F E B I Z S
K H I H H S J V O A S R P T
B W Z P F X O E B R S J F S
```

Solution on Page 314

LAMENTATIONS 3:21–29

The **reason** I **can** **still** **find** hope is that I **keep** this one **thing** in **mind**: the **Lord**'s **mercy**. We were not completely **wiped** out. His compassion is **never** **limited**. It is new **every** **morning**. His faithfulness is **great**. My **soul** can say, 'The Lord is my lot in **life**. That is why I find hope in him.' The Lord is **good** to **those** who **wait** for him, to **anyone** who **seeks** **help** **from** him. It is good to continue to hope and wait silently for the Lord to **save** us. It is good for **people** to **endure** **burdens** when they're **young**. They **should** sit **alone** and **remain** silent **because** the Lord has **laid** **these** burdens on them. They should put their **mouths** in the **dust**. **Maybe** a reason to hope **exists**. (GW)

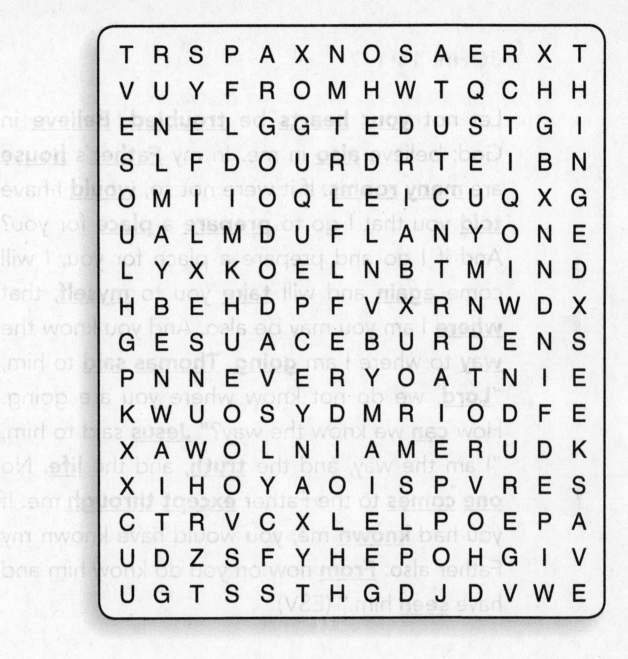

```
T R S P A X N O S A E R X T
V U Y F R O M H W T Q C H H
E N E L G G T E D U S T G I
S L F D O U R D R T E I B N
O M I I O Q L E I C U Q X G
U A L M D U F L A N Y O N E
L Y X K O E L N B T M I N D
H B E H D P F V X R N W D X
G E S U A C E B U R D E N S
P N N E V E R Y O A T N I E
K W U O S Y D M R I O D F E
X A W O L N I A M E R U D K
X I H O Y A O I S P V R E S
C T R V C X L E L P O E P A
U D Z S F Y H E P O H G I V
U G T S S T H G D J D V W E
```

Solution on Page 315

JOHN 14:1–7

Let not **your** **hearts** be **troubled**. **Believe** in God; believe **also** in me. In my **Father**'s **house** are **many** **rooms**. If it were not so, **would** I have **told** you that I go to **prepare** a **place** for you? And if I go and prepare a place for you, I will come **again** and will **take** you to **myself**, that **where** I am you may be also. And you know the **way** to where I am **going**. **Thomas** **said** to him, "**Lord**, we do not know where you are going. How **can** we know the way?" **Jesus** said to him, "I am the way, and the **truth**, and the **life**. No **one** **comes** to the Father **except** **through** me. If you had **known** me, you would have known my Father also. **From** now on you do know him and have **seen** him." (ESV)

Solution on Page 315

The Way, the Truth, and the Light

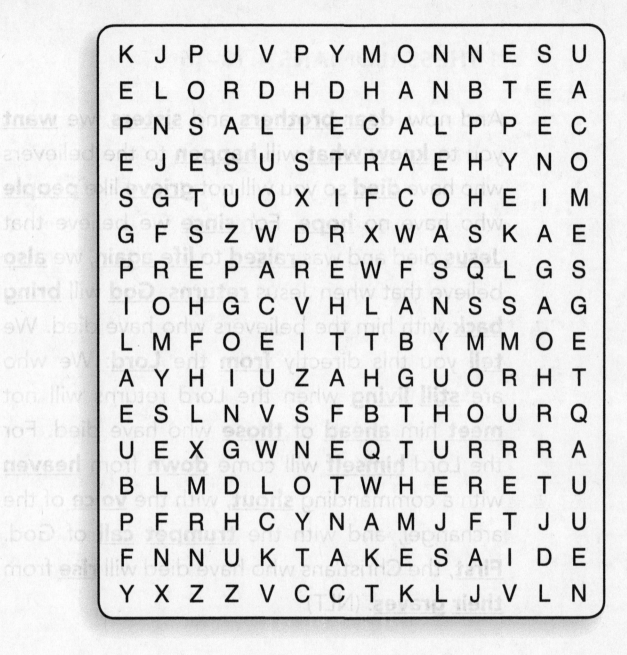

```
K J P U V P Y M O N N E S U
E L O R D H D H A N B T E A
P N S A L I E C A L P P E C
E J E S U S T R A E H Y N O
S G T U O X I F C O H E I M
G F S Z W D R X W A S K A E
P R E P A R E W F S Q L G S
I O H G C V H L A N S S A G
L M F O E I T T B Y M M O E
A Y H I U Z A H G U O R H T
E S L N V S F B T H O U R Q
U E X G W N E Q T U R R R A
B L M D L O T W H E R E T U
P F R H C Y N A M J F T J U
F N N U K T A K E S A I D E
Y X Z Z V C C T K L J V L N
```

Solution on Page 315

1 THESSALONIANS 4:13–16

And now, **dear brothers** and **sisters**, we **want** you to **know what** will **happen** to the believers who have **died** so you will not **grieve** like **people** who have no **hope**. For **since** we believe that **Jesus** died and was **raised** to **life again**, we **also** believe that when Jesus **returns**, **God** will **bring back** with him the believers who have died. We **tell** you this directly **from** the **Lord**: We who are **still living** when the Lord returns will not **meet** him **ahead** of **those** who have died. For the Lord **himself** will come **down** from **heaven** with a commanding **shout**, with the **voice** of the archangel, and with the **trumpet call** of God. **First**, the Christians who have died will **rise** from **their graves**. (NLT)

Solution on Page 315

Do Not Grieve

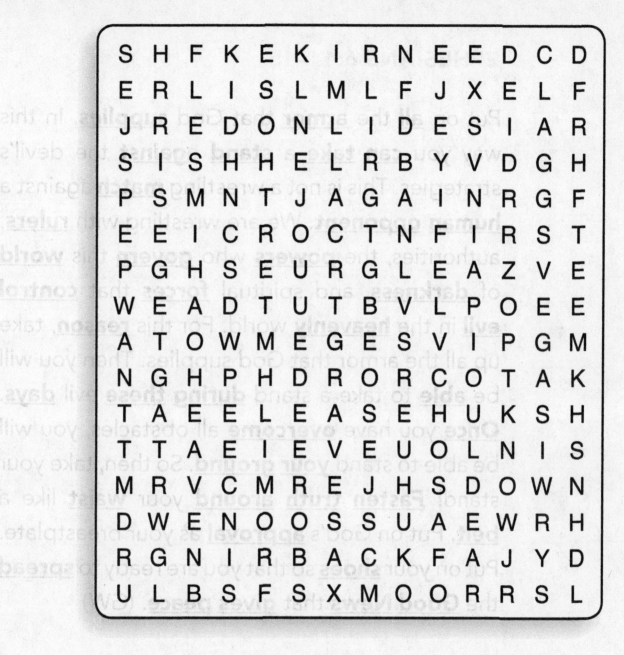

```
S H F K E K I R N E E D C D
E R L I S L M L F J X E L F
J R E D O N L I D E S I A R
S I S H H E L R B Y V D G H
P S M N T J A G A I N R G F
E E I C R O C T N F I R S T
P G H S E U R G L E A Z V E
W E A D T U T B V L P O E E
A T O W M E G E S V I P G M
N G H P H D R O R C O T A K
T A E E L E A S E H U K S H
T T A E I E V E U O L N I S
M R V C M R E J H S D O W N
D W E N O O S S U A E W R H
R G N I R B A C K F A J Y D
U L B S F S X M O O R R S L
```

Solution on Page 315

EPHESIANS 6:11–15

Put on **all** the **armor** that God **supplies**. In this way you **can** **take** a **stand** **against** the devil's strategies. This is not a wrestling **match** against a **human** **opponent**. We are wrestling with **rulers**, authorities, the **powers** who **govern** this **world** of **darkness**, and spiritual **forces** that **control** **evil** in the **heavenly** world. For this **reason**, take up all the armor that God supplies. Then you will be **able** to take a stand **during** **these** evil **days**. **Once** you have **overcome** all obstacles, you will be able to stand **your** **ground**. So then, take your stand! **Fasten** **truth** **around** your **waist** like a **belt**. Put on God's **approval** as your breastplate. Put on your **shoes** so that you are ready to **spread** the **Good** **News** that **gives** **peace**. (GW)

Put on the Armor

```
K X E W D N S B A H U M A N
M O C M O H R W E D A Y S O
S O O A P R O A E L B A E S
N W N T E W L G H N T R C A
X A T C A L O D A T T M R E
U R R H C V U C E K U O O R
X V O V E R C O M E U R F U
C N L R I A G A I N S T T L
E M N N X M V D D E N R S E
S N G S O N C E A E O U I R
E E R E D A R K N E S S A S
H T V V S D O O G L R W W E
T S E I L P P U S D Y P K O
D A X L G P O W E R S A S H
V F G R O U N D N A T S S S
R U O Y A P P R O V A L Q B
```

Solution on Page 315

JOHN 5:24–29

Truly, truly, I **say** to you, **whoever hears** my **word** and **believes** him who **sent** me has **eternal life**. He does not come **into judgment**, but has **passed from death** to life. Truly, truly, I say to you, an **hour** is **coming**, and is now **here**, when the dead will hear the **voice** of the **Son** of God, and **those** who hear will **live**. For as the **Father** has life in **himself**, so he has **granted** the Son **also** to have life in himself. And he has **given** him **authority** to **execute** judgment, **because** he is the Son of Man. Do not **marvel** at this, for an hour is coming when all who are in the **tombs** will hear his voice and come **out**, those who have **done good** to the resurrection of life, and those who have done **evil** to the resurrection of judgment. (ESV)

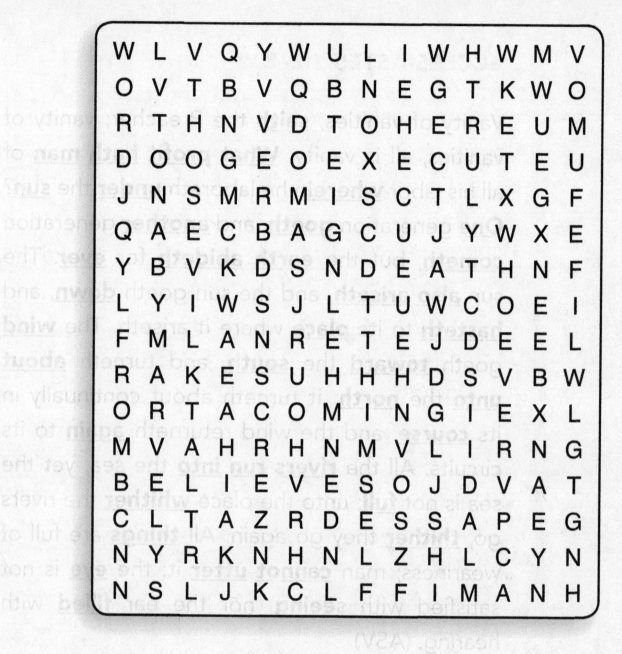

Solution on Page 316

ECCLESIASTES 1:2–8

Vanity of vanities, **saith** the Preacher; vanity of vanities, all is vanity. **What profit hath man** of all his labor **wherein** he laboreth **under** the **sun**? **One** generation **goeth**, and **another** generation **cometh**; but the **earth abideth** for **ever**. The sun **also ariseth**, and the sun goeth **down**, and **hasteth** to its **place** where it ariseth. The **wind** goeth **toward** the **south**, and turneth **about unto** the **north**; it turneth about continually in its **course**, and the wind returneth **again** to its circuits. All the **rivers run into** the sea, yet the sea is not **full**; unto the place **whither** the rivers go, **thither** they go again. All **things** are full of weariness; man **cannot utter** it: the **eye** is not satisfied with **seeing**, nor the ear **filled** with hearing. (ASV)

Solution on Page 316.

Puzzles

All Is Vanity

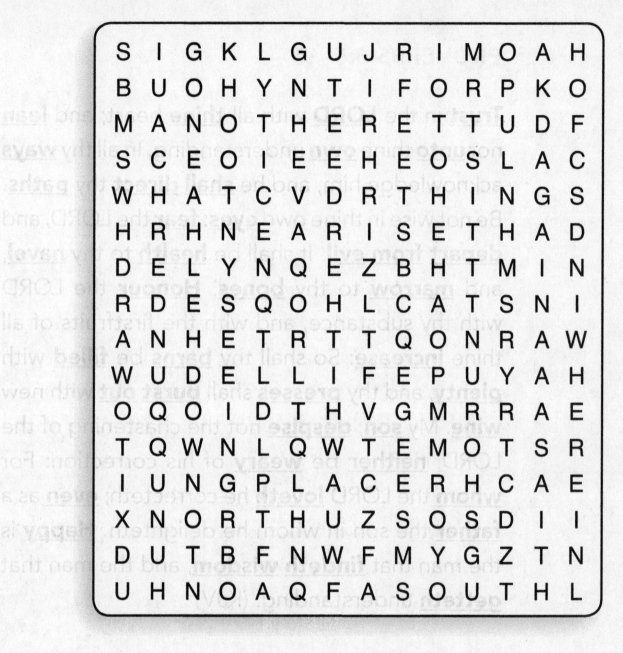

```
S  I  G  K  L  G  U  J  R  I  M  O  A  H
B  U  O  H  Y  N  T  I  F  O  R  P  K  O
M  A  N  O  T  H  E  R  E  T  T  U  D  F
S  C  E  O  I  E  E  H  E  O  S  L  A  C
W  H  A  T  C  V  D  R  T  H  I  N  G  S
H  R  H  N  E  A  R  I  S  E  T  H  A  D
D  E  L  Y  N  Q  E  Z  B  H  T  M  I  N
R  D  E  S  Q  O  H  L  C  A  T  S  N  I
A  N  H  E  T  R  T  T  Q  O  N  R  A  W
W  U  D  E  L  L  I  F  E  P  U  Y  A  H
O  Q  O  I  D  T  H  V  G  M  R  R  A  E
T  Q  W  N  L  Q  W  T  E  M  O  T  S  R
I  U  N  G  P  L  A  C  E  R  H  C  A  E
X  N  O  R  T  H  U  Z  S  O  S  D  I  I
D  U  T  B  F  N  W  F  M  Y  G  Z  T  N
U  H  N  O  A  Q  F  A  S  O  U  T  H  L
```

Solution on Page 316

PROVERBS 3:5–13

Trust in the **LORD** with all **thine** heart; and **lean** not **unto** thine **own** understanding. In all thy **ways** acknowledge him, and he **shall** **direct** thy **paths**. Be not wise in thine own **eyes**: **fear** the LORD, and **depart** **from** **evil**. It shall be **health** to thy **navel**, and **marrow** to thy **bones**. **Honour** the LORD with thy substance, and with the firstfruits of all thine **increase**: So shall thy **barns** be **filled** with **plenty**, and thy **presses** shall **burst** **out** with new **wine**. My **son**, **despise** not the chastening of the LORD; **neither** be **weary** of his correction: For **whom** the LORD **loveth** he correcteth; **even** as a **father** the son in whom he delighteth. **Happy** is the man that **findeth** **wisdom**, and the man that **getteth** understanding. (KJV)

Trust in the Lord

```
H S G P A U R N E V E N I W
F C D S F Q X D A Y Z P N J
A J H E A L T H J V S N W P
U A S H T A P X H T E V O L
F T N S H L E V T I S L R E
V R R T E A C O T C S K R N
S U Z A R G P H E Y E R A T
B S N H E A E P O E R R M Y
R T T F V R P T Y F P A I T
M U O F I N D E T H I N E D
O N O J L D B E D E Y E S W
H Y I N C R E A S E T B L W
W I S D O M B H R P O H A D
G O R T O H A D A N I Y O Q
N O N R C L D T E I S S Q V
L U F A L C X S F I L L E D
```

Solution on Page 316

PSALM 118:21–29

I give **thanks** to you, **because** you have **answered** me. You are my **savior**. The **stone** that the **builders rejected** has **become** the cornerstone. The **Lord** is responsible for this, and it is **amazing** for us to **see**. This is the day the Lord has **made**. Let's **rejoice** and be **glad today**! We beg you, O Lord, save us! We beg you, O Lord, give us **success**! **Blessed** is the one who **comes** in the **name** of the Lord. We bless you **from** the Lord's **house**. The Lord is God, and he has **given** us **light**. **March** in a **festival procession** with **branches** to the **horns** of the **altar**. You are my God, and I give thanks to you. My God, I **honor** you **highly**. Give thanks to the Lord because he is **good**, because his **mercy endures forever**. (GW)

Rejoice and Be Glad

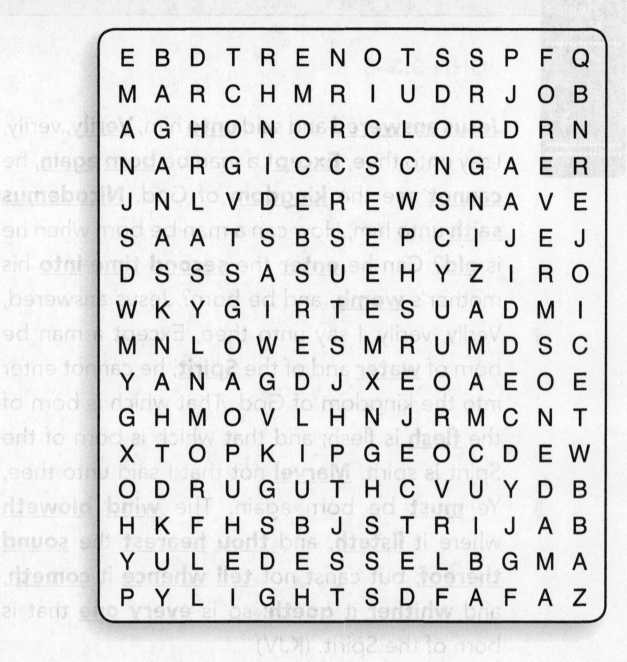

```
E B D T R E N O T S S P F Q
M A R C H M R I U D R J O B
A G H O N O R C L O R D R N
N A R G I C C S C N G A E R
J N L V D E R E W S N A V E
S A A T S B S E P C I J E J
D S S S A S U E H Y Z I R O
W K Y G I R T E S U A D M I
M N L O W E S M R U M D S C
Y A N A G D J X E O A E O E
G H M O V L H N J R M C N T
X T O P K I P G E O C D E W
O D R U G U T H C V U Y D B
H K F H S B J S T R I J A B
Y U L E D E S S E L B G M A
P Y L I G H T S D F A F A Z
```

Solution on Page 316

Holy Bible

JOHN 3:3–8

Jesus answered and said **unto** him, **Verily**, verily, I say unto thee, **Except** a man be **born again**, he **cannot** see the **kingdom** of God. **Nicodemus saith** unto him, How can a man be born when he is **old**? Can he **enter** the **second time into** his mother's **womb**, and be born? Jesus answered, Verily, verily, I say unto thee, Except a man be born of **water** and of the **Spirit**, he cannot enter into the kingdom of God. That which is born of the **flesh** is flesh; and that which is born of the Spirit is spirit. **Marvel** not that I said unto thee, Ye **must** be born again. The **wind bloweth** where it **listeth**, and **thou hearest** the **sound thereof**, but canst not **tell whence** it **cometh**, and **whither** it **goeth**: so is **every one** that is born of the Spirit. (KJV)

Solution on Page 316

Puzzles

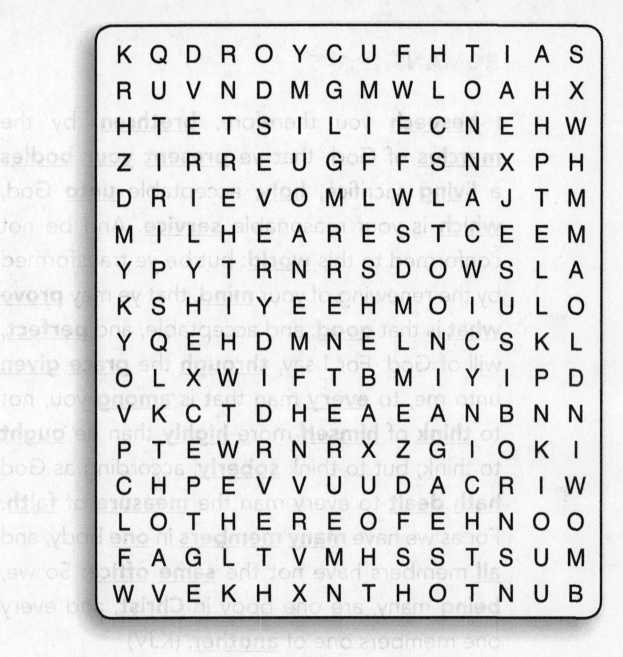

```
K Q D R O Y C U F H T I A S
R U V N D M G M W L O A H X
H T E T S I L I E C N E H W
Z I R R E U G F F S N X P H
D R I E V O M L W L A J T M
M I L H E A R E S T C E E M
Y P Y T R N R S D O W S L A
K S H I Y E E H M O I U L O
Y Q E H D M N E L N C S K L
O L X W I F T B M I Y I P D
V K C T D H E A E A N B N N
P T E W R N R X Z G I O K I
C H P E V V U U D A C R I W
L O T H E R E O F E H N O O
F A G L T V M H S S T S U M
W V E K H X N T H O T N U B
```

Solution on Page 317

ROMANS 12:1–5

I **beseech** you therefore, **brethren**, by the **mercies** of God, that ye **present your bodies** a **living** sacrifice, **holy**, acceptable **unto** God, **which** is your reasonable **service**. And be not conformed to this **world**: but be ye transformed by the renewing of your **mind**, that ye may **prove** **what** is that **good**, and acceptable, and **perfect**, will of God. For I say, **through** the **grace given** unto me, to **every** man that is **among** you, not to **think** of **himself** more **highly** than he **ought** to think; but to think **soberly**, according as God **hath dealt** to every man the **measure** of **faith**. For as we have **many members** in **one** body, and **all** members have not the **same office**: So we, **being** many, are one body in **Christ**, and every one members one of **another**. (KJV)

Living Sacrifice

```
T H U H K O S B T I B A L L
Y O S B R E T H R E N N W T
Y L H G I H I T S O F S O C
L Y U D N N X E T A A M R E
Q I O E K S E H I M S E L F
K B V P P C E T E Y R A D R
O I O I H R H I O O E S O E
G Y D I N H E T C U B U O P
G A H W D G N S E R M R G C
P N C N S U T E E A E E K H
E C I F F O Y O C N M M M A
V M H E O R B N I A T O A T
E C W T B H F E V S R A N H
R D E A L T S I R H C G Y G
Y H H H P R O V E L B N V U
G I G W C T K R S W Y W N O
```

Solution on Page 317

LUKE 13:31–35

At that **time** some Pharisees **told Jesus**, "Get out of here, and go somewhere **else**! **Herod wants** to **kill** you." Jesus **said** to them, "Tell that fox that I will **force demons** out of **people** and **heal** people **today** and **tomorrow**. I will **finish** my **work** on the **third** day. But I **must** be on my way today, tomorrow, and the **next** day. It's not possible for a prophet to **die outside** Jerusalem. Jerusalem, Jerusalem, you kill the **prophets** and **stone** to **death those sent** to you! How **often** I wanted to gather **your children** together the way a hen **gathers** her **chicks under** her **wings**! But you were not **willing**! Your **house** will be abandoned. I **can** guarantee that you will not see me **again until** you say, 'Blessed is the one who **comes** in the **name** of the Lord!'" (GW)

Solution on Page 317

A Warning for Jerusalem

```
Y E D E H E M I T S Y X J J
T Q Y I S Z F N P L T I Z T
I N R O A L E W I L L I N G
Q F H O U S E O U T S I D E
J E S U S R C R P N A C K T
G G M M S N R R T S E M O C
Q C A G W Z O O L L N T V E
P H N T C P F M P I O O F S
Q I O Y H P N O E G T L P O
W C H E I E E T I D S D B H
O K T D L P R E T X E N E T
R S A R D R H S I N I F I O
K R E I R K E D Y A D O T H
J Z D H E R O D G B N A M E
T I F T N V W A N T S U M A
E C G H G Z B S L U N T I L
```

Solution on Page 317

JOHN 14:15–21

If ye love me, keep my commandments. And I will **pray** the **Father**, and he **shall give** you **another Comforter**, that he may **abide** with you for **ever**; Even the **Spirit** of **truth**; **whom** the **world cannot receive**, **because** it **seeth** him not, **neither knoweth** him: but ye know him; for he **dwelleth** with you, and shall be in you. I will not **leave** you comfortless: I will come to you. Yet a **little while**, and the world seeth me no more; but ye see me: because I **live**, ye shall live **also**. At that **day** ye shall know that I am in my Father, and ye in me, and I in you. He that **hath** my commandments, and **keepeth** them, he it is that **loveth** me: and he that loveth me shall be loved of my Father, and I will love him, and will **manifest myself** to him. (KJV)

Solution on Page 317

Keep My Commandments

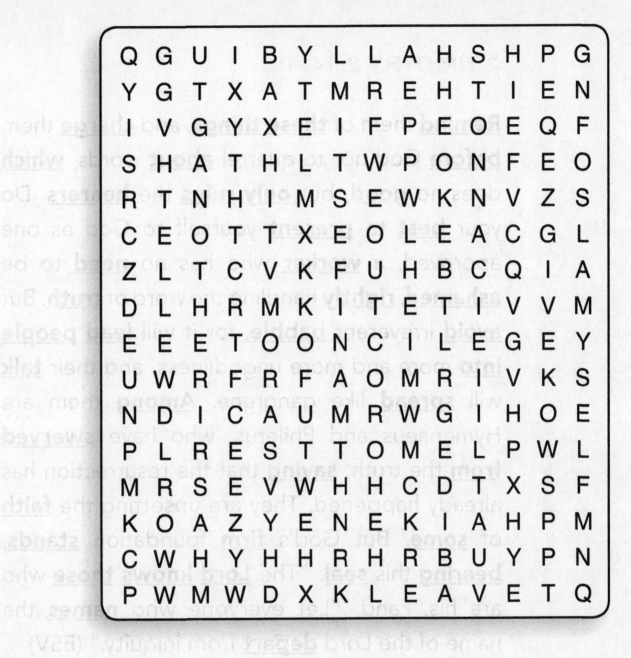

```
Q G U I B Y L L A H S H P G
Y G T X A T M R E H T I E N
I V G Y X E I F P E O E Q F
S H A T H L T W P O N F E O
R T N H I M S E W K N V Z S
C E O T T X E O L E A C G L
Z L T C V K F U H B C Q I A
D L H R M K I T E T I V V M
E E E T O O N C I L E G E Y
U W R F R F A O M R I V K S
N D I C A U M R W G I H O E
P L R E S T T O M E L P W L
M R S E V W H H C D T X S F
K O A Z Y E N E K I A H P M
C W H Y H H R H R B U Y P N
P W M W D X K L E A V E T Q
```

Solution on Page 317

2 TIMOTHY 2:14–19

Remind them of **these things**, and **charge** them **before** God not to quarrel **about** words, **which** does no **good**, but **only ruins** the **hearers**. Do your **best** to **present** yourself to God as one approved, a **worker** who has no **need** to be **ashamed**, **rightly** handling the word of **truth**. But **avoid** irreverent **babble**, for it will **lead people into** more and more ungodliness, and their **talk** will **spread** like gangrene. **Among** them are Hymenaeus and Philetus, who have **swerved from** the truth, **saying** that the resurrection has already happened. They are upsetting the **faith** of **some**. But God's **firm** foundation **stands**, **bearing** this **seal**: "The **Lord knows those** who are his," and, "Let everyone who **names** the name of the Lord **depart** from iniquity." (ESV)

Solution on Page 317

No Quarrels about Words

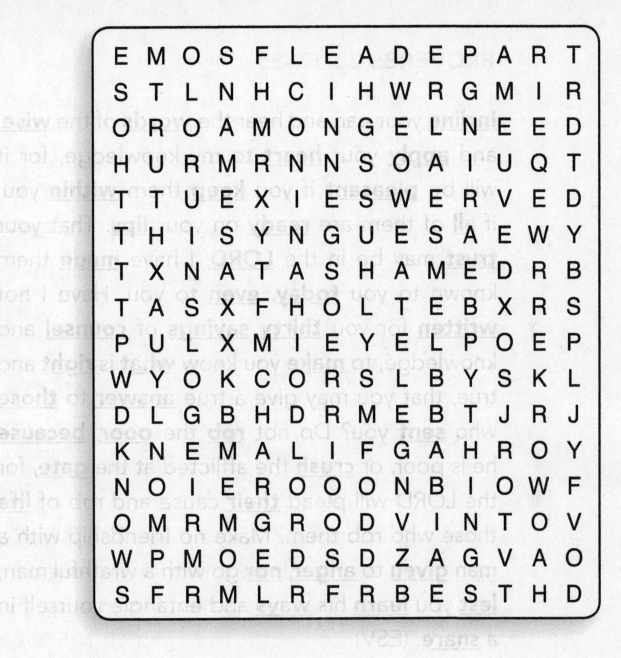

```
E M O S F L E A D E P A R T
S T L N H C I H W R G M I R
O R O A M O N G E L N E E D
H U R M R N N S O A I U Q T
T T U E X I E S W E R V E D
T H I S Y N G U E S A E W Y
T X N A T A S H A M E D R B
T A S X F H O L T E B X R S
P U L X M I E Y E L P O E P
W Y O K C O R S L B Y S K L
D L G B H D R M E B T J R J
K N E M A L I F G A H R O Y
N O I E R O O O N B I O W F
O M R M G R O D V I N T O V
W P M O E D S D Z A G V A O
S F R M L R F R B E S T H D
```

Solution on Page 318

PROVERBS 22:17–25

Incline your ear, and hear the **words** of the **wise**, and **apply** your **heart** to my knowledge, for it will be **pleasant** if you **keep** them **within** you, if **all** of them are **ready** on your **lips**. That your **trust** may be in the **LORD**, I have **made** them known to you **today**, **even** to you. Have I not **written** for you **thirty** **sayings** of **counsel** and knowledge, to **make** you know **what** is **right** and true, that you may give a true **answer** to **those** who **sent** you? Do not **rob** the **poor**, **because** he is poor, or **crush** the afflicted at the **gate**, for the LORD will plead **their** cause and rob of **life** those who rob them. Make no friendship with a man **given** to **anger**, **nor** go with a wrathful man, **lest** you **learn** his **ways** and entangle yourself in a **snare**. (ESV)

Solution on Page 318

```
S Q I I M N R A E L S P Y W
U D S A Y I N G S D L L R O
O K K Z D K W J U E I I G R
E E L R E W S N A N T P A D
B P R E G N A S C T E S T S
C N M S S P A L E N E V E Y
Z S Y Y P N I N B D H S I R
T O A L T N U N I O A S I G
P W Y H E R J O F H R M H W
O P E R E T I R C S T E S P
O I P A S M E H N U A I O L
R K D U P P D A T R W X W Y
U Y R W S E R R T C I J A A
W T H O S E S S O A C G T D
O A M T I K E F I L Z I H O
T Q L U N L F W W L S E N T
```

Solution on Page 318

MATTHEW 6:25–29

Therefore I **say unto** you, be not **anxious** for **your life**, **what** ye **shall eat**, or what ye shall **drink**; **nor** yet for your **body**, what ye shall put on. Is not the life more than the **food**, and the body than the **raiment**? **Behold** the **birds** of the heaven, that they sow not, **neither** do they **reap**, nor **gather into barns**; and your heavenly **Father feedeth** them. Are not ye of **much** more **value** then they? And **which** of you by **being** anxious **can add one cubit** unto the **measure** of his life? And why are ye anxious concerning raiment? Consider the **lilies** of the **field**, how they **grow**; they **toil** not, neither do they **spin**: yet I say unto you, that **even Solomon** in all his **glory** was not **arrayed** like one of these. (ASV)

Solution on Page 318

Be Not Anxious

```
J L S U R H X C P B O Z R L
P M V E N O T E G N I E B L
Z Q A B B Y C H Q H R G A
M P L L G U S D T T F U D H
Y W U Z B O R U I E L S R S
A S E I L I L E O I D A O O
S G T O N I N T O I I E D L
P L M K E F R T B M X M E I
I O Y G V I H E E J S N Y F
N R D I E S V N H H N T A E
O Y D G P Q T C O T R G R J
R D R P A F I E L D A E R M
A O U Q W H A T D T B F A B
W B W L W C A N H O T N U T
T I S K C U Z E I Y O U R Y
N G Q S T M R W V S R F E T
```

Solution on Page 318

LUKE 13:22–27

Jesus **went** **through** the towns and **villages**, **teaching** as he went, **always** **pressing** on toward **Jerusalem**. **Someone** **asked** him, "Lord, will **only** a **few** be saved?" He **replied**, "Work **hard** to **enter** the **narrow** **door** to God's **Kingdom**, for **many** will **try** to enter but will **fail**. When the **master** of the **house** has **locked** the door, it will be too **late**. You will **stand** **outside** **knocking** and **pleading**, 'Lord, **open** the door for us!' But he will reply, 'I don't know you or **where** you **come** **from**.' Then you will **say**, 'But we ate and **drank** with you, and you **taught** in our streets.' And he will reply, 'I **tell** you, I don't know you or where you come from. Get **away** from me, all you who do evil.'" (NLT)

Solution on Page 318

The Narrow Door

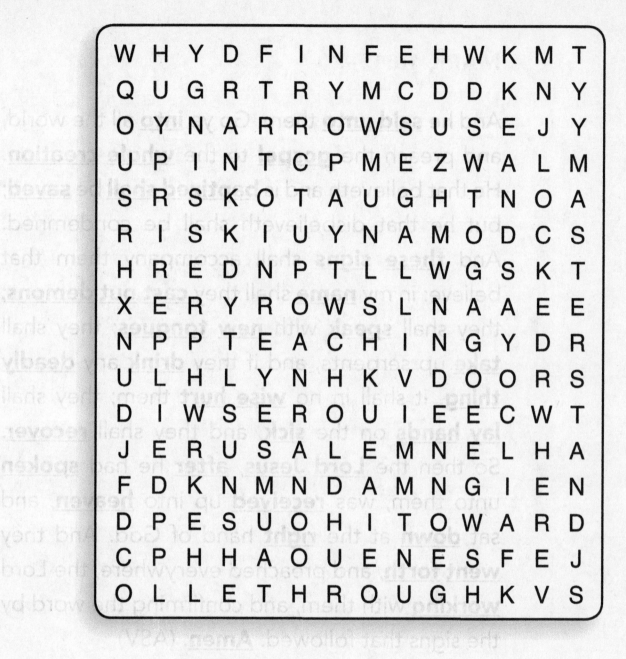

```
W H Y D F I N F E H W K M T
Q U G R T R Y M C D D K N Y
O Y N A R R O W S U S E J Y
U P I N T C P M E Z W A L M
S R S K O T A U G H T N O A
R I S K I U Y N A M O D C S
H R E D N P T L L W G S K T
X E R Y R O W S L N A A E E
N P P T E A C H I N G Y D R
U L H L Y N H K V D O O R S
D I W S E R O U I E E C W T
J E R U S A L E M N E L H A
F D K N M N D A M N G I E N
D P E S U O H I T O W A R D
C P H H A O U E N E S F E J
O L L E T H R O U G H K V S
```

Solution on Page 318

MARK 16:15–20

And he **said unto** them, Go ye **into** all the world, and preach the **gospel** to the **whole creation**. He that believeth and is **baptized shall** be **saved**; but he that disbelieveth shall be condemned. And **these signs** shall accompany them that believe: in my **name** shall they **cast out demons**; they shall **speak** with **new tongues**; they shall **take** up serpents, and if they **drink** any **deadly thing**, it shall in no **wise hurt** them; they shall **lay hands** on the **sick**, and they shall **recover**. So then the **Lord Jesus**, **after** he had **spoken** unto them, was **received** up into **heaven**, and sat **down** at the **right** hand of God. And they **went forth**, and preached everywhere, the Lord **working** with them, and confirming the word by the signs that followed. **Amen**. (ASV)

Solution on Page 318

Go Into the World

```
L W K C I S O G N I K R O W
K P A C R Y T O N G U E S W
D A F D E E L B O H U V H L
V S T S B A A D D E M O N S
A N E K O P S T A E L C D A
L H R K T D E V I E C E R V
T K S I G N S E P O D R I E
X A Z H Z A E S M S M S N D
N E V A E H O M L A Y W K F
D P G N T G T V A I N T O F
O S B D W H U R T D W Q G D
H J E S U S I U O O I W I R
G M C F I G O N E F S E K O
H L L A H S D K G W E N T L
K U U T S G A A W R N N A U
S L Y D V T K M I S U Y X T
```

Solution on Page 319

MATTHEW 10:1–7

And when he had **called unto** him his **twelve** disciples, he **gave** them **power** against unclean spirits, to **cast** them **out**, and to heal all **manner** of sickness and all manner of disease. Now the **names** of the twelve apostles are **these**; the **first**, **Simon**, who is called **Peter**, and **Andrew** his brother; **James** the **son** of Zebedee, and **John** his brother; **Philip**, and Bartholomew; **Thomas**, and **Matthew** the publican; James the son of Alphaeus, and Lebbaeus, **whose surname** was Thaddaeus; Simon the Canaanite, and **Judas** Iscariot, who **also** betrayed him. These twelve **Jesus sent forth**, and commanded them, **saying**, Go not **into** the **way** of the Gentiles, and into any **city** of the Samaritans **enter** ye not: But go **rather** to the **lost sheep** of the **house** of **Israel**. And as ye go, **preach**, saying, The kingdom of **heaven** is at **hand**. (KJV)

Instructions to the Apostles

```
B G Y H P E X E O A L S O G
W G N E C I T Y P I L I H P
H T E I J A S H Y E O M H M
O H V N Y A E U A V S O Q P
S W A T M A M R S L T N R G
E Z E O N O S E P E N T E R
F O H H X I U H S W J Z W I
O T O Y T F R T O T C N O A
E J A J O T N A S U S P P C
F W E R D N A R A R S A R H
S T T M G B M M D M I E C Z
H H C A L L E D U A T F H N
W E U N A M E S J E V A G K
B S E N T M D X P C N G Q O
K E O E T W Y Z W D G I S J
D C K R N O S P K Q L O H I
```

Solution on Page 319

2 TIMOTHY 3:12–17

Those who try to **live** a **godly** **life** **because** they **believe** in **Christ** **Jesus** will be persecuted. But **evil** **people** and **phony** preachers will go **from** **bad** to **worse** as they mislead people and are themselves **misled**. **However**, continue in **what** you have **learned** and **found** to be true. You know who **your** teachers were. From **infancy** you have **known** the **Holy** Scriptures. They have the **power** to **give** you **wisdom** so that you **can** be **saved** **through** **faith** in Christ Jesus. **Every** Scripture **passage** is inspired by God. **All** of them are **useful** for teaching, pointing **out** **errors**, correcting people, and training them for a life that has God's approval. They **equip** God's servants so that they are completely **prepared** to do **good** **things**. (GW)

Solution on Page 319

The Power of Scripture

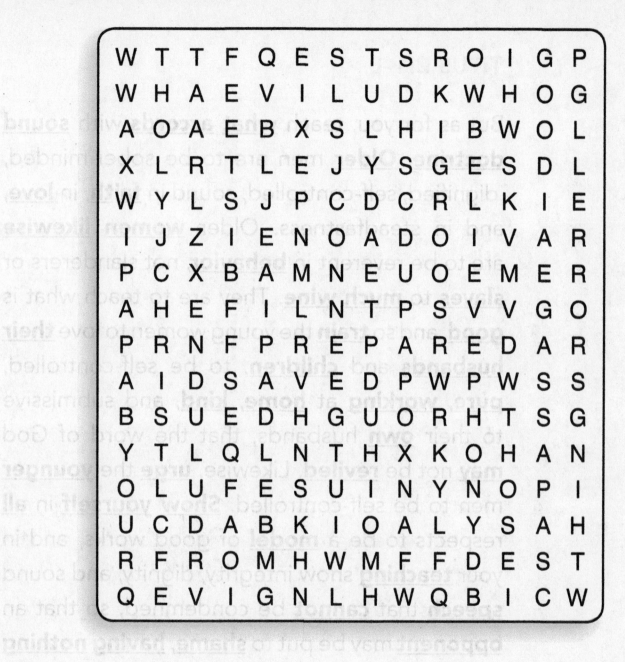

```
W T T F Q E S T S R O I G P
W H A E V I L U D K W H O G
A O A E B X S L H I B W O L
X L R T L E J Y S G E S D L
W Y L S J P C D C R L K I E
I J Z I E N O A D O I V A R
P C X B A M N E U O E M E R
A H E F I L N T P S V V G O
P R N F P R E P A R E D A R
A I D S A V E D P W P W S S
B S U E D H G U O R H T S G
Y T L Q L N T H X K O H A N
O L U F E S U I N Y N O P I
U C D A B K I O A L Y S A H
R F R O M H W M F F D E S T
Q E V I G N L H W Q B I C W
```

Solution on Page 319

TITUS 2:1–8

But as for you, teach **what accords** with **sound doctrine**. **Older** men are to be sober-minded, dignified, self-controlled, sound in **faith**, in **love**, and in steadfastness. Older **women likewise** are to be reverent in **behavior**, not slanderers or **slaves** to **much wine**. They are to teach what is **good**, and so **train** the young women to love **their husbands** and **children**, to be self-controlled, **pure**, **working** at **home**, **kind**, and submissive to their **own** husbands, that the word of God **may** not be **reviled**. Likewise, **urge** the **younger** men to be self-controlled. **Show yourself** in **all** respects to be a **model** of good works, and in your **teaching** show integrity, dignity, and sound **speech** that **cannot** be condemned, so that an **opponent** may be put to **shame**, **having nothing** evil to **say about** us. (ESV)

Solution on Page 319

Teach Sound Doctrine

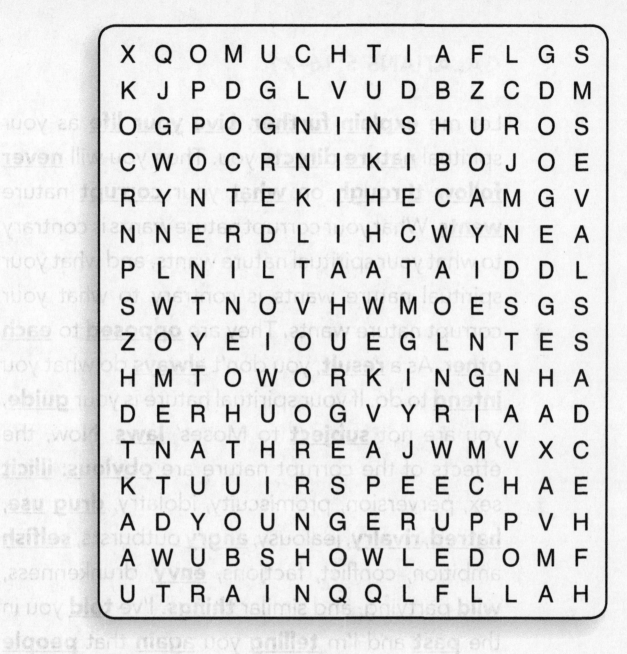

```
X Q O M U C H T I A F L G S
K J P D G L V U D B Z C D M
O G P O G N I N S H U R O S
C W O C R N I K I B O J O E
R Y N T E K I H E C A M G V
N N E R D L I H C W Y N E A
P L N I L T A A T A I D D L
S W T N O V H W M O E S G S
Z O Y E I O U E G L N T E S
H M T O W O R K I N G N H A
D E R H U O G V Y R I A A D
T N A T H R E A J W M V X C
K T U U I R S P E E C H A E
A D Y O U N G E R U P P V H
A W U B S H O W L E D O M F
U T R A I N Q Q L F L L A H
```

Solution on Page 319

GALATIANS 5:16–21

Let me **explain further**. **Live your life** as your spiritual **nature directs** you. Then you will **never follow through** on **what** your **corrupt** nature **wants**. What your corrupt nature wants is contrary to what your spiritual nature wants, and what your spiritual nature wants is contrary to what your corrupt nature wants. They are **opposed** to **each other**. As a **result**, you don't **always** do what you **intend** to do. If your spiritual nature is your **guide**, you are not **subject** to Moses' **laws**. Now, the effects of the corrupt nature are **obvious**: **illicit** sex, perversion, promiscuity, idolatry, **drug use**, **hatred**, **rivalry**, jealousy, **angry** outbursts, **selfish** ambition, conflict, factions, **envy**, drunkenness, **wild** partying, and similar **things**. I've **told** you in the **past** and I'm **telling** you **again** that **people** who do these kinds of things will not **inherit** the kingdom of **God**. (GW)

Solution on Page 319

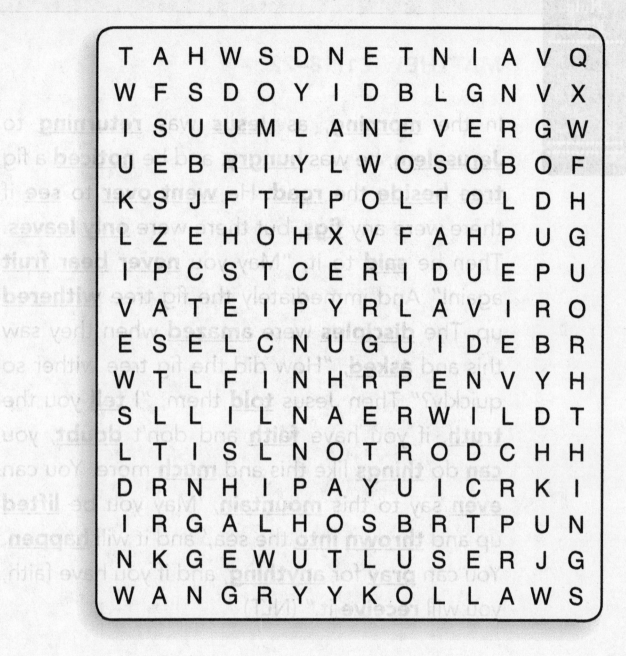

```
T A H W S D N E T N I A V Q
W F S D O Y I D B L G N V X
I S U U M L A N E V E R G W
U E B R I Y L W O S O B O F
K S J F T T P O L T O L D H
L Z E H O H X V F A H P U G
I P C S T C E R I D U E P U
V A T E I P Y R L A V I R O
E S E L C N U G U I D E B R
W T L F I N H R P E N V Y H
S L L I L N A E R W I L D T
L T I S L N O T R O D C H H
D R N H I P A Y U I C R K I
I R G A L H O S B R T P U N
N K G E W U T L U S E R J G
W A N G R Y Y K O L L A W S
```

Solution on Page 320

Holy
Bible

MATTHEW 21:18–22

In the **morning**, as **Jesus** was **returning** to **Jerusalem**, he was **hungry**, and he **noticed** a fig **tree** **beside** the **road**. He **went** **over** to **see** if there were any **figs**, but there were **only** **leaves**. Then he **said** to it, "May you **never** **bear** **fruit** again!" And immediately the fig tree **withered** up. The **disciples** were **amazed** when they saw this and **asked**, "How did the fig tree wither so quickly?" Then Jesus **told** them, "I **tell** you the **truth**, if you have **faith** and don't **doubt**, you **can** do **things** like this and **much** more. You can **even** say to this **mountain**, 'May you be **lifted** up and **thrown** **into** the sea,' and it will **happen**. You can **pray** for **anything**, and if you have faith, you will **receive** it." (NLT)

Solution on Page 320

Faith to Move Mountains

Q E S H O C R W E N T V S K
T E F U A D N E V E R E V O
E R A N U W F R U I T N F T
K T I G O D E R E H T I W T
M R T R N C Y L N O G A Q Q
H U H Y E I E Y L S N T S F
U T C I M A N Y T H I N G B
O H V H V E A R D I N U N E
S E C E D R L G O O R O I J
A E S I P O Y A T M U M H V
I W S X C B H I S D T B T H
D E T F I L C A S U E E T Q
B A M A Z E D U P L R K L U
G N O W D I S C I P L E S L
A Q N R B E A R E V E N J A
K V A P J V O D L O T N I C

Solution on Page 320

1 TIMOTHY 6:12–16

Fight the **good** fight of the **faith**. **Take** **hold** of the **eternal** **life** to **which** you were **called** and **about** which you **made** the good confession in the **presence** of **many** witnesses. I **charge** you in the presence of God, who **gives** life to all **things**, and of **Christ Jesus**, who in his testimony **before Pontius Pilate** made the good confession, to **keep** the commandment unstained and **free from** reproach **until** the appearing of our Lord Jesus Christ, which he will **display** at the **proper** time—he who is the **blessed** and **only** Sovereign, the King of **kings** and Lord of **lords**, who **alone** has immortality, who **dwells** in unapproachable **light**, **whom** no one has **ever** **seen** or can see. To him be **honor** and eternal **dominion**. **Amen**. (ESV)

The Good Fight of Faith

```
A W Y F P A E F F U P H E Z
P D K I N G S R R E N K F A
J O Q G W H O M E O A T A H
U M N H A M H K E T N G I O
X I T T W C P Y J S A O T L
O N Q U I R J L S I S L H D
D I V H O U P U L R S I I O
L O W P G B S V I H A G N P
O N E I B E A D F C Y H G P
R R V T J L I V E H N T S Q
D E C N E S E R P A A N H L
S O U A P R O S F R M A D E
E E O L L F N N S G E V E R
E C A G E L N A L E N O L A
N Y U B I Y E J L Y D Z B R
H L S L L E W D I J N H R Y
```

Solution on Page 320

ROMANS 14:1–5

As for the one who is **weak** in **faith**, welcome him, but not to **quarrel** **over** **opinions**. One **person** **believes** he may eat **anything**, **while** the weak person **eats** **only** **vegetables**. Let not the one who eats **despise** the one who **abstains**, and let not the one who abstains **pass** **judgment** on the one who eats, for **God** has **welcomed** him. Who are you to pass judgment on the **servant** of **another**? It is **before** his **own** **master** that he **stands** or **falls**. And he will be **upheld**, for the **Lord** is able to **make** him stand. One person **esteems** one day as **better** than another, while another esteems all **days** **alike**. **Each** one **should** be **fully** **convinced** in his own **mind**. (ESV)

Do Not Judge Faith

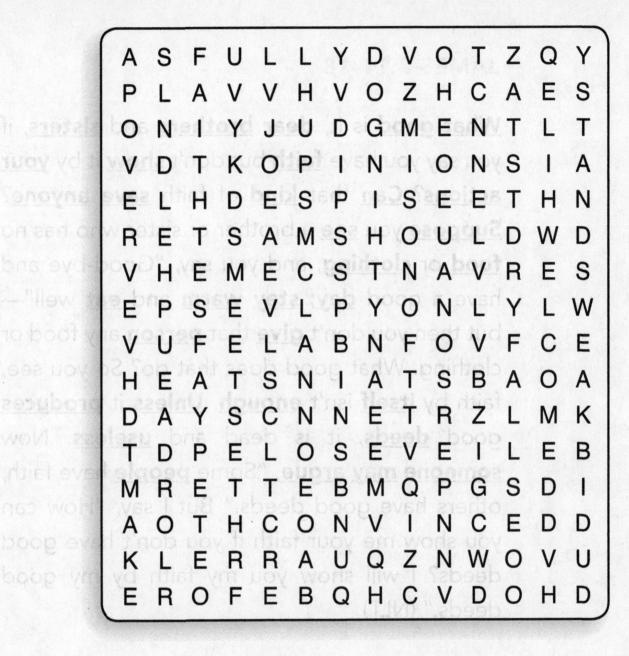

```
A  S  F  U  L  L  Y  D  V  O  T  Z  Q  Y
P  L  A  V  V  H  V  O  Z  H  C  A  E  S
O  N  I  Y  J  U  D  G  M  E  N  T  L  T
V  D  T  K  O  P  I  N  I  O  N  S  I  A
E  L  H  D  E  S  P  I  S  E  E  T  H  N
R  E  T  S  A  M  S  H  O  U  L  D  W  D
V  H  E  M  E  C  S  T  N  A  V  R  E  S
E  P  S  E  V  L  P  Y  O  N  L  Y  L  W
V  U  F  E  L  A  B  N  F  O  V  F  C  E
H  E  A  T  S  N  I  A  T  S  B  A  O  A
D  A  Y  S  C  N  N  E  T  R  Z  L  M  K
T  D  P  E  L  O  S  E  V  E  I  L  E  B
M  R  E  T  T  E  B  M  Q  P  G  S  D  I
A  O  T  H  C  O  N  V  I  N  C  E  D  D
K  L  E  R  R  A  U  Q  Z  N  W  O  V  U
E  R  O  F  E  B  Q  H  C  V  D  O  H  D
```

Solution on Page 320

JAMES 2:14–18

What **good** is it, **dear** **brothers** and **sisters**, if you say you have **faith** but don't **show** it by **your** **actions**? **Can** that **kind** of faith **save** **anyone**? **Suppose** you **see** a brother or sister who has no **food** or **clothing**, and you say, "Good-bye and have a good **day**; **stay** **warm** and **eat** well"—but then you don't **give** that **person** any food or clothing. What good does that do? So you see, faith by **itself** isn't **enough**. **Unless** it **produces** good **deeds**, it is dead and **useless**. Now **someone** **may** **argue**, "Some **people** have faith; others have good deeds." But I say, "How can you show me your faith if you don't have good deeds? I will show you my faith by my good deeds." (NLT)

Solution on Page 320

Faith Without Deeds

```
A P J O F P H G W W U Q P H
A E F S D L N G E M O P Q T
H D U O R I E C U V N D W I
B R O T H E R S N O I T C A
G G G T S M T H C N G O F
P R O D U C E S A I B E T C
U L I F P Y H N I W A R M T
C V P E P A A M O S A V E D
L L U E O M S D E E D S V E
U S V S S S W G D L M N N U
Z O K P E O P L E F O O D G
M I I L H L I R U O Y S S R
T G N S W I E T J N A R T A
Z U D D X D A S A J T E R I
O Z R P P E K J S H S P U K
Q D V W B K M M G J W C Y V
```

Solution on Page 321

ROMANS 1:17–21

For **therein** is the righteousness of God **revealed from faith** to faith: as it is **written**, the **just shall live** by faith. For the **wrath** of God is revealed from **heaven against** all ungodliness and unrighteousness of **men**, who **hold** the **truth** in unrighteousness; **Because** that **which** may be **known** of God is **manifest** in them; for God **hath shewed** it **unto** them. For the invisible **things** of him from the **creation** of the **world** are **clearly seen**, **being** understood by the things that are **made**, **even** his **eternal power** and **Godhead**; so that they are **without excuse**: Because that, when they **knew** God, they glorified him not as God, **neither** were **thankful**; but became **vain** in their imaginations, and their **foolish** heart was **darkened**. (KJV)

Solution on Page 321

Live by Faith

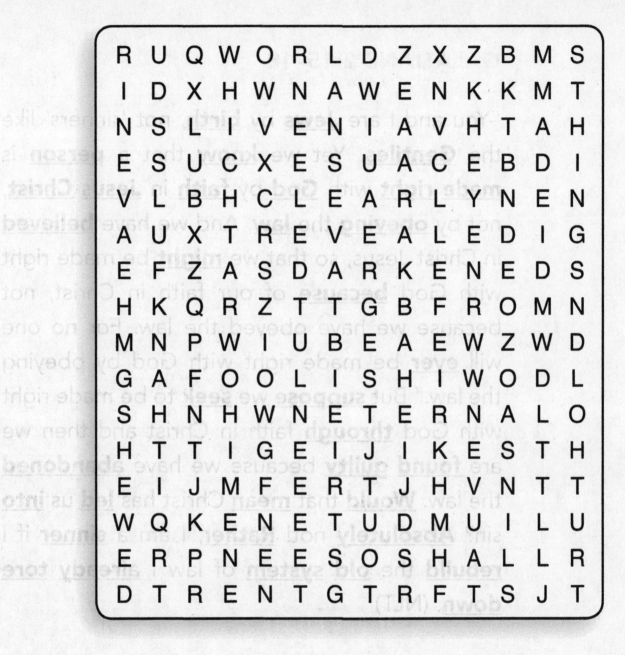

R U Q W O R L D Z X Z B M S
I D X H W N A W E N K K M T
N S L I V E N I A V H T A H
E S U C X E S U A C E B D I
V L B H C L E A R L Y N E N
A U X T R E V E A L E D I G
E F Z A S D A R K E N E D S
H K Q R Z T T G B F R O M N
M N P W I U B E A E W Z W D
G A F O O L I S H I W O D L
S H N H W N E T E R N A L O
H T T I G E I J I K E S T H
E I J M F E R T J H V N T T
W Q K E N E T U D M U I L U
E R P N E E S O S H A L L R
D T R E N T G T R F T S J T

Solution on Page 321

GALATIANS 2:15–18

"You and I are **Jews** by **birth**, not 'sinners' like the **Gentiles**. Yet we **know** that a **person** is **made right** with **God** by **faith** in **Jesus Christ**, not by **obeying** the **law**. And we have **believed** in Christ Jesus, so that we **might** be made right with God **because** of our faith in Christ, not because we have obeyed the law. For no one will **ever** be made right with God by obeying the law." But **suppose** we **seek** to be made right with God **through** faith in Christ and then we are **found guilty** because we have **abandoned** the law. **Would** that **mean** Christ has **led** us **into** sin? **Absolutely** not! **Rather**, I am a **sinner** if I **rebuild** the **old system** of law I **already tore down**. (NLT)

Solution on Page 321

Faith in Jesus

```
I D N Q I X H T I A F W T Q
Z F W O N K R T J D H H J G
Y D L Y T X A M R L G E S A
L H Y T O C T E F I S D D C
K T I L S B H T M U B E T F
S M A I E F E S S B V S H H
S W I U L T R Y M E I D G L
X O R G I A U S I R E O I N
H L E U T P G L H N T A R L
J D N B N H E C O K G L G M
N W N O E B R D N S E R O E
K O I U G C N O W W B E D A
J U S M O A A E U Q O A S N
D L Q R B F J U X G M D E L
H D Q A E V E R S N H Y G A
X Z M S U P P O S E R O T S
```

Solution on Page 321

HEBREWS 11:6–9

And **without faith** it is impossible to **please** him, for **whoever would draw near** to God **must believe** that he **exists** and that he rewards **those** who **seek** him. By faith **Noah**, **being warned** by God concerning **events** as yet **unseen**, in reverent **fear** constructed an **ark** for the **saving** of his household. By this he condemned the **world** and **became** an heir of the righteousness that **comes** by faith. By faith **Abraham obeyed** when he was **called** to go out to a **place** that he was to **receive** as an inheritance. And he **went** out, not **knowing where** he was **going**. By faith he went to live in the **land** of **promise**, as in a foreign land, **living** in **tents** with **Isaac** and **Jacob**, **heirs** with him of the **same** promise. (ESV)

```
S S C Y P L A C E O T R X B
N O J I G B I S P L V Z E W
Y O A S N R E V E O H W G V
S N A J I M E C I S A A C X
E M T H O S E C A N L C R M
E X H C G P T W E M G A O T
K I C T W L H W S I E L N I
P H S R I E H W I S V L E D
K R A B R A H A M T G E E K
K R A E F S F R O N H D S W
W O U L D E H D R E E O N E
G G N I W O N K P V B D U N
D N X E S T S I X E V L F T
G N I V A S A S Y B B R D C
V R A E N U T E N T S O L Y
J A C O B M D E N R A W K S
```

Solution on Page 321

HEBREWS 11:24–28

It was by **faith** that **Moses**, when he **grew** up, **refused** to be **called** the son of Pharaoh's daughter. He **chose** to **share** the oppression of God's **people** **instead** of **enjoying** the fleeting pleasures of **sin**. He **thought** it was **better** to **suffer** for the **sake** of **Christ** than to **own** the treasures of **Egypt**, for he was **looking** **ahead** to his great **reward**. It was by faith that Moses **left** the **land** of Egypt, not **fearing** the king's **anger**. He **kept** **right** on **going** **because** he kept his **eyes** on the **one** who is invisible. It was by faith that Moses commanded the people of **Israel** to **keep** the Passover and to **sprinkle** **blood** on the doorposts so that the angel of **death** **would** not **kill** **their** firstborn **sons**. (NLT)

Solution on Page 321

The Faith of Moses

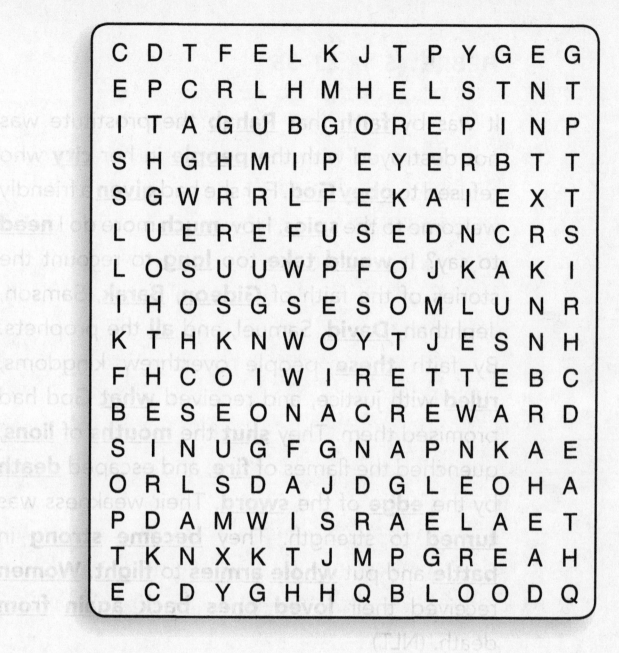

```
C D T F E L K J T P Y G E G
E P C R L H M H E L S T N T
I T A G U B G O R E P I N P
S H G H M I P E Y E R B T T
S G W R L F E K A I E X T
L U E R E F U S E D N C R S
L O S U U W P F O J K A K I
I H O S G S E S O M L U N R
K T H K N W O Y T J E S N H
F H C O I W I R E T T E B C
B E S E O N A C R E W A R D
S I N U G F G N A P N K A E
O R L S D A J D G L E O H A
P D A M W I S R A E L A E T
T K N X K T J M P G R E A H
E C D Y G H H Q B L O O D Q
```

Solution on Page 322

HEBREWS 11:31–35

It was by **faith** that **Rahab** the prostitute was not destroyed with the **people** in her **city** who refused to **obey God**. For she had **given** a friendly welcome to the **spies**. How **much** more do I **need** to say? It **would take** too **long** to recount the stories of the faith of **Gideon**, **Barak**, Samson, Jephthah, **David**, Samuel, and **all** the prophets. By faith **these** people overthrew kingdoms, **ruled** with justice, and received **what** God had promised them. They **shut** the **mouths** of **lions**, quenched the flames of **fire**, and escaped **death** by the **edge** of the **sword**. Their weakness was **turned** to strength. They **became strong** in **battle** and put **whole armies** to **flight**. **Women** received their **loved ones back again from** death. (NLT)

Solution on Page 222

The Power of Faith

```
H K C W H A T D E L U R H Y
B Z P M O N E S E H T T N K
Q U O Q Z M E D I V A D O G
D R O W S I E E C E O U V E
F B G A T B L N D V L L I Y
I A U N R P Y R E U Y O S G
L T Q O O H C U M V T E H W
F T E E N L P T E R I F L W
S L P D G E B W B P C G Q O
H E I I G S S A S K J F P U
T M I G S E H D C V V Y E L
U A I M H A W U U K U L C D
O C G H R T E Y T Y P Q C S
M E B A R A K B E A P Y R T
Y B H T I A F B E L K L A A
G R W J S N O I L L Z E M J
```

Solution on Page 322

JOHN 20:24–29

Thomas, **one** of the **twelve apostles**, who was **called Didymus**, wasn't with them when **Jesus came**. The **other** disciples **told** him, "We've **seen** the **Lord**." Thomas told them, "I **refuse** to **believe** this **unless** I see the **nail marks** in his **hands**, put my **fingers into** them, and put my hand into his **side**." A **week later** Jesus' disciples were **again** in the **house**, and Thomas was with them. **Even though** the **doors** were **locked**, Jesus stood **among** them and **said**, "Peace be with you!" Then Jesus said to Thomas, "Put **your** finger **here**, and **look** at my hands. **Take** your hand, and put it into my side. **Stop doubting**, and believe." Thomas **responded** to Jesus, "My Lord and my God!" Jesus said to Thomas, "You believe **because** you've seen me. **Blessed** are those who haven't seen me but believe." (GW)

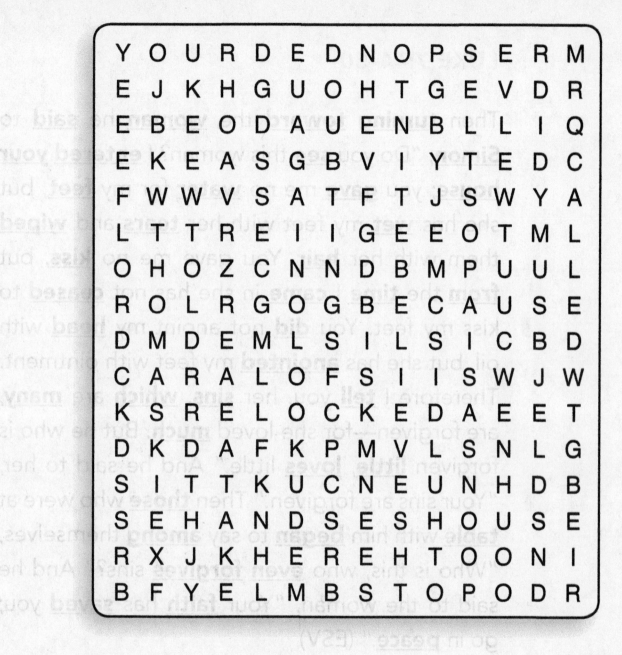

```
Y O U R D E D N O P S E R M
E J K H G U O H T G E V D R
E B E O D A U E N B L L I Q
E K E A S G B V I Y T E D C
F W W V S A T F T J S W Y A
L T T R E I I G E E O T M L
O H O Z C N N D B M P U U L
R O L R G O G B E C A U S E
D M D E M L S I L S I C B D
C A R A L O F S I I S W J W
K S R E L O C K E D A E E T
D K D A F K P M V L S N L G
S I T T K U C N E U N H D B
S E H A N D S E S H O U S E
R X J K H E R E H T O O N I
B F Y E L M B S T O P O D R
```

Solution on Page 322

LUKE 7:44–50

Then **turning** **toward** the **woman** he **said** to **Simon**, "Do you **see** this woman? I **entered** **your** **house**; you **gave** me no **water** for my **feet**, but she has **wet** my feet with her **tears** and **wiped** them with her **hair**. You gave me no **kiss**, but **from** the **time** I **came** in she has not **ceased** to kiss my feet. You **did** not anoint my **head** with oil, but she has **anointed** my feet with ointment. Therefore I **tell** you, her **sins**, **which** are **many**, are forgiven—for she loved **much**. But he who is forgiven **little**, **loves** little." And he said to her, "Your sins are forgiven." Then **those** who were at **table** with him **began** to say **among** themselves, "Who is this, who **even** **forgives** sins?" And he said to the woman, "Your **faith** has **saved** you; go in **peace**." (ESV)

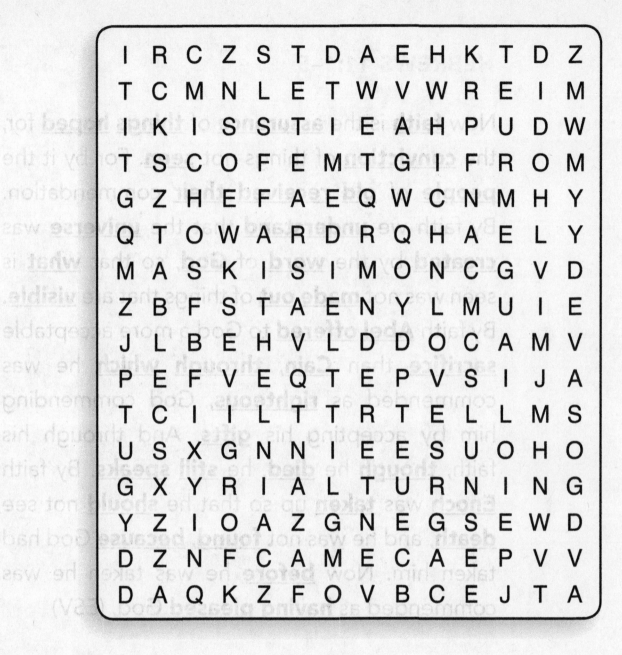

```
I R C Z S T D A E H K T D Z
T C M N L E T W V W R E I M
I K I S S T I E A H P U D W
T S C O F E M T G I F R O M
G Z H E F A E Q W C N M H Y
Q T O W A R D R Q H A E L Y
M A S K I S I M O N C G V D
Z B F S T A E N Y L M U I E
J L B E H V L D D O C A M V
P E F V E Q T E P V S I J A
T C I I L T T R T E L L M S
U S X G N N I E E S U O H O
G X Y R I A L T U R N I N G
Y Z I O A Z G N E G S E W D
D Z N F C A M E C A E P V V
D A Q K Z F O V B C E J T A
```

Solution on Page 322

HEBREWS 11:1–5

Now **faith** is the **assurance** of **things hoped** for, the **conviction** of things not **seen**. For by it the **people** of **old received their** commendation. By faith we **understand** that the **universe** was **created** by the **word** of **God**, so that **what** is seen was not **made out** of things that are **visible**. By faith **Abel offered** to God a more acceptable **sacrifice** than **Cain**, **through which** he was commended as **righteous**, God commending him by accepting his **gifts**. And through his faith, **though** he **died**, he **still speaks**. By faith **Enoch** was **taken** up so that he **should** not see **death**, and he was not **found**, **because** God had taken him. Now **before** he was taken he was commended as **having pleased** God. (ESV)

Solution on Page 322

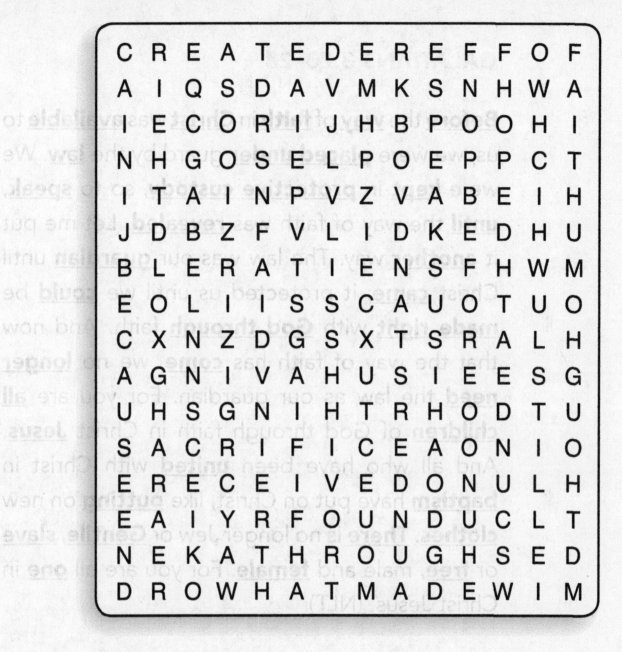

```
C R E A T E D E R E F F O F
A I Q S D A V M K S N H W A
I E C O R I J H B P O O H I
N H G O S E L P O E P P C T
I T A I N P V Z V A B E I H
J D B Z F V L I D K E D H U
B L E R A T I E N S F H W M
E O L I I S S C A U O T U O
C X N Z D G S X T S R A L H
A G N I V A H U S I E E S G
U H S G N I H T R H O D T U
S A C R I F I C E A O N I O
E R E C E I V E D O N U L H
E A I Y R F O U N D U C L T
N E K A T H R O U G H S E D
D R O W H A T M A D E W I M
```

GALATIANS 3:23–28

Before the **way** of **faith** in **Christ** was **available** to us, we were **placed under** guard by the **law**. We were **kept** in **protective custody**, so to **speak**, **until** the way of faith was **revealed**. Let me put it **another** way. The law was our **guardian** until Christ **came**; it protected us until we **could** be **made right** with **God through** faith. And now that the way of faith has **come**, we no **longer need** the law as our guardian. For you are **all children** of God through faith in Christ **Jesus**. And all who have been **united** with Christ in **baptism** have put on Christ, like **putting** on new **clothes**. **There** is no longer Jew or **Gentile**, **slave** or **free**, male and **female**. For you are all **one** in Christ Jesus. (NLT)

Solution on Page 323

Children of God Through Faith

```
T Y H H M S I T P A B B Z X
X G C S V P Y G D N E E D O
S E S D I S E H T O L C K N
G V W E C H R I S T G L A V
F A I T H R O U G H H I K G
Y L S I F E M A L E D T E G
K S W N C H I L D R E N P Y
I O R U J P R L A L T U T D
Z O N E C I L U B I M D E O
R H S F G G G A L A L L R T
F U R H E N L E C V A U O S
S E T D E I O P U E W O F U
E X A R A T N L V O D C E C
D M E V I T C E T O R P B O
I H A O P U R E D N U K Q M
T H T C S P E A K C X X R E
```

Solution on Page 323

EXODUS 2:3–6

When she couldn't **hide** him any **longer**, she **took** a **basket made** of **papyrus plants** and **coated** it with tar and **pitch**. She put the **baby** in it and set it **among** the papyrus plants **near** the **bank** of the **Nile River**. The baby's **sister stood** at a **distance** to see **what would happen** to him. **While** Pharaoh's **daughter came** to the Nile to **take** a **bath**, her servants **walked along** the bank of the river. She saw the basket among the papyrus plants and **sent** her **slave girl** to get it. Pharaoh's daughter **opened** the basket, **looked** at the baby, and saw it was a **boy**. He was **crying**, and she **felt sorry** for him. She **said**, "This is **one** of the **Hebrew** children." (GW)

The Baby in the Basket

```
O X W H A T S D A T L E F Y
Z Z W H T C L W M O Y H Z E
E L I N I U A Y O O I C K Y
H D Y K O L V K N K O Y O E
E E W W K W E C G S R B S T
A Q C E N D B P C R T A K E
I G D O R A I O O R R B C A
B E I W S B L S A E Y P V L
O P V K U A E I T S M I L O
D I E H R T Z H E A O O N N
O T P L Y H G N D B N E X G
B C R L P U T E A G P C R I
O H I C A D E N E P O S E R
W N V D P N K R A D C A M L
L N E A R G T H H G I I A E
A Z R E T S I S T O O D C L
```

Solution on Page 323

LUKE 3:15–20

And as the **people** were in expectation, and all **men** reasoned in their **hearts** concerning **John**, whether **haply** he were the **Christ**; John answered, **saying unto** them all, I **indeed** baptize you with **water**; but there **cometh** he that is mightier than I, the **latchet** of **whose shoes** I am not **worthy** to **unloose**: he **shall** baptize you in the **Holy Spirit** and in **fire**: whose **fan** is in his **hand**, thoroughly to cleanse his threshing-floor, and to **gather** the wheat **into** his **garner**; but the **chaff** he will **burn** up with unquenchable fire. With **many other** exhortations therefore preached he **good** tidings unto the people; but Herod the tetrarch, **being** reproved by him for Herodias his brother's **wife**, and for all the **evil things which** Herod had **done**, **added** this **also** to them all, that he **shut** up John in **prison**. (ASV)

Solution on Page 325

John the Baptist

A V V Z J I D R F D O N E W
D K V U B Z Q M E I B D S C
A C H P S H A L L U D O O G
Q R T L T S P I R I T V H U
Y R M D D O D N A H G U W M
C E E Y E N L O H A L N H R
E T N P D E S A T E N L I F
Q A T W D L D H T E M O C I
M W U H A E E N S C H O H R
Z N O S I R P T I A H S R E
J S W R Z N H U R S Y E V O
O Y I H T H G H H T N I T Z
H O F F A H C S C R L N N S
N O E P F Q Y V A A I O A G
Y J L B E I N G S E O H S F
F Y P Y U N T O T H E R C Q

Solution on Page 324

GENESIS 11:5–9

And the **LORD** **came** **down** to **see** the **city** and the **tower**, **which** the **children** of man had built. And the LORD **said**, "**Behold**, they are one **people**, and they have all one **language**, and this is **only** the **beginning** of **what** they will do. And **nothing** that they **propose** to do will now be **impossible** for them. **Come**, let us go down and there confuse their language, so that they **may** not **understand** one another's **speech**." So the LORD **dispersed** them **from** there **over** the **face** of all the **earth**, and they **left off building** the city. **Therefore** its **name** was **called** Babel, **because** there the LORD **confused** the language of all the earth. And from there the LORD dispersed them over the face of all the earth. (ESV)

Solution on Page 324

The Tower of Babel

O C R D I D W D O W N C W Q
B E Y E M A C A L L E D H T
F M T E L B I S S O P M I K
U A I H H S P E E C H U C U
P N C P E O P L E O M E H L
S X D E S R E P S I D G B U
G S E E I R E V O D I A S B
J W S F R O M F P N O U E A
U O U H W S E E O F F G M B
Q T F T F S T T R R I N O E
H L N R U O H A P N E A C L
L B O A W I Y L N O F L G E
G O C E N C H I L D R E N F
L E R G X G N I D L I U B T
B H E D I G T W X W H A T Y
E O Z B U X Z M A Y I R P T

Solution on Page 324

GENESIS 6:14–18

Make **yourself** an **ark** of **gopher** **wood**. Make **rooms** in the ark, and cover it **inside** and **out** with **pitch**. This is how you are to make it: the **length** of the ark 300 **cubits**, its **breadth** 50 cubits, and its **height** 30 cubits. Make a roof for the ark, and **finish** it to a cubit **above**, and set the **door** of the ark in its side. Make it with **lower**, **second**, and **third** **decks**. For **behold**, I will **bring** a **flood** of **waters** **upon** the **earth** to **destroy** all **flesh** in **which** is the breath of **life** **under** **heaven**. Everything that is on the earth **shall** **die**. But I will establish my **covenant** with you, and you shall **come** **into** the ark, you, your **sons**, your **wife**, and your sons' **wives** with you. (ESV)

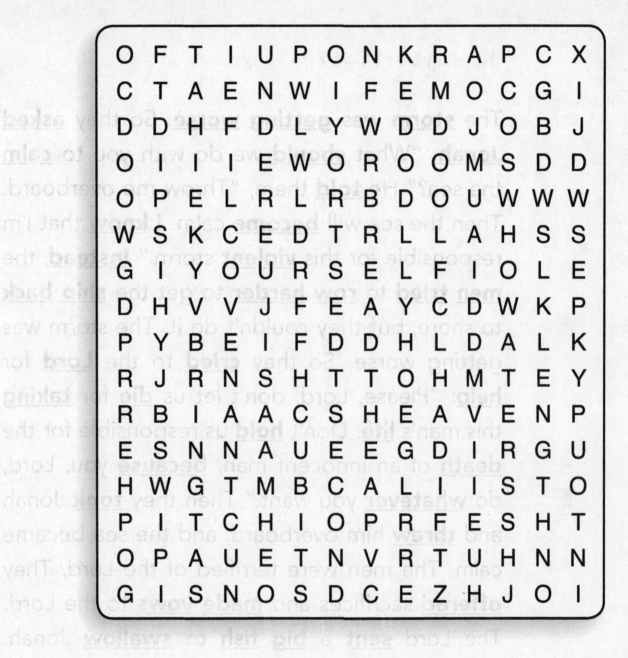

```
O F T I U P O N K R A P C X
C T A E N W I F E M O C G I
D D H F D L Y W D D J O B J
O I I E W O R O O M S D D
O P E L R L R B D O U W W W
W S K C E D T R L L A H S S
G I Y O U R S E L F I O L E
D H V V J F E A Y C D W K P
P Y B E I F D D H L D A L K
R J R N S H T T O H M T E Y
R B I A A C S H E A V E N P
E S N N A U E E G D I R G U
H W G T M B C A L I I S T O
P I T C H I O P R F E S H T
O P A U E T N V R T U H N N
G I S N O S D C E Z H J O I
```

JONAH 1:11–17

The **storm** was **getting worse**. So they **asked** Jonah, "What **should** we do with you to **calm** the sea?" He **told** them, "Throw me overboard. Then the sea will **become** calm. I **know** that I'm responsible for this **violent** storm." **Instead**, the **men tried** to **row harder** to get the **ship back** to shore, but they couldn't do it. The storm was getting worse. So they **cried** to the **Lord** for **help**: "Please, Lord, don't let us **die** for **taking** this man's **life**. Don't **hold** us responsible for the **death** of an innocent man, **because** you, Lord, do **whatever** you want." Then they **took** Jonah and **threw** him overboard, and the sea became calm. The men were terrified of the Lord. They **offered** sacrifices and **made vows** to the Lord. The Lord **sent** a **big fish** to **swallow** Jonah. Jonah was **inside** the fish for three **days** and three **nights**. (GW)

Solution on Page 324.

Jonah and the Whale

Then the **LORD** **rained** **upon** **Sodom** and upon Gomorrah brimstone and **fire** **from** the LORD **out** of **heaven**; And he overthrew **those** **cities**, and **all** the **plain**, and all the inhabitants of the cities, and that **which** **grew** upon the **ground**. But his **wife** **looked** **back** from **behind** him, and she **became** a **pillar** of **salt**. And **Abraham** **gat** up **early** in the **morning** to the place **where** he **stood** **before** the LORD: And he looked **toward** Sodom and Gomorrah, and toward all the **land** of the plain, and **beheld**, and, lo, the **smoke** of the **country** **went** up as the smoke of a **furnace**. And it came to **pass**, when God destroyed the cities of the plain, that God remembered Abraham, and **sent** Lot out of the **midst** of the overthrow, when he overthrew the cities in the which Lot **dwelt**. (KJV)

Sodom and Gomorrah

E B D A M E G G E M A C E B
I R R K H L E C T C O I O E
S T O O D R C C N U M T E H
D N L F M B A L N P O I A E
B E W B E O N T L L G E E L
M S F H A B R A H A M S N D
J I I M R Y U N X I M L V X
D N R U L S F S I N F O M M
D N E R P M B T D N U O R G
R E A V J O N A H T G K A F
A E N L A K N V C O S E L T
W S X I S E W E I K S D L R
O E S S A P H M H U E E I U
T I N C L R E R W P W D P M
A E I T T Y R M O D O S X W
G U E F I W E R G S S A C C

Solution on Page 325

JOSHUA 6:1–6

Jericho was **bolted** and **barred shut** because the **people** were **afraid** of the Israelites. No one **could enter** or **leave**. The **Lord said** to **Joshua**, "I am **about** to **hand** Jericho, its **king**, and its warriors **over** to you. All the soldiers will **march around** the **city once** a day for **six days**. Seven priests will **carry** rams' **horns ahead** of the ark. But on the seventh day you **must** march around the city seven **times while** the priests **blow their** horns. When you **hear** a **long blast** on the horn, all the **troops** must **shout very loudly**. The **wall** around the city will collapse. Then the troops must **charge** straight ahead **into** the city." Joshua, son of **Nun**, summoned the priests. He said to them, "Pick up the ark of the promise, and have seven priests carry seven rams' horns ahead of the Lord's ark." (GW)

The Battle of Jericho

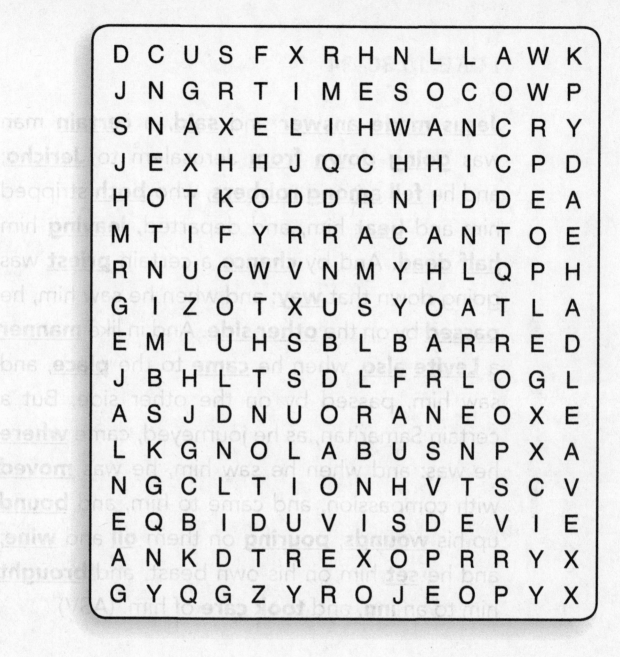

```
D C U S F X R H N L L A W K
J N G R T I M E S O C O W P
S N A X E L I H W A N C R Y
J E X H H J Q C H H I C P D
H O T K O D D R N I D D E A
M T I F Y R R A C A N T O E
R N U C W V N M Y H L Q P H
G I Z O T X U S Y O A T L A
E M L U H S B L B A R R E D
J B H L T S D L F R L O G L
A S J D N U O R A N E O X E
L K G N O L A B U S N P X A
N G C L T I O N H V T S C V
E Q B I D U V I S D E V I E
A N K D T R E X O P R R Y X
G Y Q G Z Y R O J E O P Y X
```

Solution on Page 325

LUKE 10:30–34

Jesus **made** **answer** and **said**, a **certain** man was **going** **down** **from** Jerusalem to **Jericho**; and he **fell** **among** **robbers**, who **both** stripped him and **beat** him, and departed, **leaving** him **half** **dead**. And by **chance** a certain **priest** was going down that **way**: and when he saw him, he **passed** by on the **other** **side**. And in like **manner** a **Levite** **also**, when he **came** to the **place**, and saw him, passed by on the other side. But a certain Samaritan, as he journeyed, came **where** he was: and when he saw him, he was **moved** with compassion, and came to him, and **bound** up his **wounds**, **pouring** on them **oil** and **wine**; and he **set** him on his own beast, and **brought** him to an **inn**, and **took** **care** of him. (ASV)

The Good Samaritan

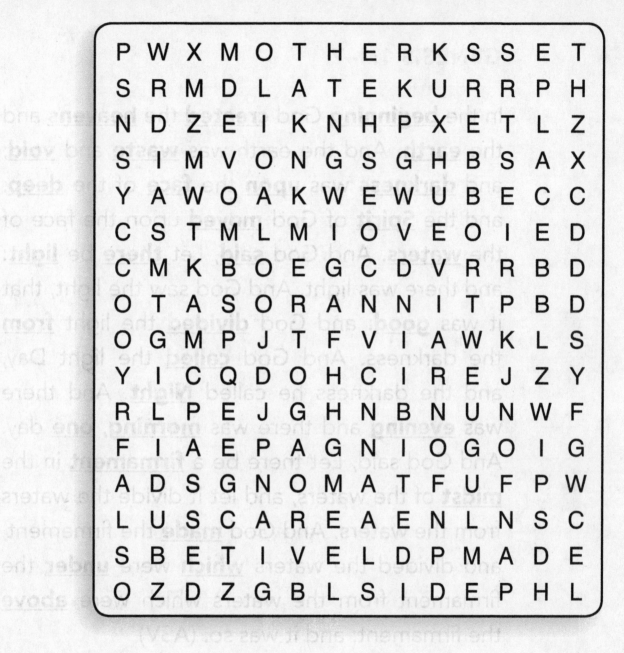

```
P W X M O T H E R K S S E T
S R M D L A T E K U R R P H
N D Z E I K N H P X E T L Z
S I M V O N G S G H B S A X
Y A W O A K W E W U B E C C
C S T M L M I O V E O I E D
C M K B O E G C D V R R B D
O T A S O R A N N I T P B D
O G M P J T F V I A W K L S
Y I C Q D O H C I R E J Z Y
R L P E J G H N B N U N W F
F I A E P A G N I O G O I G
A D S G N O M A T F U F P W
L U S C A R E A E N L N S C
S B E T I V E L D P M A D E
O Z D Z G B L S I D E P H L
```

Solution on Page 325

GENESIS 1:1–7

In the **beginning** God **created** the **heavens** and the **earth**. And the earth was **waste** and **void**; and **darkness** was **upon** the **face** of the **deep**: and the **Spirit** of God **moved** upon the face of the **waters**. And God **said**, Let **there** be **light**: and there was light. And God saw the light, that it was **good**: and God **divided** the light **from** the darkness. And God **called** the light Day, and the darkness he called **Night**. And there was **evening** and there was **morning**, **one** day. And God said, Let there be a **firmament** in the **midst** of the waters, and let it divide the waters from the waters. And God **made** the firmament, and divided the waters **which** were **under** the firmament from the waters which were **above** the firmament: and it was so. (ASV)

Creation

```
B M I M P A G T H L V Y U M
B R U Q R C S U F P E E D A
X B E G I N N I N G R R T D
F X E D D A R K N E S S O E
T R Q C N M D V H T N E Z T
C F O K A U F T D D E N P S
F R D M L F P M O E V O B A
E V E N I N G O L L A O B W
H N V A M X G R N S E V I X
T U O O T A D N G P H A Z D
R C M M D E D I V I D I T N
A Z X E L I D N S R E T A W
E M P L J C A G N I G H T S
G T A F B S Z S W T S G L Q
H C I H W L V P T S D I M F
J R F Q D M E R T P Y L C E
```

Solution on Page 325

MATTHEW 2:7–11

Then **Herod** summoned the **wise** **men** secretly and ascertained **from** them **what** **time** the **star** had appeared. And he **sent** them to Bethlehem, **saying**, "Go and **search** diligently for the **child**, and when you have **found** him, **bring** me word, that I too may **come** and worship him." **After** listening to the **king**, they **went** on **their** **way**. And behold, the star that they had **seen** when it **rose** went **before** them **until** it **came** to **rest** **over** the **place** **where** the child was. When they saw the star, they rejoiced exceedingly with **great** **joy**. And **going** **into** the **house** they saw the child with **Mary** his **mother**, and they **fell** **down** and worshiped him. Then, opening their treasures, they offered him **gifts**, **gold** and frankincense and **myrrh**. (ESV)

Solution on Page 328

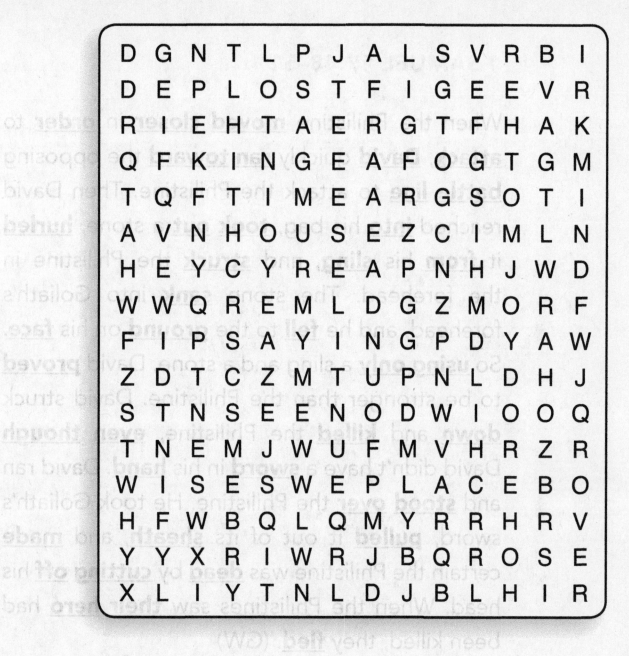

```
D G N T L P J A L S V R B I
D E P L O S T F I G E E V R
R I E H T A E R G T F H A K
Q F K I N G E A F O G T G M
T Q F T I M E A R G S O T I
A V N H O U S E Z C I M L N
H E Y C Y R E A P N H J W D
W W Q R E M L D G Z M O R F
F I P S A Y I N G P D Y A W
Z D T C Z M T U P N L D H J
S T N S E E N O D W I O O Q
T N E M J W U F M V H R Z R
W I S E S W E P L A C E B O
H F W B Q L Q M Y R R H R V
Y Y X R I W R J B Q R O S E
X L I Y T N L D J B L H I R
```

Solution on Page 326

1 SAMUEL 17:48–51

When the Philistine **moved closer** in **order** to **attack**, **David** quickly **ran toward** the opposing **battle line** to attack the Philistine. Then David reached **into** his bag, **took out** a stone, **hurled** it **from** his **sling**, and **struck** the Philistine in the forehead. The stone **sank** into Goliath's forehead, and he **fell** to the **ground** on his **face**. So **using only** a sling and a stone, David **proved** to be stronger than the Philistine. David struck **down** and **killed** the Philistine, **even though** David didn't have a **sword** in his **hand**. David ran and **stood over** the Philistine. He took Goliath's sword, **pulled** it out of its **sheath**, and **made** certain the Philistine was **dead** by **cutting off** his head. When the Philistines saw **their hero** had been killed, they **fled**. (GW)

David and Goliath

G J L E I S T N H K K S N H
Q N K H Y Z D S L I N G L Q
D G A L T A L P L A E A Y A
G N N R V A D L Y D V B S R
D O C I T D E V O M E L O F
E T D E T D L H X V L L F D
O R E H W T R O S E E U F I
T E A T R W U K F W B R N X
N V D E H F H C R A O D W E
I E D D U D L A T O C R O S
K R N O E O S T U H M E D Z
O A U V S L L T O D O O T S
O E O E L E L A R W P U R K
T R R G N I S U W U A G G F
P L G E K P N P P Y C R F H
M H B C M A D E X S O K D Q

Solution on Page 326

JUDGES 16:15–18

Delilah **said** to **Samson**, "How **can** you say that you **love** me when **your** **heart** isn't **mine**? You've **made** **fun** of me **three** **times** now, but you **still** haven't **told** me **what** **makes** you so strong." Every **day** she made his **life** miserable with her questions. She pestered him **until** he **wished** he were **dead**. **Finally**, he told her the **truth**. He told her, "Because I'm a Nazirite, no one has ever **cut** the **hair** on my head. I was dedicated to **God** **before** I was **born**. If my hair is ever **shaved** **off**, my strength will **leave** me. Then I'll be like any **other** man." When Delilah realized that he had told her everything, she **sent** a message to the Philistine **rulers**, "Come **here** **once** more." (She did this because Samson had told her everything.) So the Philistine rulers **arrived** with the **money** in **their** **hands**. (GW)

Solution on Page 326

Samson and Delilah

```
A V T E Z E Q V E J N B R X
J T H R E E Z S D I G Y E U
S Q B C A N I A A T C O Z B
A C M O N E Y E Q I D U O Y
M X L Y F S H A V E D R T J
S R E L U R A P H A N D S Q
O C Y L J B L S K R E N I M
N I G A R R I V E D T L W B
F G T N H W L R G S H P A M
Q L L I T S E R O F E B R A
H I N F M H D G T D I K I D
G T E U F E I B H O R O A E
O N V F F K S T E X L E H M
Y U O I N I U A R C D D U A
M U L H T R W H S E N T O A
Y W Q S T R Q W Z Z M O H G
```

Solution on Page 326

GENESIS 4:8–13

Cain **spoke** to **Abel** his **brother**. And when they were in the **field**, Cain **rose** up **against** his brother Abel and **killed** him. Then the **LORD** **said** to Cain, "**Where** is Abel **your** brother?" He said, "I do not **know**; am I my brother's **keeper**?" And the LORD said, "**What** have you **done**? The **voice** of your brother's **blood** is **crying** to me **from** the **ground**. And now you are **cursed** from the ground, **which** has **opened** its **mouth** to **receive** your brother's blood from your **hand**. When you **work** the ground, it **shall** no **longer** **yield** to you its **strength**. You shall be a **fugitive** and a **wanderer** on the **earth**." Cain said to the LORD, "My **punishment** is **greater** than I can **bear**." (ESV)

Solution on Page 326

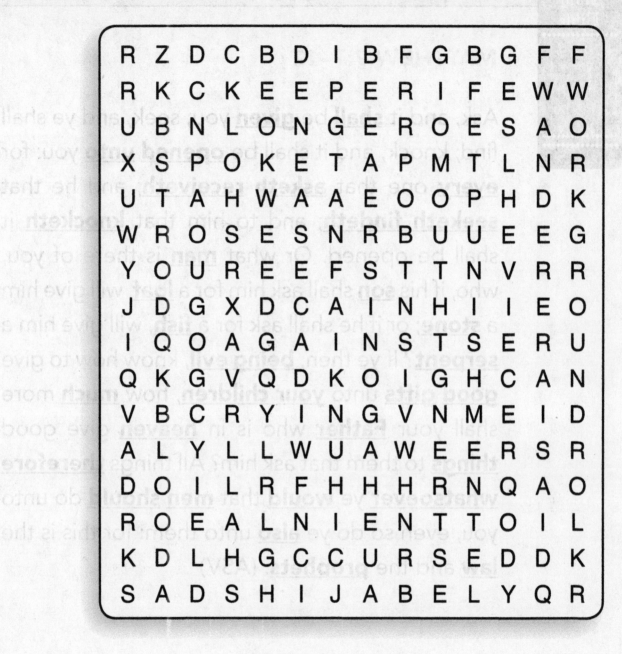

R Z D C B D I B F G B G F F
R K C K E E P E R I F E W W
U B N L O N G E R O E S A O
X S P O K E T A P M T L N R
U T A H W A A E O O P H D K
W R O S E S N R B U U E E G
Y O U R E E F S T T N V R R
J D G X D C A I N H I I E O
I Q O A G A I N S T S E R U
Q K G V Q D K O I G H C A N
V B C R Y I N G V N M E I D
A L Y L L W U A W E E R S R
D O I L R F H H H R N Q A O
R O E A L N I E N T T O I L
K D L H G C C U R S E D D K
S A D S H I J A B E L Y Q R

Solution on Page 326

MATTHEW 7:7–12

Ask, and it **shall** be **given** you; seek, and ye shall find; knock, and it shall be **opened** **unto** you: for **every** one that **asketh** **receiveth**; and he that **seeketh** **findeth**; and to him that **knocketh** it shall be opened. Or what **man** is there of you, who, if his **son** shall ask him for a **loaf**, will give him a **stone**; or if he shall ask for a **fish**, will give him a **serpent**? If ye then, **being** **evil**, know how to give **good** **gifts** unto **your** **children**, how **much** more shall your **Father** who is in **heaven** give good **things** to them that ask him? All things **therefore** **whatsoever** ye **would** that **men** **should** do unto you, even so do ye **also** unto them: for this is the **law** and the **prophets**. (ASV)

Ask and You Shall Receive

```
S P N O S H T E K S A N B G
D D E H S Q H C D X A L I B
W W R T O P E N E D E V S V
L A D E Y P R O P H E T S O
P K L D V R E P E N O T S K
G F I N D E F A A C Z S W E
G P H I G C O M T H I N G S
T A C F R E R S E E K E T H
Q N A U I I E A T Q W N Y A
X O O I V V F M A E M O L
L Y R E V E A U S P H X W L
H G V U N T C B R H V W T A
S F W M H H T E K C O N K T
L I V E Q P S I Q D L U O W
V S R N W U U N T O H K L U
N H G Q D O O G I F T S G D
```

Solution on Page 327

1 TIMOTHY 2:1–7

I **urge** you, **first** of **all**, to **pray** for all **people**. **Ask** God to **help** them; intercede on their **behalf**, and **give** **thanks** for them. Pray this way for **kings** and all who are in authority so that we **can** live peaceful and **quiet** **lives** **marked** by godliness and **dignity**. This is **good** and **pleases** God our **Savior**, who **wants** everyone to be saved and to understand the **truth**. For **there** is **only** one God and one **Mediator** who can reconcile God and humanity—the man **Christ** **Jesus**. He **gave** his **life** to purchase **freedom** for everyone. This is the **message** God gave to the **world** at **just** the **right** **time**. And I have been **chosen** as a preacher and **apostle** to **teach** the Gentiles this message **about** **faith** and truth. I'm not exaggerating—just **telling** the truth. (NLT)

Pray for All People

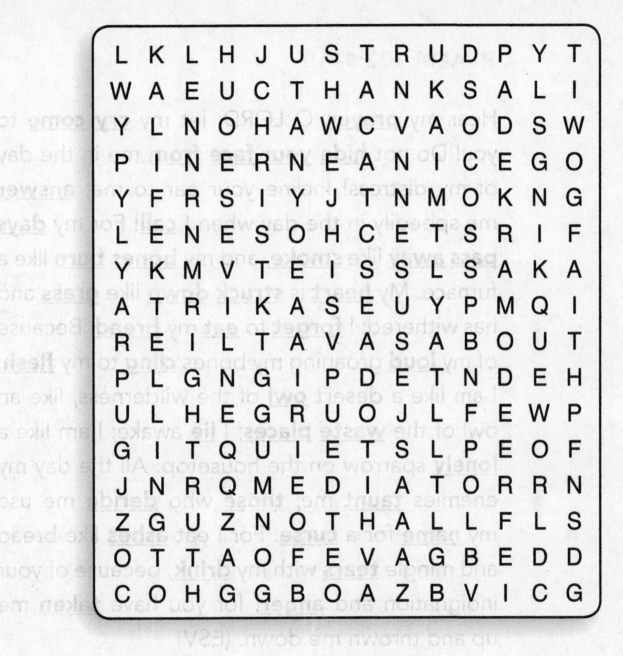

```
L K L H J U S T R U D P Y T
W A E U C T H A N K S A L I
Y L N O H A W C V A O D S W
P I N E R N E A N I C E G O
Y F R S I Y J T N M O K N G
L E N E S O H C E T S R I F
Y K M V T E I S S L S A K A
A T R I K A S E U Y P M Q I
R E I L T A V A S A B O U T
P L G N G I P D E T N D E H
U L H E G R U O J L F E W P
G I T Q U I E T S L P E O F
J N R Q M E D I A T O R R N
Z G U Z N O T H A L L F L S
O T T A O F E V A G B E D D
C O H G G B O A Z B V I C G
```

Solution on Page 327

PSALM 102:1–10

Hear my **prayer**, O LORD; let my **cry** **come** to you! Do not **hide** **your** **face** **from** me in the day of my distress! Incline your ear to me; **answer** me speedily in the day when I **call**! For my **days** **pass** **away** like **smoke**, and my **bones** **burn** like a furnace. My **heart** is **struck** **down** like **grass** and has withered; I **forget** to **eat** my **bread**. Because of my **loud** groaning my bones **cling** to my **flesh**. I am like a desert **owl** of the wilderness, like an owl of the **waste** **places**; I **lie** awake; I am like a **lonely** sparrow on the housetop. All the day my enemies **taunt** me; **those** who **deride** me use my **name** for a **curse**. For I eat **ashes** like bread and mingle **tears** with my **drink**, because of your indignation and **anger**; for you have **taken** me up and thrown me down. (ESV)

Prayer for the Afflicted

```
I K N S R I S T R U C K B J
F S L O U D A E R B P A L J
V A Q L M Y Y H R N K I I Y
F V C P L A C E S M O K E E
Z R K E R P G C T E S O H T
F U N P H N N R U B L F Z S
Y O I P A L A Y D N R F L A
L Y R B S E L A T O N O W W
E J D G H D Y A M Z W Y T O
A O Q I E S R U C L G N A K
N O D R S T E Y Y S U Q O Z
S E I A E G P A R A R V I E
W D R M N E K A T Q W A M U
E G O I O D E N S I R A Q S
R C L Y B T H R H S N X U A
Q C S R X S A P Z E W C Z A
```

Solution on Page 327

JAMES 1:5–11

If any of you **lacks wisdom**, let him **ask God**, who **gives** generously to all **without** reproach, and it will be given him. But let him ask in **faith**, with no **doubting**, for the **one** who doubts is like a **wave** of the **sea** that is **driven** and **tossed** by the **wind**. For that **person must** not **suppose** that he will **receive** anything **from** the **Lord**; he is a double-minded **man**, **unstable** in all his **ways**. Let the **lowly brother boast** in his exaltation, and the **rich** in his humiliation, **because** like a **flower** of the **grass** he will **pass away**. For the sun **rises** with its scorching **heat** and **withers** the grass; its flower **falls**, and its **beauty** perishes. So **also** will the rich man **fade** away in the **midst** of his pursuits. (ESV)

Solution on Page 327

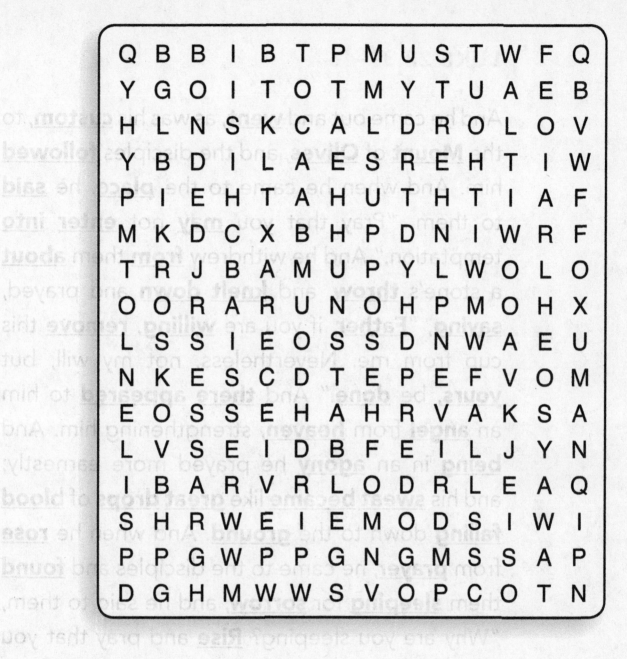

Q B B I B T P M U S T W F Q
Y G O I T O T M Y T U A E B
H L N S K C A L D R O L O V
Y B D I L A E S R E H T I W
P I E H T A H U T H T I A F
M K D C X B H P D N I W R F
T R J B A M U P Y L W O L O
O O R A R U N O H P M O H X
L S S I E O S S D N W A E U
N K E S C D T E P E F V O M
E O S S E H A H R V A K S A
L V S E I D B F E I L J Y N
I B A R V R L O D R L E A Q
S H R W E I E M O D S I W I
P P G W P P G N G M S S A P
D G H M W W S V O P C O T N

Solution on Page 327

LUKE 22:39–46

And he came out and **went**, as was his **custom**, to the **Mount** of **Olives**, and the disciples **followed** him. And when he came to the **place**, he **said** to them, "Pray that you **may** not **enter** **into** temptation." And he withdrew **from** them **about** a stone's **throw**, and **knelt** **down** and prayed, **saying**, "**Father**, if you are **willing**, **remove** this cup from me. Nevertheless, not my will, but **yours**, be **done**." And **there** **appeared** to him an **angel** from **heaven**, strengthening him. And **being** in an **agony** he prayed more earnestly; and his **sweat** **became** like **great** **drops** of **blood** **falling** down to the **ground**. And when he **rose** from **prayer**, he came to the disciples and **found** them **sleeping** for **sorrow**, and he said to them, "Why are you sleeping? **Rise** and pray that you may not enter into temptation." (ESV)

Prayer on the Mount of Olives

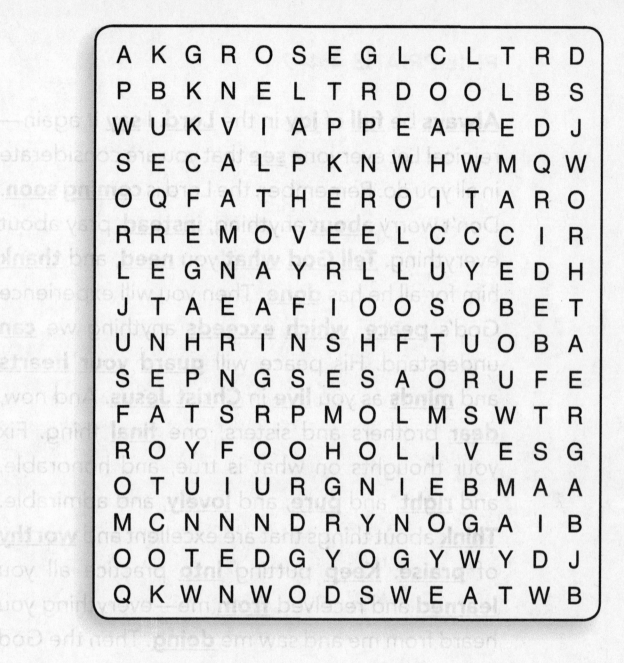

```
A K G R O S E G L C L T R D
P B K N E L T R D O O L B S
W U K V I A P P E A R E D J
S E C A L P K N W H W M Q W
O Q F A T H E R O I T A R O
R R E M O V E E L C C C I R
L E G N A Y R L L U Y E D H
J T A E A F I O O S O B E T
U N H R I N S H F T U O B A
S E P N G S E S A O R U F E
F A T S R P M O L M S W T R
R O Y F O O H O L I V E S G
O T U I U R G N I E B M A A
M C N N N D R Y N O G A I B
O O T E D G Y O G Y W Y D J
Q K W N W O D S W E A T W B
```

Solution on Page 328

PHILIPPIANS 4:4–9

Always be **full** of **joy** in the **Lord**. I **say** it again—rejoice! Let everyone **see** that you are considerate in all you do. Remember, the Lord is **coming soon**. Don't worry **about** anything; **instead**, pray about everything. **Tell God what** you **need**, and **thank** him for all he has **done**. Then you will experience God's **peace**, **which exceeds** anything we **can** understand. His peace will **guard your hearts** and **minds** as you **live** in **Christ Jesus**. And now, **dear** brothers and sisters, one **final** thing. Fix your thoughts on what is true, and honorable, and **right**, and **pure**, and **lovely**, and admirable. **Think** about things that are excellent and **worthy** of **praise**. **Keep** putting **into** practice all you **learned** and received **from** me—everything you heard from me and saw me **doing**. Then the God of peace will be with you. (NLT)

Solution on Page 328

Pray about Everything

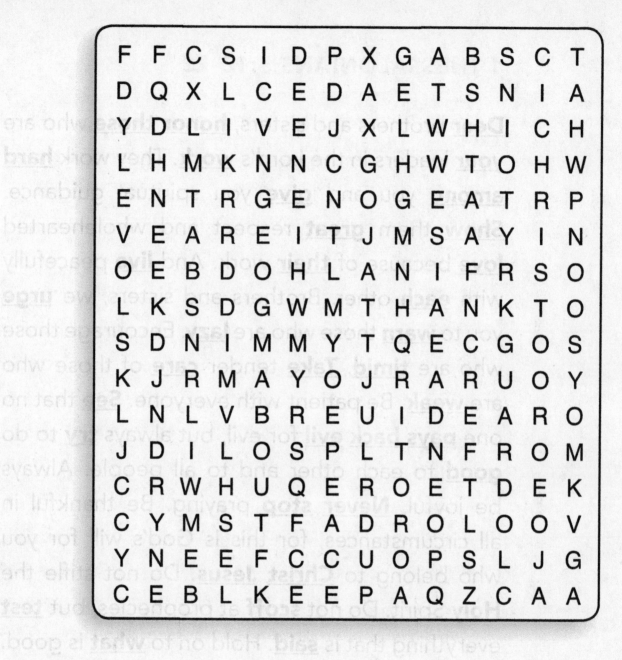

```
F F C S I D P X G A B S C T
D Q X L C E D A E T S N I A
Y D L I V E J X L W H I C H
L H M K N N C G H W T O H W
E N T R G E N O G E A T R P
V E A R E I T J M S A Y I N
O E B D O H L A N I F R S O
L K S D G W M T H A N K T O
S D N I M M Y T Q E C G O S
K J R M A Y O J R A R U O Y
L N L V B R E U I D E A R O
J D I L O S P L T N F R O M
C R W H U Q E R O E T D E K
C Y M S T F A D R O L O O V
Y N E E F C C U O P S L J G
C E B L K E E P A Q Z C A A
```

Solution on Page 328

1 THESSALONIANS 5:12–22

Dear brothers and sisters, **honor those** who are **your** leaders in the Lord's **work**. They work **hard among** you and **give** you spiritual guidance. **Show** them **great** respect and wholehearted **love** because of **their** work. And **live** peacefully with **each** other. Brothers and sisters, we **urge** you to **warn** those who are **lazy**. Encourage those who are **timid**. **Take** tender **care** of those who are **weak**. Be patient with everyone. **See** that no one **pays back evil** for evil, but always **try** to do **good** to each other and to all people. Always be joyful. **Never stop** praying. Be thankful in all circumstances, for this is God's will for you who belong to **Christ Jesus**. Do not stifle the **Holy** Spirit. Do not **scoff** at prophecies, but **test** everything that is **said**. Hold on to **what** is good. **Stay away from** every **kind** of evil. (NLT)

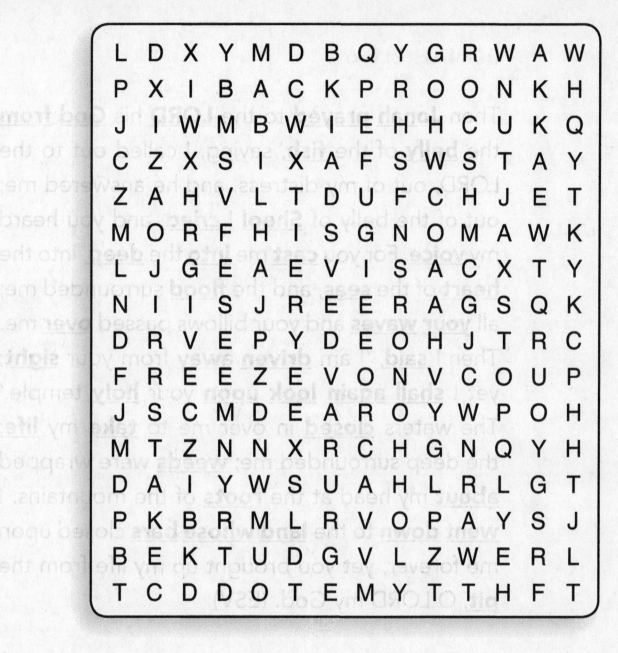

```
L D X Y M D B Q Y G R W A W
P X I B A C K P R O O N K H
J I W M B W I E H H C U K Q
C Z X S I X A F S W S T A Y
Z A H V L T D U F C H J E T
M O R F H I S G N O M A W K
L J G E A E V I S A C X T Y
N I I S J R E E R A G S Q K
D R V E P Y D E O H J T R C
F R E E Z E V O N V C O U P
J S C M D E A R O Y W P O H
M T Z N N X R C H G N Q Y H
D A I Y W S U A H L R L G T
P K B R M L R V O P A Y S J
B E K T U D G V L Z W E R L
T C D D O T E M Y T T H F T
```

Solution on Page 328

JONAH 2:1–6

Then **Jonah** **prayed** to the **LORD** his **God** **from** the **belly** of the **fish**, saying, I called out to the LORD, out of my distress, and he answered me; out of the belly of **Sheol** I **cried**, and you heard my **voice**. For you **cast** me **into** the **deep**, into the **heart** of the **seas**, and the **flood** surrounded me; all **your** **waves** and your billows passed **over** me. Then I **said**, 'I am **driven** **away** from your **sight**; yet I **shall** **again** **look** **upon** your **holy** temple.' The waters **closed** in over me to **take** my **life**; the deep surrounded me; **weeds** were wrapped **about** my head at the **roots** of the mountains. I **went** **down** to the **land** **whose** **bars** closed upon me forever; yet you brought up my life from the **pit**, O LORD my God. (ESV)

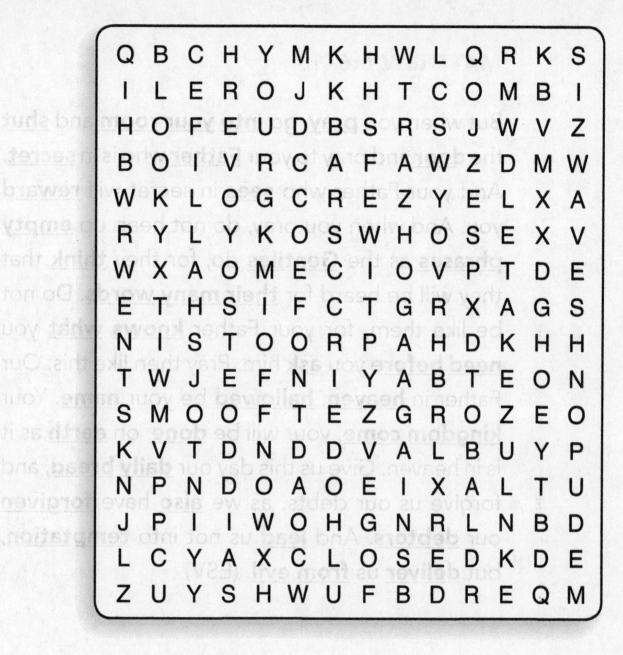

```
Q B C H Y M K H W L Q R K S
I L E R O J K H T C O M B I
H O F E U D B S R S J W V Z
B O I V R C A F A W Z D M W
W K L O G C R E Z Y E L X A
R Y L Y K O S W H O S E X V
W X A O M E C I O V P T D E
E T H S I F C T G R X A G S
N I S T O O R P A H D K H H
T W J E F N I Y A B T E O N
S M O O F T E Z G R O Z E O
K V T D N D D V A L B U Y P
N P N D O A O E I X A L T U
J P I I W O H G N R L N B D
L C Y A X C L O S E D K D E
Z U Y S H W U F B D R E Q M
```

Solution on Page 328

MATTHEW 6:6–13

But when you **pray**, go **into your room** and **shut** the **door** and pray to your **Father** who is in **secret**. And your Father who **sees** in secret will **reward** you. And when you pray, do not heap up **empty phrases** as the **Gentiles** do, for they **think** that they will be heard for **their many words**. Do not be like them, for your Father **knows what** you **need before** you **ask** him. Pray then like this: Our Father in **heaven**, **hallowed** be your **name**. Your **kingdom come**, your will be **done**, on **earth** as it is in heaven. Give us this day our **daily bread**, and forgive us our debts, as we **also** have **forgiven** our **debtors**. And **lead** us not into **temptation**, but **deliver** us **from evil**. (ESV)

The Lord's Prayer

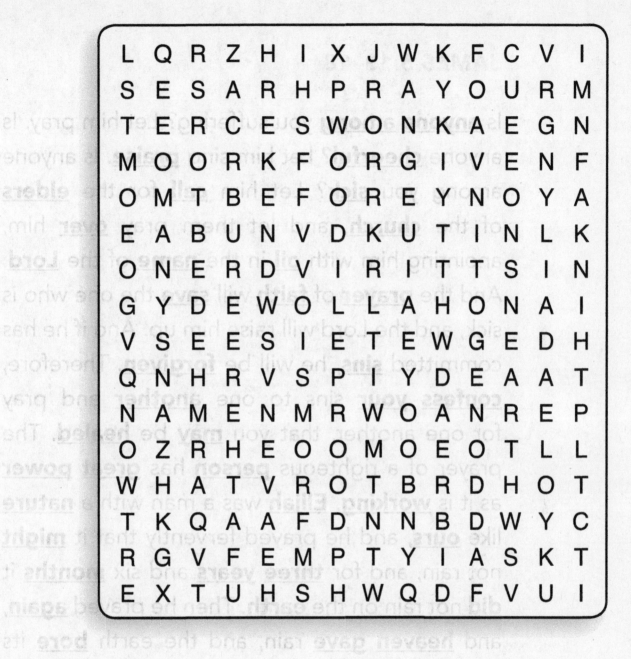

```
L Q R Z H I X J W K F C V I
S E S A R H P R A Y O U R M
T E R C E S W O N K A E G N
M O O R K F O R G I V E N F
O M T B E F O R E Y N O Y A
E A B U N V D K U T I N L K
O N E R D V I R I T T S I N
G Y D E W O L L A H O N A I
V S E E S I E T E W G E D H
Q N H R V S P I Y D E A A T
N A M E N M R W O A N R E P
O Z R H E O O M O E O T L L
W H A T V R O T B R D H O T
T K Q A A F D N N B D W Y C
R G V F E M P T Y I A S K T
E X T U H S H W Q D F V U I
```

Solution on Page 329

JAMES 5:13–18

Is **anyone among** you suffering? Let him pray. Is anyone **cheerful**? Let him sing **praise**. Is anyone among you **sick**? Let him **call** for the **elders** of the **church**, and let them pray **over** him, anointing him with **oil** in the **name** of the **Lord**. And the **prayer** of **faith** will **save** the one who is sick, and the Lord will raise him up. And if he has committed **sins**, he will be **forgiven**. Therefore, **confess** **your** sins to one **another** and pray for one another, that you **may** be **healed**. The prayer of a righteous **person** has **great** **power** as it is **working**. **Elijah** was a man with a **nature** like **ours**, and he prayed fervently that it **might** not rain, and for **three** **years** and six **months** it **did** not rain on the **earth**. Then he prayed **again**, and **heaven** **gave** rain, and the earth **bore** its **fruit**. (ESV)

Solution on Page 329

The Prayer of Faith

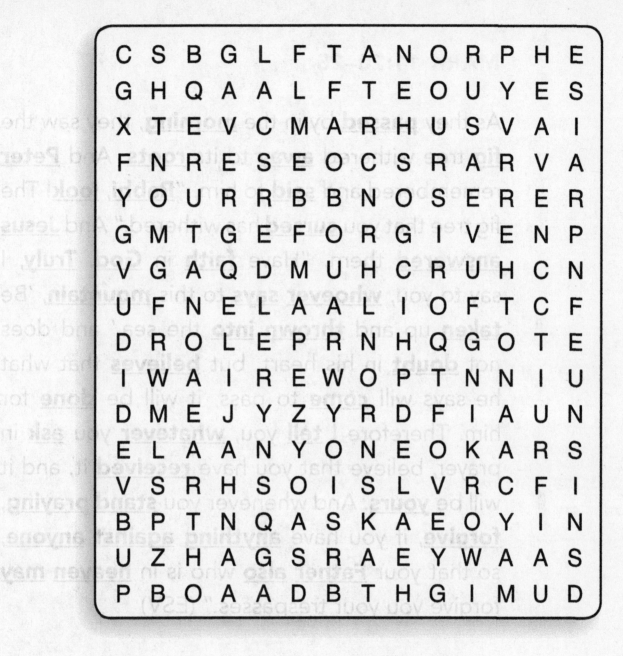

```
C S B G L F T A N O R P H E
G H Q A A L F T E O U Y E S
X T E V C M A R H U S V A I
F N R E S E O C S R A R V A
Y O U R R B B N O S E R E R
G M T G E F O R G I V E N P
V G A Q D M U H C R U H C N
U F N E L A A L I O F T C F
D R O L E P R N H Q G O T E
I W A I R E W O P T N N I U
D M E J Y Z Y R D F I A U N
E L A A N Y O N E O K A R S
V S R H S O I S L V R C F I
B P T N Q A S K A E O Y I N
U Z H A G S R A E Y W A A S
P B O A A D B T H G I M U D
```

Solution on Page 329

MARK 11:20–25

As they **passed** by in the **morning**, they saw the **fig** tree withered **away** to its **roots**. And **Peter** remembered and **said** to him, "**Rabbi**, **look**! The fig tree that you **cursed** has withered." And **Jesus** **answered** them, "Have **faith** in **God**. **Truly**, I say to you, **whoever** **says** to this **mountain**, 'Be **taken** up and **thrown** **into** the sea,' and does not **doubt** in his heart, but **believes** that what he says will **come** to pass, it will be **done** for him. Therefore I **tell** you, **whatever** you **ask** in prayer, believe that you have **received** it, and it will be **yours**. And whenever you **stand praying**, **forgive**, if you have **anything** **against** **anyone**, so that your **Father** **also** who is in **heaven** **may** forgive you your trespasses." (ESV)

Solution on Page 229

```
Y D N Z D I A S G L O O K D
P M E I E G S F V P E T E R
D C Q S A J A E X W J V T I
O U E I S T F G V K I H U B
U R N V H A N S W E R E D B
B S N E I I P U C G I F O A
T E R T H G W E O K L L N R
R D H T H W R J I M L A E R
G E Y F T H R O W N L V K B
Y N V P J O P O F S E S A X
A C I E D C C R O T T A T L
W V S N O T N I A T N K R J
A U A C R H Y H G Y S B U X
S T D R O O W G O A I A L T
S R U O Y M M N U M S N Y G
G A R U G N E V A E H X G S
```

PSALM 17:1–7

O **Lord**, hear my **plea** for justice. **Listen** to my cry for **help**. Pay attention to my prayer, for it comes **from** **honest** **lips**. Declare me innocent, for you see those who do **right**. You have **tested** my thoughts and examined my **heart** in the **night**. You have scrutinized me and **found** nothing **wrong**. I am determined not to **sin** in **what** I **say**. I have followed **your** commands, **which** **keep** me from following **cruel** and **evil** **people**. My **steps** have **stayed** on your **path**; I have not **wavered** from following you. I am praying to you because I **know** you will **answer**, O **God**. **Bend** **down** and listen as I pray. **Show** me your unfailing **love** in wonderful **ways**. By your **mighty** **power** you **rescue** those who **seek** **refuge** from **their** enemies. (NLT)

Solution on Page 329

A Prayer of David

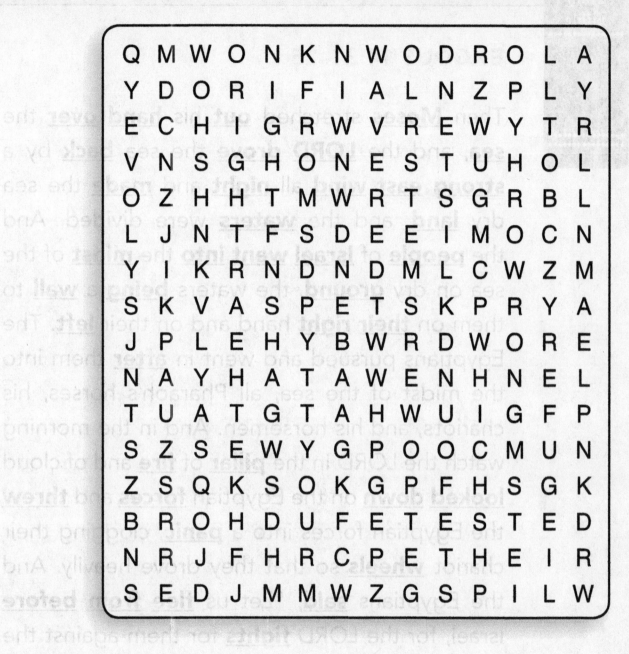

```
Q M W O N K N W O D R O L A Y
Y D O R I F I A L N Z P L Y
E C H I G R W V R E W Y T R
V N S G H O N E S T U H O L
O Z H H T M W R T S G R B L
L J N T F S D E E I M O C N
Y I K R N D N D M L C W Z M
S K V A S P E T S K P R Y A
J P L E H Y B W R D W O R E
N A Y H A T A W E N H N E L
T U A T G T A H W U I G F P
S Z S E W Y G P O O C M U N
Z S Q K S O K G P F H S G K
B R O H D U F E T E S T E D
N R J F H R C P E T H E I R
S E D J M M W Z G S P I L W
```

Solution on Page 329

Holy
Bible

EXODUS 14:21–25

Then **Moses** stretched **out** his **hand over** the **sea**, and the **LORD drove** the sea **back** by a **strong east wind** all **night** and **made** the sea dry **land**, and the **waters** were divided. And the **people** of **Israel went into** the **midst** of the sea on dry **ground**, the waters **being** a **wall** to them on **their right** hand and on their **left**. The Egyptians pursued and went in **after** them into the midst of the sea, all Pharaoh's horses, his chariots, and his horsemen. And in the morning watch the LORD in the **pillar** of **fire** and of cloud **looked down** on the Egyptian **forces** and **threw** the Egyptian forces into a **panic**, clogging their chariot **wheels** so that they drove heavily. And the Egyptians **said**, "Let us **flee from before** Israel, for the LORD **fights** for them against the Egyptians." (ESV)

Solution on Page 329

```
X W V C A P W E R H T T I O
J Y I S M L A E V Q H W J J
X P D W E N T N I G V F T O
D Q J W C F E H I Z G H Y K
S G M D A L R R G C E K W L
J F O X P L S R D I F I R E
L Y S O A S L E R N N R A F
O V E R T W K V W D H S O T
M P S R G O D O R A T T U M
D U O D O N D R N Y S W T E
F N L L U F I D A Z D P D I
G O O O M I E E F D I A S X
A I R L W G S B B L M N B G
O G D C W H E E L S E T T T
N K T A E T B A C K F E E O
P I D M I S R A E L A N D M
```

Solution on Page 330

EXODUS 7:8–13

Then the **LORD** **said** to **Moses** and **Aaron**, "When **Pharaoh** **says** to you, 'Prove **yourselves** by **working** a miracle,' then you **shall** say to Aaron, 'Take your staff and **cast** it **down** **before** Pharaoh, that it may **become** a serpent.'" So Moses and Aaron **went** to Pharaoh and **did** **just** as the LORD **commanded**. Aaron cast down his staff before Pharaoh and his **servants**, and it **became** a serpent. Then Pharaoh **summoned** the **wise** **men** and the **sorcerers**, and they, the **magicians** of **Egypt**, **also** did the **same** by **their** **secret** **arts**. For **each** man cast down his staff, and they became **serpents**. But Aaron's staff **swallowed** up their **staffs**. **Still** Pharaoh's **heart** was **hardened**, and he **would** not **listen** to them, as the LORD had said. (ESV)

Solution on Page 330

A Staff Becomes a Serpent

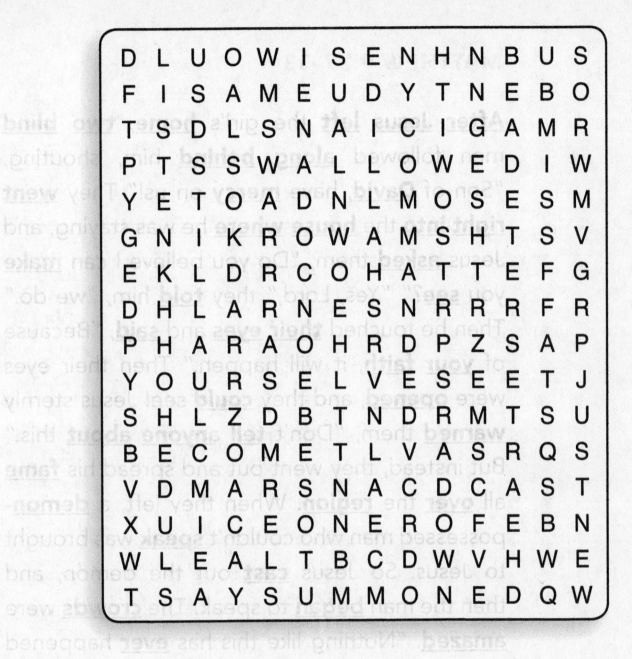

```
D L U O W I S E N H N B U S
F I S A M E U D Y T N E B O
T S D L S N A I C I G A M R
P T S S W A L L O W E D I W
Y E T O A D N L M O S E S M
G N I K R O W A M S H T S V
E K L D R C O H A T T E F G
D H L A R N E S N R R R F R
P H A R A O H R D P Z S A P
Y O U R S E L V E S E E T J
S H L Z D B T N D R M T S U
B E C O M E T L V A S R Q S
V D M A R S N A C D C A S T
X U I C E O N E R O F E B N
W L E A L T B C D W V H W E
T S A Y S U M M O N E D Q W
```

Solution on Page 330

MATTHEW 9:27–33

After **Jesus** **left** the girl's **home**, **two** **blind** men followed **along** **behind** him, shouting, "Son of **David**, have **mercy** on us!" They **went** **right** **into** the **house** **where** he was staying, and Jesus **asked** them, "Do you believe I can **make** you **see**?" "Yes, Lord," they **told** him, "we do." Then he touched **their** **eyes** and **said**, "Because of **your** **faith**, it will happen." Then their eyes were **opened**, and they **could** see! Jesus sternly **warned** them, "Don't **tell** **anyone** **about** this." But instead, they went out and spread his **fame** all **over** the **region**. When they left, a **demon**-possessed man who couldn't **speak** was brought to Jesus. So Jesus **cast** out the demon, and then the man **began** to speak. The **crowds** were **amazed**. "Nothing like this has **ever** happened in Israel!" they exclaimed. (NLT)

Solution on Page 330

The Blind See

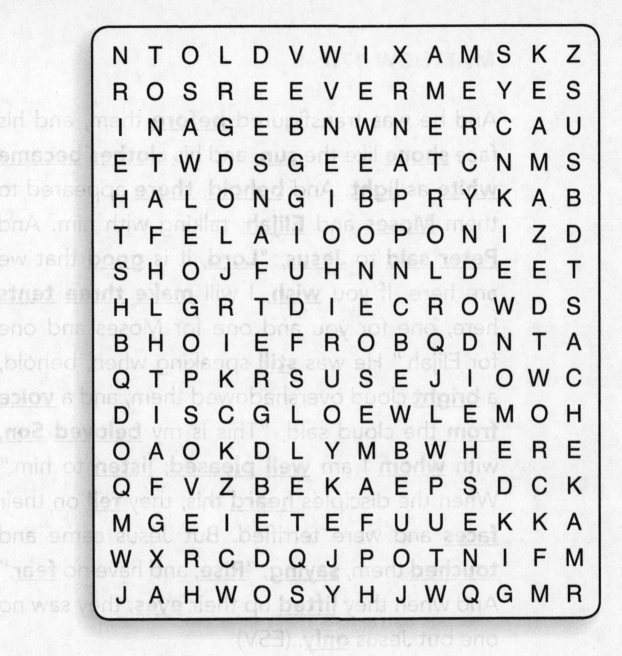

```
N T O L D V W I X A M S K Z
R O S R E E V E R M E Y E S
I N A G E B N W N E R C A U
E T W D S G E E A T C N M S
H A L O N G I B P R Y K A B
T F E L A I O O P O N I Z D
S H O J F U H N N L D E E T
H L G R T D I E C R O W D S
B H O I E F R O B Q D N T A
Q T P K R S U S E J I O W C
D I S C G L O E W L E M O H
O A O K D L Y M B W H E R E
Q F V Z B E K A E P S D C K
M G E I E T E F U U E K K A
W X R C D Q J P O T N I F M
J A H W O S Y H J W Q G M R
```

Solution on Page 330

MATTHEW 17:2–8

And he was transfigured **before** them, and his face **shone** like the **sun**, and his **clothes became white** as **light**. And **behold**, **there** appeared to them **Moses** and **Elijah**, talking with him. And **Peter said** to **Jesus**, "**Lord**, it is **good** that we are here. If you **wish**, I will **make three tents** here, one for you and one for Moses and one for Elijah." He was **still** speaking when, behold, a **bright** cloud overshadowed them, and a **voice from** the cloud said, "This is my **beloved Son**, with **whom** I am **well pleased**; **listen** to him." When the disciples **heard** this, they **fell** on their **faces** and were terrified. But Jesus came and **touched** them, **saying**, "**Rise**, and have no **fear**." And when they **lifted** up their **eyes**, they saw no one but Jesus **only**. (ESV)

The Transfiguration

```
K N A J W H I T E S I R X Z
G B R D B T A V H R U S L X
E P Z E H I X O E G T N X F
F T Y E M D F T G N I Y A S
D E R F A C E S E E L L E F
S E A X Z P N T R T O J S B
Q R V R Z I O I F S U S E J
H H H O C N H L E I Z D G L
S T Y E L C S L A L L M O L
I L T Y O E E T P O S O O E
W H O M T B B L H E A R D W
Z U U M H S E E I G D F L S
W Y C O E A B C F J I U R J
A Y H S S I Z J A O A R V Z
M P E E O D E K A M R H B V
F Z D S M N V O I C E E Z S
```

Solution on Page 330

EXODUS 3:1–5

One **day** **Moses** was tending the **flock** of his father-in-law, **Jethro**, the **priest** of **Midian**. He led the flock **far** **into** the wilderness and **came** to **Sinai**, the mountain of **God**. **There** the **angel** of the **Lord** appeared to him in a **blazing fire** **from** the **middle** of a **bush**. Moses **stared** in amazement. **Though** the bush was engulfed in **flames**, it didn't burn up. "This is amazing," Moses **said** to **himself**. "Why isn't that bush **burning** up? I **must** go **see** it." When the Lord saw Moses **coming** to **take** a **closer** **look**, God **called** to him from the middle of the bush, "Moses! Moses!" "Here I am!" Moses **replied**. "Do not come any closer," the Lord **warned**. "Take **off** **your** **sandals**, for you are standing on **holy** **ground**." (NLT)

The Burning Bush

```
M Y E K A T W G N K Z B E V
A L G R N D E R A T S S F X
F O M R E T S E I R P A Y R
Z H G U O H T M D N R I Q L
T Y Y A S U T H I U C D B L
S V O S Y T N E M D K R D Q
Z I C A L L E D R C D O F F
E O C L O S E R O H G L L J
L G U J G I U L O O K E E I
O N A C L N F H S Z G T N A
P I V P A Y I L I N H V O N
Z N E Y T M A M A R D K K I
F R O M S D E D O M O S E S
L U D E N R A W T C E R I F
R B L A Z I N G N K H S U B
R F S M V F A F I P N E V Z
```

Solution on Page 331

JOHN 6:15–21

Jesus therefore perceiving that they were **about** to **come** and **take** him by **force**, to **make** him king, **withdrew** **again** **into** the mountain **himself** **alone**. And when **evening** **came**, his disciples went **down** **unto** the **sea**; and they **entered** into a **boat**, and were **going** **over** the sea unto Capernaum. And it was now **dark**, and Jesus had not yet come to them. And the sea was **rising** by **reason** of a **great** **wind** that **blew**. When therefore they had **rowed** about **five** and **twenty** or **thirty** furlongs, they **behold** Jesus **walking** on the sea, and **drawing** **nigh** unto the boat: and they were **afraid**. But he **saith** unto them, It is I; be not afraid. They were **willing** therefore to **receive** him into the boat: and straightway the boat was at the **land** **whither** they were going. (ASV)

Solution on Page 331

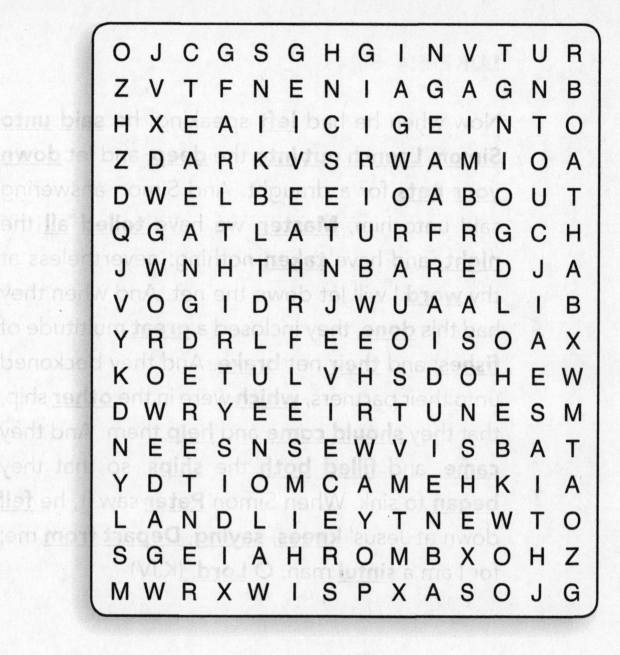

```
O J C G S G H G I N V T U R
Z V T F N E N I A G A G N B
H X E A I I C I G E I N T O
Z D A R K V S R W A M I O A
D W E L B E E I O A B O U T
Q G A T L A T U R F R G C H
J W N H T N B A R E D J A
V O G I D R J W U A A L I B
Y R D R L F E E O I S O A X
K O E T U L V H S D O H E W
D W R Y E E I R T U N E S M
N E E S N S E W V I S B A T
Y D T I O M C A M E H K I A
L A N D L I E Y T N E W T O
S G E I A H R O M B X O H Z
M W R X W I S P X A S O J G
```

Solution on Page 331

LUKE 5:4–8

Now when he had **left** speaking, he **said unto** Simon, **Launch out into** the **deep**, and let **down your nets** for a draught. And Simon answering said unto him, **Master**, we have **toiled all** the **night**, and have **taken** nothing: nevertheless at thy **word** I will let down the net. And when they had this **done**, they inclosed a **great** multitude of **fishes**: and **their** net **brake**. And they beckoned unto their partners, **which** were in the **other** ship, that they **should come** and **help** them. And they **came**, and **filled both** the **ships**, so that they **began** to sink. When Simon **Peter** saw it, he **fell** down at Jesus' **knees**, **saying**, **Depart from** me; for I am a **sinful** man, O **Lord**. (KJV)

Solution on Page 331

Good Fishing

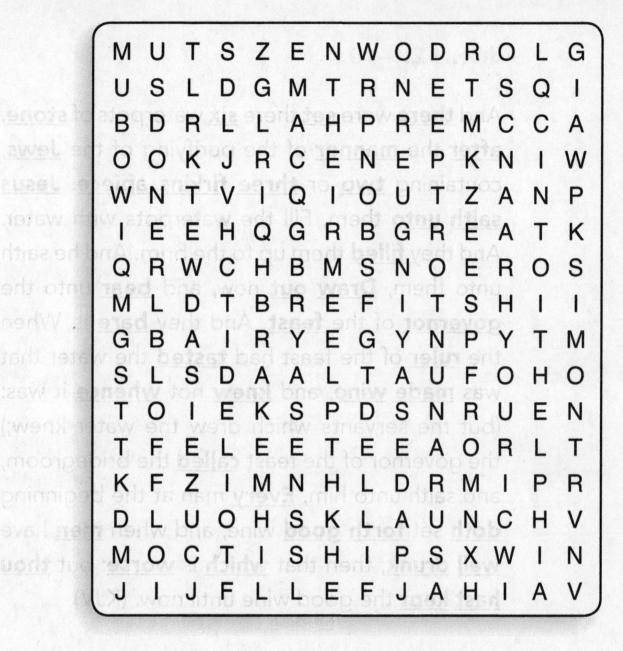

```
M U T S Z E N W O D R O L G
U S L D G M T R N E T S Q I
B D R L L A H P R E M C C A
O O K J R C E N E P K N I W
W N T V I Q I O U T Z A N P
I E E H Q G R B G R E A T K
Q R W C H B M S N O E R O S
M L D T B R E F I T S H I I
G B A I R Y E G Y N P Y T M
S L S D A A L T A U F O H O
T O I E K S P D S N R U E N
T F E L E E T E E A O R L T
K F Z I M N H L D R M I P R
D L U O H S K L A U N C H V
M O C T I S H I P S X W I N
J I J F L L E F J A H I A V
```

Solution on Page 331

JOHN 2:6–10

And **there** were **set** there **six** waterpots of **stone**, **after** the **manner** of the purifying of the **Jews**, containing **two** or **three firkins apiece**. **Jesus saith unto** them, Fill the waterpots with water. And they **filled** them up to the brim. And he saith unto them, **Draw out** now, and **bear** unto the **governor** of the **feast**. And they **bare** it. When the **ruler** of the feast had **tasted** the water that was **made wine**, and **knew** not **whence** it was: (but the servants which drew the water knew;) the governor of the feast **called** the bridegroom, and saith unto him, **Every** man at the beginning **doth** set **forth good** wine; and when **men** have **well drunk**, then that **which** is **worse**: but **thou hast kept** the good wine until now. (KJV)

Water to Wine

```
Q F U N X T S W E J H M B Y
K V C D R I H E D A M E C I
W K G F Y I S R K K A N M O
C T W O C R T H E R E N I W
H V E H O V O T P E K N T S
L L E W Z D N J B D F K S Y
M W G E W F E A R I I H A A
T E A I O S R U L E R A E A
V N G R U E N L R E O S F E
Y K T S D K E I M C V T E S
O H V A K D C C K A E E N M
U U H P S G O V E R N O R U
W O T A H T O D A I I N V Y
F H I Z W H E N C E P F E I
D T B B N U C D E L L A C R
H Z S A T T B C I R T R P I
```

Solution on Page 331

MATTHEW 15:32–37

And **Jesus** **called** **unto** him his disciples, and **said**, I have compassion on the multitude, **because** they continue with me now **three** **days** and have **nothing** to eat: and I **would** not **send** them **away** fasting, **lest** **haply** they **faint** on the way. And the disciples say unto him, **Whence** **should** we have so **many** **loaves** in a **desert** **place** as to fill so **great** a multitude? And Jesus said unto them, How many loaves have ye? And they said, **Seven**, and a **few** **small** **fishes**. And he commanded the multitude to **sit** **down** on the **ground**; and he **took** the seven loaves and the fishes; and he **gave** **thanks** and **brake**, and gave to the disciples, and the disciples to the multitudes. And they all **ate**, and were **filled**: and they took up that **which** remained **over** of the **broken** **pieces**, seven **baskets** **full**. (ASV)

Feeding the Multitude

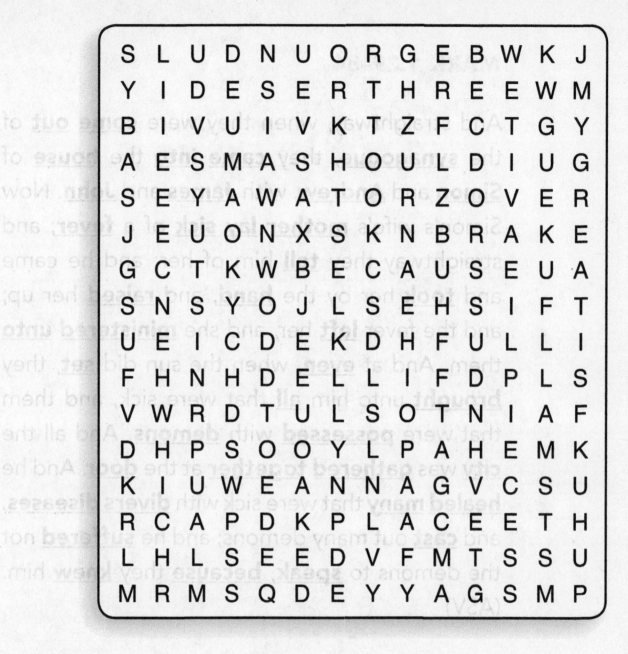

```
S L U D N U O R G E B W K J
Y I D E S E R T H R E E W M
B I V U I V K T Z F C T G Y
A E S M A S H O U L D I U G
S E Y A W A T O R Z O V E R
J E U O N X S K N B R A K E
G C T K W B E C A U S E U A
S N S Y O J L S E H S I F T
U E I C D E K D H F U L L I
F H N H D E L L I F D P L S
V W R D T U L S O T N I A F
D H P S O O Y L P A H E M K
K I U W E A N N A G V C S U
R C A P D K P L A C E E T H
L H L S E E D V F M T S S U
M R M S Q D E Y Y A G S M P
```

Solution on Page 332

MARK 1:29–34

And straightway, when they were **come** **out** of the **synagogue**, they **came** **into** the **house** of **Simon** and **Andrew**, with **James** and **John**. Now Simon's wife's **mother** **lay** **sick** of a **fever**; and straightway they **tell** him of her: and he came and **took** her by the **hand**, and **raised** her up; and the fever **left** her, and she **ministered** **unto** them. And at **even**, when the sun did **set**, they **brought** unto him **all** that were sick, and them that were **possessed** with **demons**. And all the **city** was **gathered** **together** at the **door**. And he **healed** **many** that were sick with **divers** **diseases**, and **cast** out many demons; and he **suffered** not the demons to **speak**, **because** they **knew** him. (ASV)

Solution on Page 332

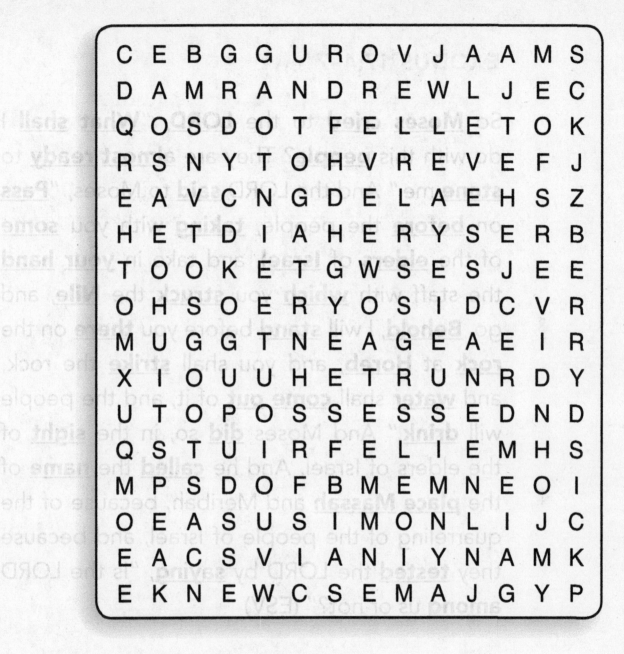

```
C E B G G U R O V J A A M S
D A M R A N D R E W L J E C
Q O S D O T F E L L E T O K
R S N Y T O H V R E V E F J
E A V C N G D E L A E H S Z
H E T D I A H E R Y S E R B
T O O K E T G W S E S J E E
O H S O E R Y O S I D C V R
M U G G T N E A G E A E I R
X I O U U H E T R U N R D Y
U T O P O S S E S S E D N D
Q S T U I R F E L I E M H S
M P S D O F B M E M N E O I
O E A S U S I M O N L I J C
E A C S V I A N I Y N A M K
E K N E W C S E M A J G Y P
```

Solution on Page 332

EXODUS 17:4–7

So **Moses** **cried** to the **LORD**, "**What** **shall** I do with this **people**? They are **almost** **ready** to **stone** me." And the LORD **said** to Moses, "**Pass** on **before** the people, **taking** with you **some** of the **elders** of **Israel**, and take in **your** **hand** the staff with **which** you **struck** the **Nile**, and go. **Behold**, I will **stand** before you **there** on the **rock** at **Horeb**, and you shall **strike** the rock, and **water** shall **come** **out** of it, and the people will **drink**." And Moses **did** so, in the **sight** of the elders of Israel. And he **called** the **name** of the **place** **Massah** and Meribah, because of the quarreling of the people of Israel, and because they **tested** the LORD by **saying**, "Is the LORD **among** us or not?" (ESV)

Solution on Page 332

Water from a Rock

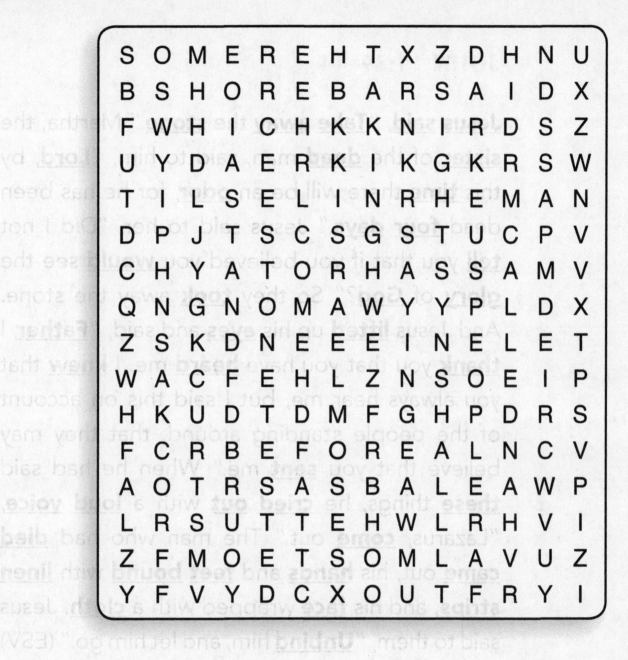

```
S O M E R E H T X Z D H N U
B S H O R E B A R S A I D X
F W H I C H K K N I R D S Z
U Y D A E R K I K G K R S W
T I L S E L I N R H E M A N
D P J T S C S G S T U C P V
C H Y A T O R H A S S A M V
Q N G N O M A W Y Y P L D X
Z S K D N E E E I N E L E T
W A C F E H L Z N S O E I P
H K U D T D M F G H P D R S
F C R B E F O R E A L N C V
A O T R S A S B A L E A W P
L R S U T T E H W L R H V I
Z F M O E T S O M L A V U Z
Y F V Y D C X O U T F R Y I
```

Solution on Page 332

JOHN 11:39–44

Jesus **said**, "**Take** **away** the **stone**." Martha, the **sister** of the **dead** man, said to him, "**Lord**, by this **time** there will be an **odor**, for he has been dead **four** **days**." Jesus said to her, "Did I not **tell** you that if you believed you **would** see the **glory** of **God**?" So they **took** away the stone. And Jesus **lifted** up his **eyes** and said, "**Father**, I **thank** you that you have **heard** me. I **knew** that you always hear me, but I said this on account of the people standing around, that they may believe that you **sent** me." When he had said **these** things, he **cried** **out** with a **loud** **voice**, "Lazarus, **come** out." The man who had **died** **came** out, his **hands** and **feet** **bound** with **linen** **strips**, and his **face** wrapped with a **cloth**. Jesus said to them, "**Unbind** him, and let him go." (ESV)

Solution on Page 332

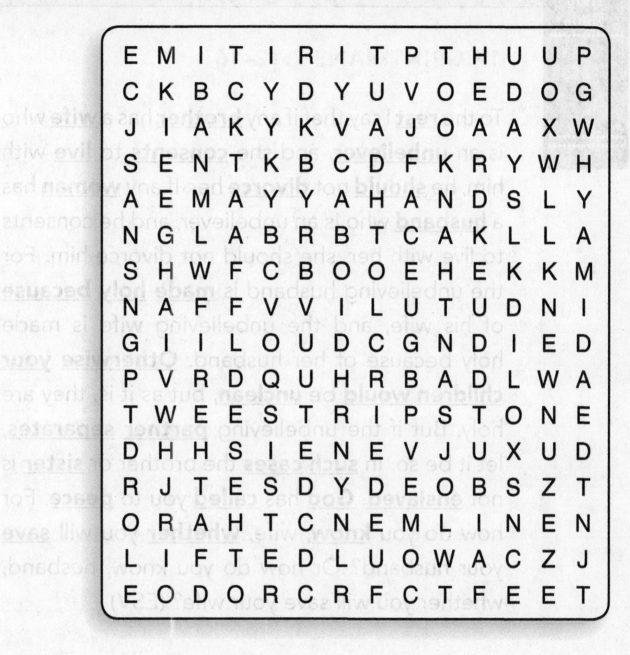

E M I T I R I T P T H U U P
C K B C Y D Y U V O E D O G
J I A K Y K V A J O A A X W
S E N T K B C D F K R Y W H
A E M A Y Y A H A N D S L Y
N G L A B R B T C A K L L A
S H W F C B O O E H E K K M
N A F F V V I L U T U D N I
G I I L O U D C G N D I E D
P V R D Q U H R B A D L W A
T W E E S T R I P S T O N E
D H H S I E N E V J U X U D
R J T E S D Y D E O B S Z T
O R A H T C N E M L I N E N
L I F T E D L U O W A C Z J
E O D O R C R F C T F E E T

Solution on Page 332

Holy
Bible

1 CORINTHIANS 7:12–16

To the **rest** I say that if any **brother** has a **wife** who is an **unbeliever**, and she **consents** to **live** with him, he **should** not **divorce** her. If any **woman** has a **husband** who is an unbeliever, and he consents to live with her, she should not divorce him. For the unbelieving husband is **made** **holy** **because** of his wife, and the unbelieving wife is made holy because of her husband. **Otherwise** **your** **children** **would** be **unclean**, but as it is, they are holy. But if the unbelieving **partner** **separates**, let it be so. In **such** **cases** the brother or **sister** is not **enslaved**. **God** has **called** you to **peace**. For how do you **know**, wife, **whether** you will **save** your husband? Or how do you know, husband, whether you will save your wife? (ESV)

Solution on Page 332

```
V X X G K M D B R A S B I R
R U O Y P D C V U K O Z D G
S D N E Q R E H T E H W L H
A R A B W D L I V E O U C
V C E R E D A M L L C N O O
E T L O Y L A K N A D K H N
F W C T L J I T B Q C R S S
I D N H O T H E R W I S E E
W S U E H H C H V W V N T N
B A Z R H A S C O E S O A T
X M G Z U I H U V L R T R S
J B Z S S B L S A S E S A C
T Y E T B D I V O R C E P N
T S E R A R E N T R A P E V
A R W F N D N A M O W T S E
Z O S U D R M D T U H C S R
```

Solution on Page 333

EZEKIEL 45:1–5

Divide the **land** by **drawing** **lots** for the **property** you will **inherit**. Set **aside** an **area** 43,750 **feet** long and 35,000 feet **wide** for the **Lord**. The **entire** area will be **holy**. An area of 875 feet **square** will be for the holy **place** with an **open** area 87½ feet wide. **Measure** **off** an area 43,750 feet long and 17,500 feet wide. The holy place, that is, the **most** holy place, will be in this area. This holy **part** of the land will **belong** to the **priests** who **serve** in the holy place, the priests who **come** **near** to serve the Lord. They will **use** this place for **their** **homes**, and it will be the **location** for the holy place. An area 43,750 feet long and 17,500 feet wide will belong to the **Levites** who serve in the **temple**. (GW)

```
N M H M S O D I S G Z O N H
S Q K H B J V S U U D I U E
S P A X W E B U C T N N N D
T R A P M X V M Z H K T A E
O C A B G M J S E T I V E L
S P M E A N W R V N S X X O
T T I V N I I A E V Q E Z T
P O S R D T R W E U Y M T S
K I Y E I L O C A T I O N D
M E F S I E M R R R T H J N
A M S G T R E E U A D T Y T
E O J U N L P D A L R H X G
E C A L P O W Y I S T E E F
T S O M R K L V F S U I A R
B R E P P O I E W F A R E B
D T K X H J G M B N O P E N
```

Solution on Page 333

ROMANS 11:16–20

If the **first** **handful** of **dough** is **holy**, the **whole** **batch** of dough is holy. If the root is holy, the **branches** are holy. But **some** of the **olive** branches have been **broken** **off**, and you, a **wild** olive branch, have been **grafted** in **their** **place**. You get **your** nourishment **from** the **roots** of the olive **tree**. So don't brag **about** **being** **better** than the **other** branches. If you brag, **remember** that you don't support the root, the root **supports** you. "Well," you **say**, "Branches were **cut** off so that I **could** be grafted **onto** the tree." That's **right**! They were broken off **because** they didn't **believe**, but you **remain** on the tree because you do believe. Don't **feel** **arrogant**, but be **afraid**. (GW)

Solution on Page 332

Holy Root

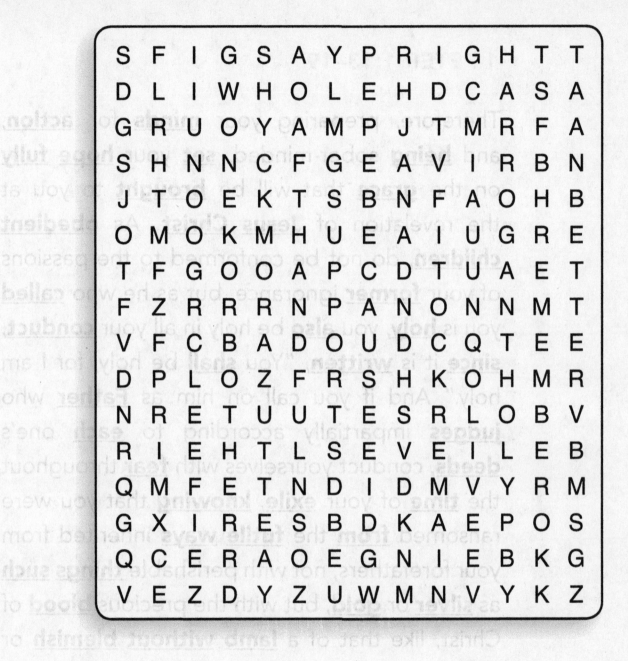

S F I G S A Y P R I G H T T
D L I W H O L E H D C A S A
G R U O Y A M P J T M R F A
S H N N C F G E A V I R B N
J T O E K T S B N F A O H B
O M O K M H U E A I U G R E
T F G O O A P C D T U A E T
F Z R R R N P A N O N N M T
V F C B A D O U D C Q T E E
D P L O Z F R S H K O H M R
N R E T U U T E S R L O B V
R I E H T L S E V E I L E B
Q M F E T N D I D M V Y R M
G X I R E S B D K A E P O S
Q C E R A O E G N I E B K G
V E Z D Y Z U W M N V Y K Z

Solution on Page 333

1 PETER 1:13–19

Therefore, preparing your **minds** for **action**, and **being** sober-minded, **set** your **hope fully** on the **grace** that will be **brought** to you at the revelation of **Jesus Christ**. As **obedient children**, do not be conformed to the passions of your **former** ignorance, but as he who **called** you is **holy**, you **also** be holy in all your **conduct**, **since** it is **written**, "You **shall** be holy, for I am holy." And if you call on him as **Father** who **judges** impartially according to **each** one's **deeds**, conduct yourselves with **fear** throughout the **time** of your **exile**, **knowing** that you were ransomed **from** the **futile ways** inherited from your forefathers, not with perishable **things such** as **silver** or **gold**, but with the precious **blood** of Christ, like that of a **lamb without blemish** or **spot**. (ESV)

Solution on Page 333

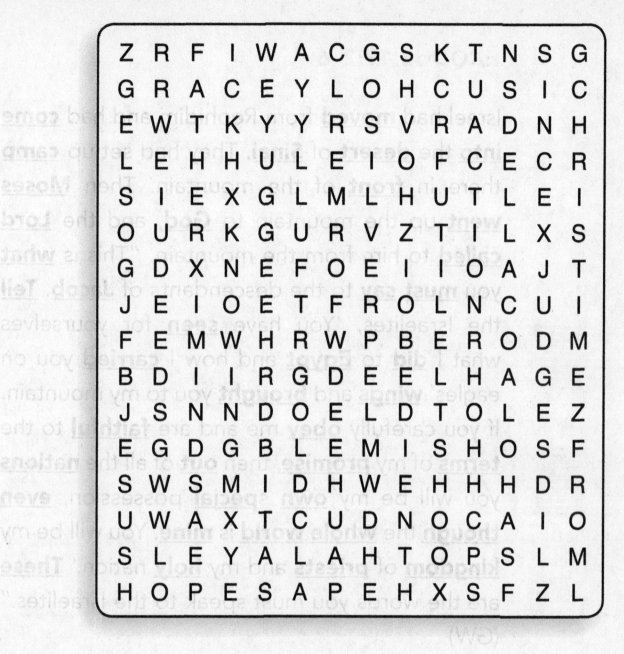

```
Z R F I W A C G S K T N S G
G R A C E Y L O H C U S I C
E W T K Y Y R S V R A D N H
L E H H U L E I O F C E C R
S I E X G L M L H U T L E I
O U R K G U R V Z T I L X S
G D X N E F O E I I O A J T
J E I O E T F R O L N C U I
F E M W H R W P B E R O D M
B D I I R G D E E L H A G E
J S N N D O E L D T O L E Z
E G D G B L E M I S H O S F
S W S M I D H W E H H H D R
U W A X T C U D N O C A I O
S L E Y A L A H T O P S L M
H O P E S A P E H X S F Z L
```

Solution on Page 333

EXODUS 19:2–6

Israel had **moved** from Rephidim and had **come into** the **desert** of **Sinai**. They had set up **camp** there in **front** of the mountain. Then **Moses went** up the mountain to **God**, and the **Lord called** to him from the mountain, "This is **what** you **must say** to the descendants of **Jacob**. **Tell** the Israelites, 'You have **seen** for yourselves what I **did** to **Egypt** and how I **carried** you on eagles' **wings** and **brought** you to my mountain. If you carefully **obey** me and are **faithful** to the **terms** of my **promise**, then **out** of all the **nations** you will be my **own special** possession, **even though** the **whole world** is **mine**. You will be my **kingdom** of **priests** and my **holy** nation.' **These** are the words you must speak to the Israelites." (GW)

Solution on Page 333

```
M H Q S O C L V I S X Q I W
C V T B A W O R L D T D N E
G P C P A D T M C H E V E N
I B R O Y O O F E L O V J T
A T H O U G H S L Z S L O Y
M A M B M T E A P M A C Y M
A H O E N I C T R T P E G T
D W D Y D A S E S G I J E K
U X G B R E T E A O A T J X
L X N R R T S I Y C N W T O
O D I O S O E E O O I E W W
R E K U M T I B R N S N U I
D T M G N X R F G T S I T S
E L O H W Q P S E D F M E O
F A I T H F U L A I C E P S
S X W H Q D L E J D N I O E
```

Solution on Page 334

LEVITICUS 11:41–45

"**Every** **swarming** **thing** that swarms on the **ground** is **detestable**; it **shall** not be **eaten**. **Whatever** **goes** on its **belly**, and whatever goes on all **fours**, or whatever has **many feet**, any swarming thing that swarms on the ground, you shall not eat, for they are detestable. You shall not **make yourselves** detestable with any swarming thing that swarms, and you shall not **defile** yourselves with them, and **become** **unclean through** them. For I am the **LORD** your God. **Consecrate** yourselves **therefore**, and be **holy**, for I am holy. You shall not defile yourselves with any swarming thing that **crawls** on the ground. For I am the LORD who **brought** you up **out** of the **land** of **Egypt** to be your God. You shall therefore be holy, for I am holy." (ESV)

240

```
X Y H A H F H H M J N W G A
R I S R I V R Y X A L H D P
X F C E Z G G R O U N D J G
M W O V V Y O T U O E Y G L
D O N E P L L F H T P N D J
A Y S T O L E O E I I O F E
G Y E A V E M S E M N F T A
M W C H T B T B R O U G H T
Y H R W J A A A O U N G R E
E K A M B A W E F A O X O N
M V T L C S B C E L T Y U B
I H E G S Y E L R L C D G S
F O U R S E C L E A I C H L
M H O L Y N O C H H W F A A
I A S E U R M G T S L L E N
M F Y L D U E G Y P T J S D
```

Solution on Page 334

1 SAMUEL 21:3–6

Now then, what do you have on **hand**? **Give** me **five** **loaves** of **bread**, or **whatever** is **here**. And the **priest** **answered** **David**, "I have no **common** bread on hand, but there is **holy** bread— if the **young** men have **kept** **themselves** **from** **women**." And David answered the priest, "**Truly** women have been kept from us as **always** when I go on an **expedition**. The **vessels** of the young men are holy **even** when it is an **ordinary** **journey**. How **much** more **today** will their vessels be holy?" So the priest **gave** him the holy bread, for there was no bread there but the bread of the **Presence**, **which** is **removed** from **before** the **LORD**, to be **replaced** by hot bread on the day it is **taken** **away**. (ESV)

Holy Bread

```
N H W G A G P O D N A H E D
N K C J A Q R T H O L Y E A
W E D U F E I H K Y W C G E
F N M I M Y E E W E V A N R
P I O O V R S M E L Y D U B
Y E V I W A T S P I S E O D
L E P E T N D E G T R A Y T
D I N A T I R L I E H C A B
J R K R R D D V V Z A O W E
L E O N U R H E E H N M A F
N O F L L O T S P M S M A O
J Q A H Y A J N O X W O H R
D M Z V H A P R E S E N C E
Q C O W E H F C F V R C I V
Z Q O E R S L E S S E V H A
F R T P E K M W R A D O W G
```

Solution on Page 334

ACTS 10:43–48

To him **give** all the **prophets** **witness**, that **through** his **name** whosoever believeth in him **shall** receive remission of **sins**. **While** **Peter** yet **spake** **these** **words**, the **Holy** **Ghost** **fell** on all them which **heard** the word. And they of the circumcision which believed were astonished, as **many** as **came** with Peter, **because** that on the **Gentiles** **also** was **poured** **out** the **gift** of the Holy Ghost. For they heard them **speak** with **tongues**, and **magnify** **God**. Then **answered** Peter, Can any man **forbid** **water**, that these **should** not be **baptized**, which have **received** the Holy Ghost as **well** as we? And he commanded them to be baptized in the name of the **Lord**. Then **prayed** they him to **tarry** **certain** **days**. (KJV)

The Holy Ghost

Solution on Page 334

EZEKIEL 39:7–10

And my **holy** **name** I will **make** **known** in the **midst** of my **people** Israel, and I will not let my holy name be profaned **anymore**. And the nations **shall** know that I am the **LORD**, the Holy **One** in Israel. **Behold**, it is **coming** and it will be **brought** **about**, declares the Lord **GOD**. That is the **day** of **which** I have **spoken**. Then **those** who **dwell** in the **cities** of Israel will go out and make **fires** of the **weapons** and **burn** them, **shields** and bucklers, **bow** and **arrows**, **clubs** and **spears**; and they will make fires of them for **seven** **years**, so that they will not **need** to **take** **wood** out of the **field** or **cut** **down** any out of the **forests**, for they will make **their** fires of the weapons. (ESV)

Solution on Page 334

Holy Name

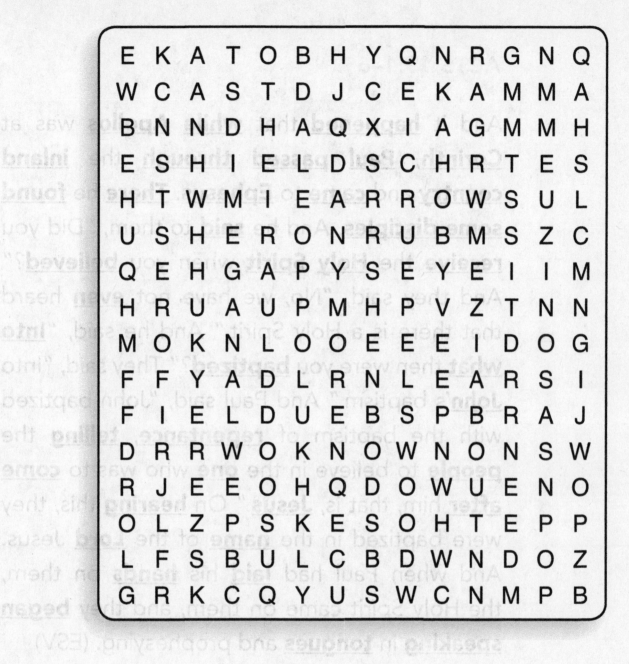

```
E K A T O B H Y Q N R G N Q
W C A S T D J C E K A M M A
B N N D H A Q X I A G M M H
E S H I E L D S C H R T E S
H T W M I E A R R O W S U L
U S H E R O N R U B M S Z C
Q E H G A P Y S E Y E I M M
H R U A U P M H P V Z T N N
M O K N L O O E E E I D O G
F F Y A D L R N L E A R S I
F I E L D U E B S P B R A J
D R R W O K N O W N O N S W
R J E E O H Q D O W U E N O
O L Z P S K E S O H T E P P
L F S B U L C B D W N D O Z
G R K C Q Y U S W C N M P B
```

Solution on Page 335

ACTS 19:1–6

And it **happened** that **while Apollos** was at **Corinth**, **Paul passed through** the **inland country** and **came** to **Ephesus**. **There** he **found some disciples**. And he **said** to them, "Did you **receive** the **Holy Spirit** when you **believed**?" And they said, "No, we have not **even** heard that there is a Holy Spirit." And he said, "**Into what** then were you **baptized**?" They said, "Into **John**'s baptism." And Paul said, "John baptized with the baptism of **repentance**, **telling** the **people** to believe in the **one** who was to **come after** him, that is, **Jesus**." On **hearing** this, they were baptized in the **name** of the **Lord** Jesus. And when Paul had **laid** his **hands** on them, the Holy Spirit came on them, and they **began speaking** in **tongues** and prophesying. (ESV)

Solution on Page 335

```
L I E X W P A U L G B N F W
O F R E T F A A F Q H A O H
R T S E L P I C S I D G U A
D O H W P D L D C A M E N T
L N O R D E Z I T P A B D P
E G A C O U N T R Y Z E S K
P U F L H U M T U P S B D J
H E P O N A G U A S G E N E
E S E W E I P H A N V L A S
S J O H O L Y P I I C I H U
U S P I R I T K E O E E J S
S O L L O P A C R N A V L O
N K E E Y E E I O R E E I M
L E M R P R N D I A S D N E
O O V S D T G N I L L E T I
C E R E H T G E M A N H O J
```

NEHEMIAH 8:9–12

And **Nehemiah**, who was the **governor**, and **Ezra** the **priest** and **scribe**, and the **Levites** who **taught** the **people said** to **all** the people, "This **day** is **holy** to the **LORD your** God; do not **mourn** or **weep**." For all the people **wept** as they **heard** the **words** of the **Law**. Then he said to them, "Go your **way**. Eat the **fat** and **drink sweet wine** and **send** portions to **anyone** who has **nothing ready**, for this day is holy to our Lord. And do not be **grieved**, for the **joy** of the LORD is your **strength**." So the Levites **calmed** all the people, **saying**, "Be **quiet**, for this day is holy; do not be grieved." And all the people **went their** way to eat and drink and to send portions and to **make great** rejoicing, **because** they had understood the words that were declared to them. (ESV)

Solution on Page 335

250

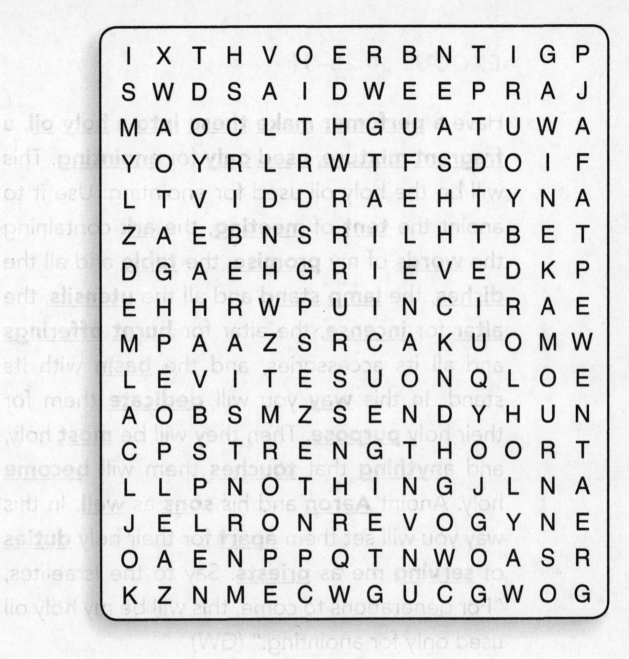

```
I X T H V O E R B N T I G P
S W D S A I D W E E P R A J
M A O C L T H G U A T U W A
Y O Y R L R W T F S D O I F
L T V I D D R A E H T Y N A
Z A E B N S R I L H T B E T
D G A E H G R I E V E D K P
E H H R W P U I N C I R A E
M P A A Z S R C A K U O M W
L E V I T E S U O N Q L O E
A O B S M Z S E N D Y H U N
C P S T R E N G T H O O R T
L L P N O T H I N G J L N A
J E L R O N R E V O G Y N E
O A E N P P Q T N W O A S R
K Z N M E C W G U C G W O G
```

Solution on Page 335

EXODUS 30:25–31

Have a **perfumer** **make** **these** **into** a **holy** **oil**, a **fragrant** **mixture**, **used** **only** for **anointing**. This will be the holy oil used for anointing. Use it to anoint the **tent** of **meeting**, the **ark** containing the **words** of my **promise**, the **table** and all the **dishes**, the **lamp** **stand** and all the **utensils**, the **altar** for **incense**, the altar for **burnt** **offerings** and all its accessories, and the **basin** with its stand. In this **way** you will **dedicate** them for their holy **purpose**. Then they will be **most** holy, and **anything** that **touches** them will **become** holy. Anoint **Aaron** and his **sons** as **well**. In this way you will set them **apart** for their holy **duties** of **serving** me as **priests**. Say to the Israelites, "For generations to come, this will be my holy oil used only for anointing." (GW)

```
F L M X C G K T W S O N S M
T L G Y P U R P O S E A B I
H E U T E N S I L S V A D X
E W N S R I N C E N S E N T
S B Y T F A Y A P I D K N U
E G L S U H P M N I W A Y R
X N N E M O A A C S R M A E
E I O I E L N A E G G T S Z
Z P T R R R Y T H A N L I Y J
O N A P T E C R I A M B D S
M I A H B U F V X O E U T D
O O I L O B R F R C T A A R
G N I T E E M P O I N A B O
G A N Q S O O M E D R P L W
F I D I S H E S S K U S E D
X L I T Y Z J O G V B Y O L
```

Solution on Page 335

Holy
Bible

LUKE 16:19–24

There was a **rich man** who was clothed in **purple** and fine **linen** and who feasted sumptuously **every day**. And at his **gate** was **laid** a **poor** man **named** Lazarus, covered with **sores**, who **desired** to be fed with **what fell from** the rich man's **table**. Moreover, even the **dogs came** and **licked** his sores. The poor man **died** and was carried by the **angels** to Abraham's **side**. The rich man **also** died and was **buried**, and in **Hades**, **being** in torment, he **lifted** up his **eyes** and **saw** Abraham **far off** and Lazarus at his side. And he **called out**, "Father Abraham, have **mercy** on me, and **send** Lazarus to dip the end of his **finger** in **water** and **cool** my **tongue**, for I am in anguish in this flame." (ESV)

Solution on Page 335

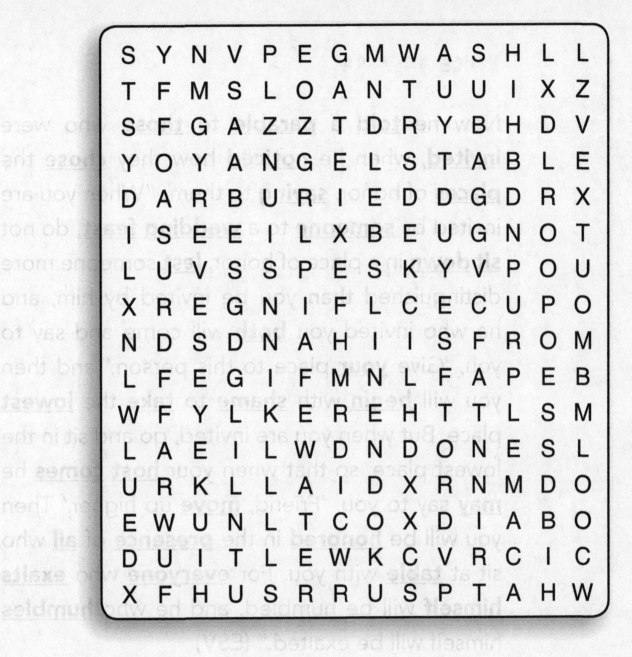

```
S Y N V P E G M W A S H L L
T F M S L O A N T U U I X Z
S F G A Z Z T D R Y B H D V
Y O Y A N G E L S T A B L E
D A R B U R I E D D G D R X
I S E E I L X B E U G N O T
L U V S S P E S K Y V P O U
X R E G N I F L C E C U P O
N D S D N A H I I S F R O M
L F E G I F M N L F A P E B
W F Y L K E R E H T T L S M
L A E I L W D N D O N E S L
U R K L L A I D X R N M D O
E W U N L T C O X D I A B O
D U I T L E W K C V R C I C
X F H U S R R U S P T A H W
```

Solution on Page 336

LUKE 14:7–11

Now he **told** a **parable** to **those** who were **invited**, when he **noticed** how they **chose** the **places** of honor, **saying** to them, "When you are invited by **someone** to a **wedding feast**, do not **sit down** in a place of honor, **lest** someone more distinguished than you be invited by him, and he who invited you **both** will come and say to you, 'Give **your** place to this person,' and then you will **begin** with **shame** to **take** the **lowest** place. But when you are invited, go and sit in the lowest place, so that when your **host comes** he **may** say to you, 'Friend, **move** up higher.' Then you will be **honored** in the **presence** of **all** who sit at **table** with you. For **everyone** who **exalts himself** will be humbled, and he who **humbles** himself will be exalted." (ESV)

Solution on Page 336

A Wedding Feast

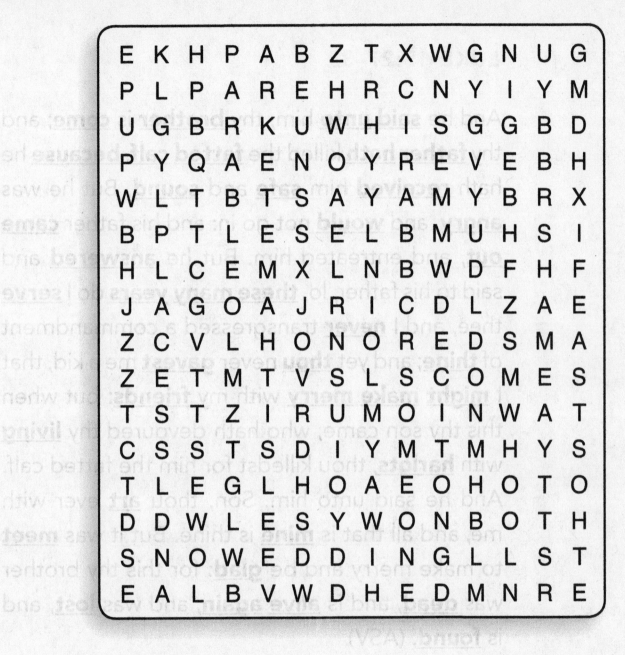

```
E K H P A B Z T X W G N U G
P L P A R E H R C N Y I Y M
U G B R K U W H I S G G B D
P Y Q A E N O Y R E V E B H
W L T B T S A Y A M Y B R X
B P T L E S E L B M U H S I
H L C E M X L N B W D F H F
J A G O A J R I C D L Z A E
Z C V L H O N O R E D S M A
Z E T M T V S L S C O M E S
T S T Z I R U M O I N W A T
C S S T S D I Y M T M H Y S
T L E G L H O A E O H O T O
D D W L E S Y W O N B O T H
S N O W E D D I N G L L S T
E A L B V W D H E D M N R E
```

Solution on Page 336

LUKE 15:27–32

And he **said** **unto** him, thy **brother** is **come**; and thy **father** **hath** killed the **fatted** **calf**, **because** he hath **received** him **safe** and **sound**. But he was **angry**, and **would** not go in: and his father **came** **out**, and entreated him. But he **answered** and said to his father, lo, **these** **many** **years** do I **serve** thee, and I **never** transgressed a commandment of **thine**; and yet **thou** never **gavest** me a kid, that I **might** **make** **merry** with my **friends**: but when this thy son came, who hath devoured thy **living** with **harlots**, thou killedst for him the fatted calf. And he said unto him, Son, thou **art** ever with me, and all that is **mine** is thine. But it was **meet** to make merry and be **glad**: for this thy brother was **dead**, and is **alive** **again**; and was **lost**, and is **found**. (ASV)

The Prodigal Son

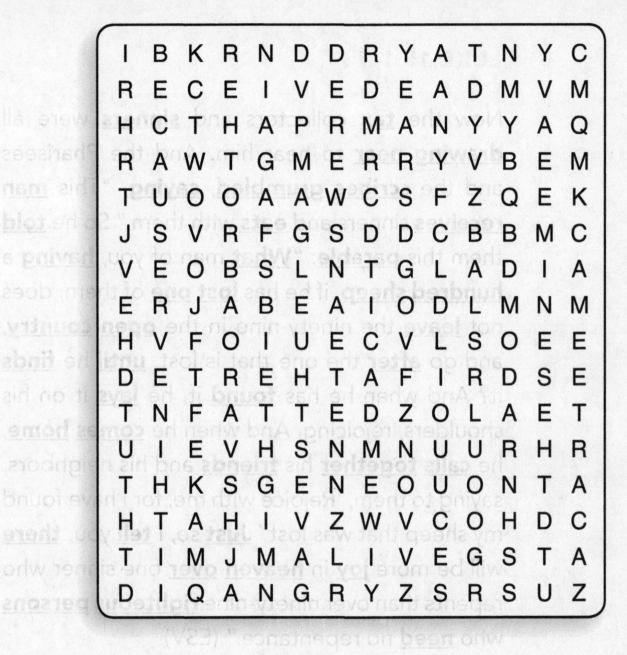

I B K R N D D R Y A T N Y C
R E C E I V E D E A D M V M
H C T H A P R M A N Y Y A Q
R A W T G M E R R Y V B E M
T U O O A A W C S F Z Q E K
J S V R F G S D D C B B M C
V E O B S L N T G L A D I A
E R J A B E A I O D L M N M
H V F O I U E C V L S O E E
D E T R E H T A F I R D S E
T N F A T T E D Z O L A E T
U I E V H S N M N U U R H R
T H K S G E N E O U O N T A
H T A H I V Z W V C O H D C
T I M J M A L I V E G S T A
D I Q A N G R Y Z S R S U Z

Solution on Page 336

LUKE 15:1–7

Now the **tax** collectors and **sinners** were all **drawing near** to hear him. And the Pharisees and the **scribes grumbled**, **saying**, "This **man receives** sinners and **eats** with them." So he **told** them this **parable**: "**What** man of you, **having** a **hundred sheep**, if he has **lost one** of them, does not **leave** the ninety-nine in the **open country**, and go **after** the one that is lost, **until** he **finds** it? And when he has **found** it, he **lays** it on his shoulders, rejoicing. And when he **comes home**, he **calls together** his **friends** and his neighbors, saying to them, 'Rejoice with me, for I have found my sheep that was lost.' **Just** so, I **tell** you, **there** will be more **joy** in **heaven over** one sinner who repents than over ninety-nine **righteous persons** who **need** no repentance." (ESV)

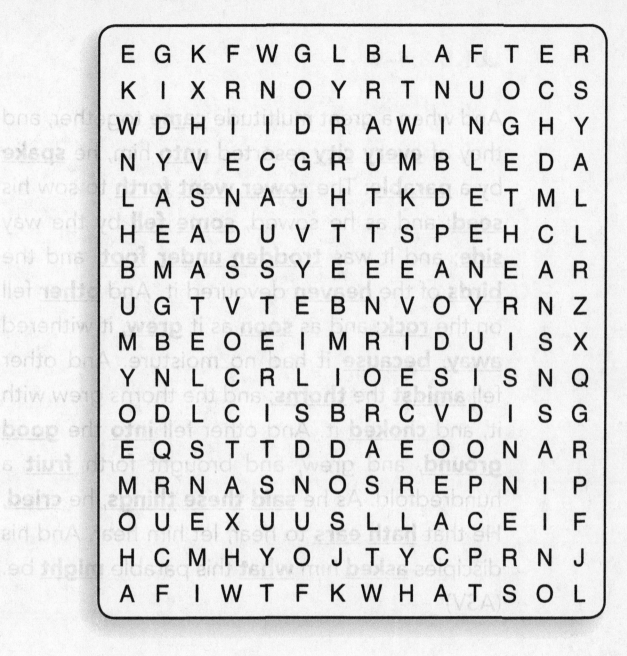

```
E G K F W G L B L A F T E R
K I X R N O Y R T N U O C S
W D H I I D R A W I N G H Y
N Y V E C G R U M B L E D A
L A S N A J H T K D E T M L
H E A D U V T T S P E H C L
B M A S S Y E E E A N E A R
U G T V T E B N V O Y R N Z
M B E O E I M R I D U I S X
Y N L C R L I O E S I S N Q
O D L C I S B R C V D I S G
E Q S T T D D A E O O N A R
M R N A S N O S R E P N I P
O U E X U U S L L A C E I F
H C M H Y O J T Y C P R N J
A F I W T F K W H A T S O L
```

LUKE 8:4–9

And when a great multitude **came** together, and they of **every** **city** resorted **unto** him, he **spake** by a **parable**: The **sower** **went** **forth** to sow his **seed**: and as he sowed, **some** **fell** by the way **side**; and it was **trodden** **under** **foot**, and the **birds** of the **heaven** devoured it. And **other** fell on the **rock**; and as **soon** as it **grew**, it withered **away**, **because** it had no moisture. And other fell **amidst** the **thorns**; and the thorns grew with it, and **choked** it. And other fell **into** the **good** **ground**, and grew, and brought forth **fruit** a hundredfold. As he **said** **these** **things**, he **cried**, He that **hath** **ears** to hear, let him hear. And his disciples **asked** him **what** this parable **might** be. (ASV)

Scattering Seed

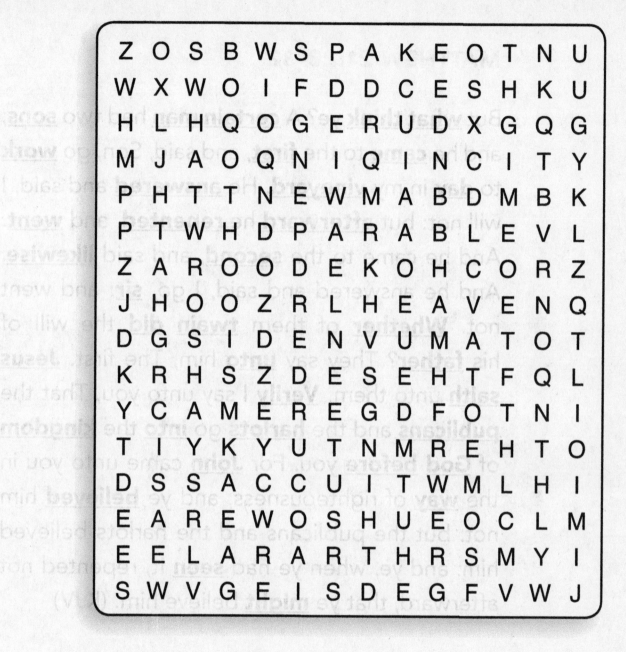

```
Z O S B W S P A K E O T N U
W X W O I F D D C E S H K U
H L H Q O G E R U D X G Q G
M J A O Q N I Q I N C I T Y
P H T T N E W M A B D M B K
P T W H D P A R A B L E V L
Z A R O O D E K O H C O R Z
J H O O Z R L H E A V E N Q
D G S I D E N V U M A T O T
K R H S Z D E S E H T F Q L
Y C A M E R E G D F O T N I
T I Y K Y U T N M R E H T O
D S S A C C U I T W M L H I
E A R E W O S H U E O C L M
E E L A R A R T H R S M Y I
S W V G E I S D E G F V W J
```

Solution on Page 337

MATTHEW 21:28–32

But **what think** ye? A **certain man** had two **sons**; and he **came** to the **first**, and said, Son, go **work** to **day** in my **vineyard**. He **answered** and said, I will not: but **afterward** he **repented**, and **went**. And he came to the **second**, and said **likewise**. And he answered and said, I go, **sir**: and went not. **Whether** of them **twain did** the will of his **father**? They say **unto** him, The first. **Jesus saith** unto them, **Verily** I say unto you, That the **publicans** and the **harlots** go **into** the **kingdom** of **God before** you. For **John** came unto you in the **way** of righteousness, and ye **believed** him not: but the publicans and the harlots believed him: and ye, when ye had **seen** it, repented not afterward, that ye **might** believe him. (KJV)

Solution on Page 337

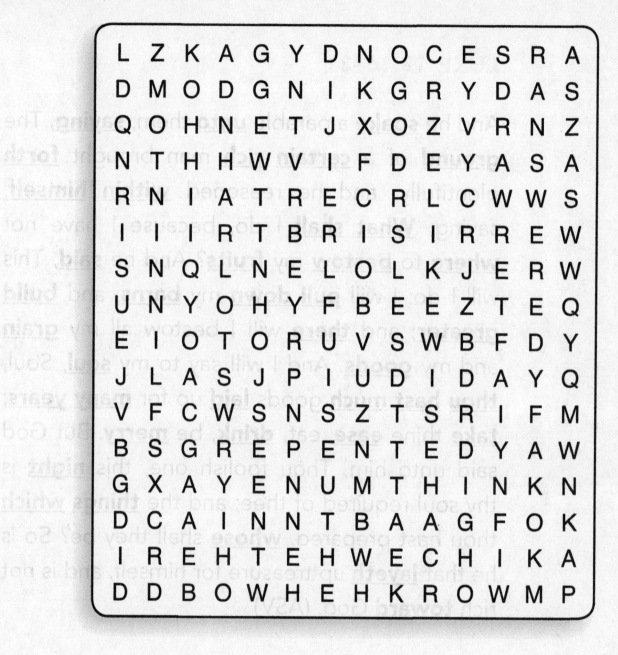

```
L Z K A G Y D N O C E S R A
D M O D G N I K G R Y D A S
Q O H N E T J X O Z V R N Z
N T H H W V I F D E Y A S A
R N I A T R E C R L C W W S
I I I R T B R I S I R R E W
S N Q L N E L O L K J E R W
U N Y O H Y F B E E Z T E Q
E I O T O R U V S W B F D Y
J L A S J P I U D I D A Y Q
V F C W S N S Z T S R I F M
B S G R E P E N T E D Y A W
G X A Y E N U M T H I N K N
D C A I N N T B A A G F O K
I R E H T E H W E C H I K A
D D B O W H E H K R O W M P
```

Solution on Page 337

LUKE 12:16–21

And he **spake** a parable **unto** them, **saying**, The **ground** of a **certain** **rich** man brought **forth** plentifully: and he reasoned **within** **himself**, saying, **What** **shall** I do, because I have not **where** to **bestow** my **fruits**? And he **said**, This will I do: I will **pull** **down** my **barns**, and **build** **greater**; and **there** will I bestow all my **grain** and my **goods**. And I will say to my **soul**, Soul, **thou** **hast** **much** goods **laid** up for **many** **years**; **take** thine **ease**, eat, **drink**, be **merry**. But God said unto him, Thou foolish one, this **night** is thy soul required of thee; and the **things** **which** thou hast prepared, **whose** shall they be? So is he that **layeth** up treasure for himself, and is not rich **toward** God. (ASV)

```
K N Y K Y W S A F G Y C Z R
T Y B E N H F N T H E R E R
P R A A A E S G R O U N D T
C R W L M R R T T A W B Y H
S E L F L E S M I H B A C O
Z M R T A H W S D U I I R U
U B H T E Y A L I F R N A D
P H E S A Y G L A O D F G E
E R O S I I D O L R R Z C S
Z H Y N T T N I H T I W V A
W W G S D O O G D H N F G E
C G H L D O W N I I K E S K
L Y A I V F E K A P S P M A
H N S H C U M R S L U O S T
U N T O T H G I N N K L Q D
Z O O K B R B Q X B Z K L Q
```

Solution on Page 337

MATTHEW 13:24–29

He put **another parable before** them, **saying**, "The **kingdom** of **heaven** may be **compared** to a man who **sowed good seed** in his **field**, but **while** his **men** were **sleeping**, his **enemy came** and sowed **weeds among** the **wheat** and **went away**. So when the **plants** came up and **bore grain**, then the weeds **appeared also**. And the **servants** of the **master** of the **house** came and **said** to him, 'Master, **did** you not sow good seed in **your** field? How then does it have weeds?' He said to them, 'An enemy has **done** this.' So the servants said to him, 'Then do you **want** us to go and gather them?' But he said, 'No, **lest** in **gathering** the weeds you **root** up the wheat **along** with them.'" (ESV)

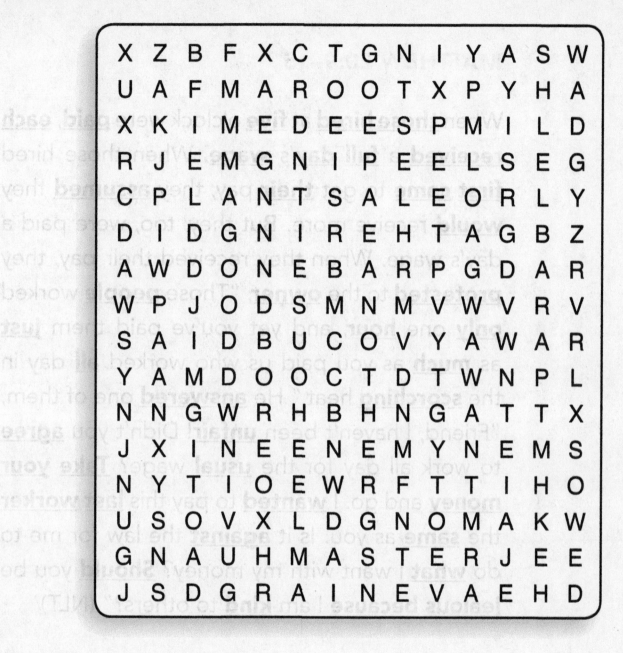

```
X Z B F X C T G N I Y A S W
U A F M A R O O T X P Y H A
X K I M E D E E S P M I L D
R J E M G N I P E E L S E G
C P L A N T S A L E O R L Y
D I D G N I R E H T A G B Z
A W D O N E B A R P G D A R
W P J O D S M N M V W V R V
S A I D B U C O V Y A W A R
Y A M D O O C T D T W N P L
N N G W R H B H N G A T T X
J X I N E E N E M Y N E M S
N Y T I O E W R F T T I H O
U S O V X L D G N O M A K W
G N A U H M A S T E R J E E
J S D G R A I N E V A E H D
```

Solution on Page 337

MATTHEW 20:9–15

When **those** **hired** at **five** o'clock were **paid**, **each** **received** a **full** **day**'s **wage**. When those hired **first** **came** to get **their** pay, they **assumed** they **would** receive more. But they, too, were paid a day's wage. When they received their pay, they **protested** to the **owner**, "Those **people** worked **only** one **hour**, and yet you've paid them **just** as **much** as you paid us who worked **all** day in the **scorching** heat." He **answered** one of them, "Friend, I haven't been **unfair**! Didn't you **agree** to work all day for the **usual** wage? **Take** **your** **money** and go. I **wanted** to pay this **last** **worker** the **same** as you. Is it **against** the law for me to do **what** I want with my money? **Should** you be **jealous** **because** I am **kind** to others?" (NLT)

Vineyard Workers

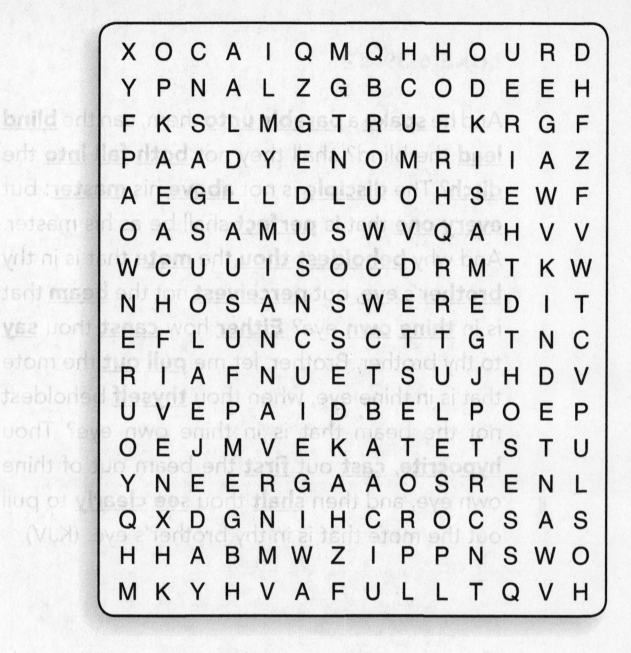

```
X O C A I Q M Q H H O U R D D
Y P N A L Z G B C O D E E H
F K S L M G T R U E K R G F
P A A D Y E N O M R I I A Z
A E G L L D L U O H S E W F
O A S A M U S W V Q A H V V
W C U U I S O C D R M T K W
N H O S A N S W E R E D I T
E F L U N C S C T T G T N C
R I A F N U E T S U J H D V
U V E P A I D B E L P O E P
O E J M V E K A T E T S T U
Y N E E R G A A O S R E N L
Q X D G N I H C R O C S A S
H H A B M W Z I P P N S W O
M K Y H V A F U L L T Q V H
```

Solution on Page 338

LUKE 6:39–42

And he **spake** a **parable unto** them, can the **blind** **lead** the blind? shall they not **both fall into** the **ditch**? The **disciple** is not **above** his **master**: but **every one** that is **perfect** shall be as his master. And why **beholdest thou** the **mote** that is in thy **brother**'s **eye**, but **perceivest** not the **beam** that is in **thine own** eye? **Either** how **canst** thou **say** to thy brother, Brother, let me **pull out** the mote that is in thine eye, when thou **thyself** beholdest not the beam that is in thine own eye? Thou **hypocrite**, **cast** out **first** the beam out of thine own eye, and then **shalt** thou **see clearly** to pull out the mote that is in thy brother's eye. (KJV)

Solution on Page 338

The Blind Leading the Blind

```
A Q Q H G T H J U O H T R F
C K R P X U N T O I S E A G
U P R I Y Q D P O R R L E L
L P B E V E R Y I B L I N D
S S E C H E D F R E T S A M
B Y A R E T Y M L H J L D X
Q S M K C S O E E E T I O C
T D A O N E A R H G S T M M
K P J C E D I Y B C N Y T P
S E V L D L P V I I A A H O
I R G E Y O B P E L C S R T
T F V A C H L A U S H A L T
H E V R X E C L R O T M T S
I C I L G B G T U A B O V E
N T S Y D F B T I P P T W E
E B V E P B N G L D B E C N
```

Solution on Page 338

LUKE 21:29-36

Then he **gave** them this illustration: "Notice the **fig tree**, or any **other** tree. When the leaves come out, you **know** without **being told** that summer is **near**. In the **same way**, when you **see** all **these things** taking **place**, you can know that the Kingdom of **God** is near. I **tell** you the **truth**, this generation will not **pass from** the **scene until** all these things have taken place. Heaven and **earth** will disappear, but my words will **never** disappear. Watch out! Don't let **your hearts** be dulled by carousing and drunkenness, and by the worries of this **life**. Don't let that **day catch** you unaware, like a **trap**. For that day will come **upon** everyone **living** on the earth. **Keep alert** at all **times**. And **pray** that you **might** be strong enough to **escape** these coming horrors and **stand before** the **Son** of Man." (NLT)

Solution on Page 338

The Fig Tree

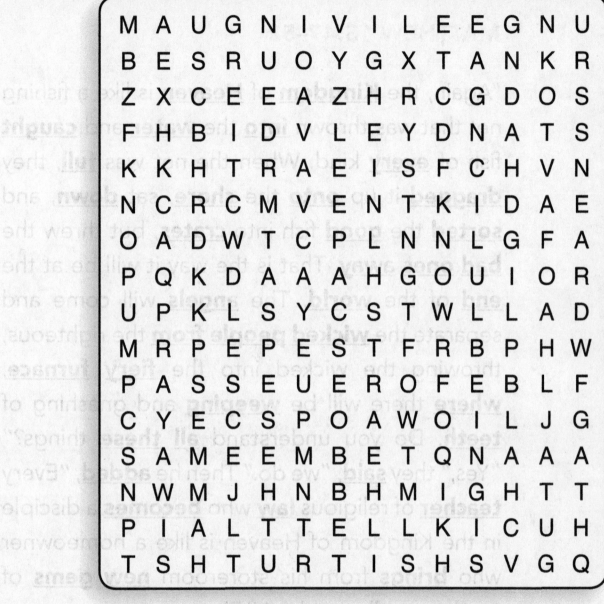

Solution on Page 338

"Again, the **Kingdom** of **Heaven** is like a fishing net that was thrown **into** the **water** and **caught** fish of **every** kind. When the net was **full**, they **dragged** it up **onto** the **shore**, sat **down**, and **sorted** the **good** fish into **crates**, but threw the **bad** **ones** **away**. That is the way it will be at the **end** of the **world**. The **angels** will come and separate the **wicked** **people** **from** the righteous, throwing the wicked into the **fiery** **furnace**, **where** there will be **weeping** and gnashing of **teeth**. Do you understand **all** **these** things?" "Yes," they **said**, "we do." Then he **added**, "Every **teacher** of religious **law** who **becomes** a disciple in the Kingdom of Heaven is like a homeowner who **brings** from his storeroom **new** **gems** of **truth** as **well** as old." (NLT)

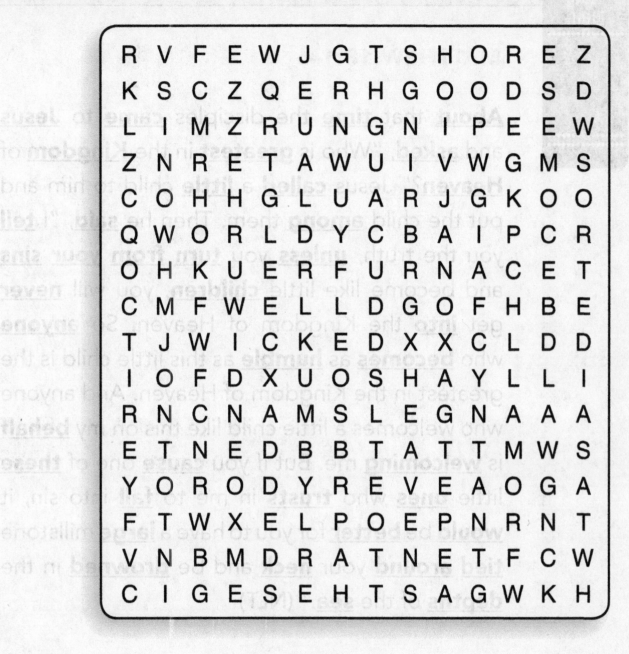

```
R V F E W J G T S H O R E Z
K S C Z Q E R H G O O D S D
L I M Z R U N G N I P E E W
Z N R E T A W U I V W G M S
C O H H G L U A R J G K O O
Q W O R L D Y C B A I P C R
O H K U E R F U R N A C E T
C M F W E L L D G O F H B E
T J W I C K E D X X C L D D
I O F D X U O S H A Y L L I
R N C N A M S L E G N A A A
E T N E D B B T A T T M W S
Y O R O D Y R E V E A O G A
F T W X E L P O E P N R N T
V N B M D R A T N E T F C W
C I G E S E H T S A G W K H
```

Holy
Bible

MATTHEW 18:1–6

About that **time** the disciples **came** to **Jesus** and **asked**, "Who is **greatest** in the **Kingdom** of **Heaven**?" Jesus **called** a **little** child to him and put the child **among** them. Then he **said**, "I **tell** you the truth, **unless** you **turn** **from** **your** **sins** and become like little **children**, you will **never** get **into** the Kingdom of Heaven. So **anyone** who **becomes** as **humble** as this little child is the greatest in the Kingdom of Heaven. And anyone who welcomes a little child like this on my **behalf** is **welcoming** me. But if you **cause** one of **these** little **ones** who **trusts** in me to **fall** into sin, it **would** be **better** for you to have a **large** millstone **tied** **around** your **neck** and be **drowned** in the **depths** of the **sea**." (NLT)

Solution on Page 338

Puzzles

Solution on Page 339

2 CHRONICLES 7:1–5

Now when **Solomon** had **made** an end of **praying**, the **fire came down from heaven**, and consumed the **burnt offering** and the sacrifices; and the **glory** of the **LORD filled** the **house**. And the **priests could** not **enter into** the house of the LORD, **because** the glory of the LORD had filled the LORD's house. And when **all** the **children** of **Israel** saw how the fire came down, and the glory of the LORD **upon** the house, they **bowed** themselves with their **faces** to the **ground** upon the pavement, and worshipped, and **praised** the LORD, **saying**, for he is **good**; for his **mercy endureth** for **ever**. Then the **king** and all the **people** offered sacrifices **before** the LORD. And king Solomon offered a sacrifice of **twenty** and two **thousand oxen**, and an **hundred** and twenty thousand **sheep**: so the king and all the people dedicated the house of God. (KJV)

Fire from Heaven

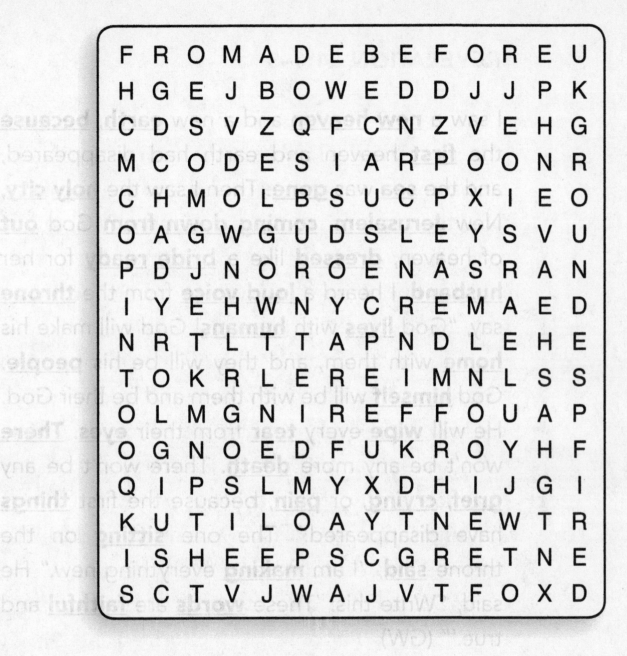

```
F R O M A D E B E F O R E U
H G E J B O W E D D J J P K
C D S V Z Q F C N Z V E H G
M C O D E S I A R P O O N R
C H M O L B S U C P X I E O
O A G W G U D S L E Y S V U
P D J N O R O E N A S R A N
I Y E H W N Y C R E M A E D
N R T L T T A P N D L E H E
T O K R L E R E I M N L S S
O L M G N I R E F F O U A P
O G N O E D F U K R O Y H F
Q I P S L M Y X D H I J G I
K U T I L O A Y T N E W T R
I S H E E P S C G R E T N E
S C T V J W A J V T F O X D
```

Solution on Page 339

REVELATION 21:1–5

I saw a **new** **heaven** and a new **earth**, **because** the **first** heaven and earth had disappeared, and the **sea** was **gone**. Then I saw the **holy** **city**, New **Jerusalem**, **coming** **down** **from** God **out** of heaven, **dressed** like a **bride** **ready** for her **husband**. I heard a **loud** **voice** from the **throne** say, "God **lives** with **humans**! God will make his **home** with them, and they will be his **people**. God **himself** will be with them and be their God. He will **wipe** every **tear** from their **eyes**. **There** won't be any more **death**. There won't be any **grief**, **crying**, or **pain**, because the first **things** have disappeared." The one **sitting** on the throne **said**, "I am **making** everything new." He said, "Write this: 'These **words** are **faithful** and true.'" (GW)

Solution on Page 339

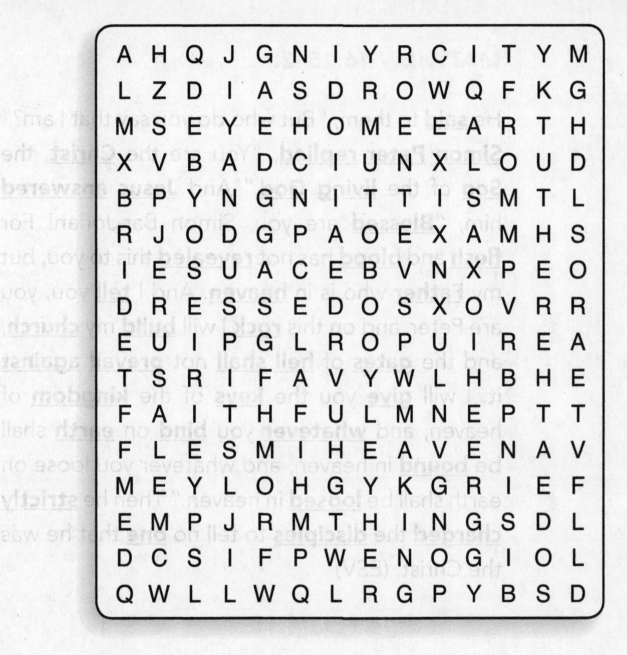

```
A H Q J G N I Y R C I T Y M
L Z D I A S D R O W Q F K G
M S E Y E H O M E E A R T H
X V B A D C I U N X L O U D
B P Y N G N I T T I S M T L
R J O D G P A O E X A M H S
I E S U A C E B V N X P E O
D R E S S E D O S X O V R R
E U I P G L R O P U I R E A
T S R I F A V Y W L H B H E
F A I T H F U L M N E P T T
F L E S M I H E A V E N A V
M E Y L O H G Y K G R I E F
E M P J R M T H I N G S D L
D C S I F P W E N O G I O L
Q W L L W Q L R G P Y B S D
```

Solution on Page 339

MATTHEW 16:15–20

He **said** to them, "But who do you say that I am?" **Simon** **Peter** **replied**, "You are the **Christ**, the **Son** of the **living** **God**." And **Jesus** **answered** him, "**Blessed** are you, Simon Bar-Jonah! For **flesh** and **blood** has not **revealed** this to you, but my **Father** who is in **heaven**. And I **tell** you, you are Peter, and on this **rock** I will **build** my **church**, and the **gates** of **hell** **shall** not **prevail** **against** it. I will **give** you the **keys** of the **kingdom** of heaven, and **whatever** you **bind** on **earth** shall be **bound** in heaven, and whatever you loose on earth shall be **loosed** in heaven." Then he **strictly** **charged** the **disciples** to tell no **one** that he was the Christ. (ESV)

The Keys of Heaven

L S Y D N W N U K W R Y E X
T T E D E O H E A V E N S R
S R B L M S Y A G M O H R O
K I N I P S O X T S I R H C
W C S U N I K O T E A H W K
L T T B A D C S L I V I N G
I L G K L A N S W E R E D D
K Y I I I I C O I F V E R N
J P V N A W H E S D L U T U
E E E G V G A R D A T T H O
S T A D E C R D E S S E L B
U E R O R H G V I H E L L S
S R T M P U E B L G T O H L
Y C H A W R D H P N O A M L
D A O B G C R R E D L D F Z
E F L E S H U Y R L C L R R

Solution on Page 339

REVELATION 12:7–10

Now **war arose** in **heaven**, **Michael** and his **angels fighting against** the **dragon**. And the dragon and his angels **fought back**, but he was **defeated**, and **there** was no **longer** any **place** for them in heaven. And the **great** dragon was **thrown down**, that **ancient serpent**, who is **called** the **devil** and **Satan**, the **deceiver** of the **whole** world—he was thrown down to the **earth**, and his angels were thrown down with him. And I heard a **loud voice** in heaven, **saying**, "Now the **salvation** and the **power** and the **kingdom** of our **God** and the **authority** of his **Christ** have **come**, for the accuser of our **brothers** has been thrown down, who **accuses** them **day** and **night before** our God." (ESV)

Solution on Page 339

A War in Heaven

```
E R E H T M T H R O W N N L
L O U D A H Y S H H T R A E
Y H X M O D G N I K W R T D
G B E F O R E I W R O E A C
N O G A R D D F N S H Y S O
E P D G F O E L E A H C I M
V O F A O W L C Q A G Y S E
A W G I U N L C E B T K C T
E E A N G T A B R I W E N A
H R C S H H C O R E V E D E
G E C T T A T O C W I E N R
N G U S N H H I D C A H R G
I N S G E T O T N E P R E S
Y O E R U V M A D G V K A U
A L S A L V A T I O N I L V
S B A C K W H O L E C A L P
```

Solution on Page 340

GENESIS 28:10–14

__Meanwhile__, __Jacob__ __left__ Beersheba and __traveled__ __toward__ Haran. At __sundown__ he __arrived__ at a __good__ __place__ to __set__ up __camp__ and __stopped__ __there__ for the __night__. Jacob __found__ a stone to __rest__ his head __against__ and __lay__ down to sleep. As he __slept__, he __dreamed__ of a __stairway__ that __reached__ __from__ the __earth__ up to __heaven__. And he saw the __angels__ of God __going__ up and down the stairway. At the top of the stairway stood the __Lord__, and he __said__, "I am the Lord, the God of __your__ grandfather __Abraham__, and the God of your __father__, __Isaac__. The __ground__ you are __lying__ on __belongs__ to you. I am __giving__ it to you and your descendants. Your descendants will be as __numerous__ as the __dust__ of the earth!" (NLT)

Stairway to Heaven

```
G L O Y D V F R S S L T L A R
R N E I U B T G E H A R A N C
C E I F S L N C A A S I E I N
N R T Y T O W A R D C V D G T
T E D P L A C E V M A H M H S
S H D E V I R R A E J Z E T G
G T B E M S M A H A R B A D O
O B P G L A S U N D O W N E I
I V M E N E E A R T H U W P N
N D G F L I V R Q L M L H P G
G N O R A S V A D E J A I O A
A R T O S T A I R W A Y L T P
P O O M G J H O G T C Y E S M
M F O U N D U E U L O R D E A
A G A I N S T F R U B W Y R C
C Y N S E D C X R E T J O B
```

Solution on Page 340

ACTS 1:7–11

Jesus **told** them, "You don't **need** to **know** **about** **times** or **periods** that the **Father** has determined by his **own** authority. But you will **receive** **power** when the **Holy** **Spirit** **comes** to you. Then you will be my witnesses to testify about me in Jerusalem, throughout **Judea** and Samaria, and to the **ends** of the earth." **After** he had **said** this, he was **taken** to **heaven**. A cloud **hid** him so that they **could** no **longer** **see** him. They were **staring** **into** the **sky** as he departed. Suddenly, **two** **men** in **white** **clothes** **stood** **near** them. They **asked**, "Why are you men **from** **Galilee** standing **here** **looking** at the sky? Jesus, who was taken from you to heaven, will come **back** in the same **way** that you saw him go to heaven." (GW)

Jesus Ascends to Heaven

```
G L B N Y I B Y K S B P T J
S U P L C A O F G M E H U U
D O O T S A R M N R N E O D
K H W K J E G W I X R J B G
N E E D T U H O K P F A A M
N D R F F I D T O R N L E E
V K A D T S I D O S I S R N
T C I E H R T M L L E E E I
L A H R I E F A E U C M H I
S B K P A G A E R E O O I H
S U S E J N T V I I O C Y T
E N D S N O H V E N N U A L
A U I L V L E O W N T G I A
J O H Y O B R V U K N O W Z
O S N U X T W O R X Q A X V
F R G P L U B K Z W Y S Z C
```

Solution on Page 340

JOHN 6:30–35

So they **said** to him, "Then **what sign** do you do, that we may **see** and believe you? What work do you **perform**? Our **fathers ate** the **manna** in the **wilderness**; as it is **written**, 'He **gave** them **bread from heaven** to eat.'" **Jesus** then said to them, "**Truly**, truly, I say to you, it was not **Moses** who gave you the bread from heaven, but my Father **gives** you the true bread from heaven. For the bread of **God** is he who **comes down** from heaven and gives **life** to the **world**." They said to him, "Sir, give us this bread **always**." Jesus said to them, "I am the bread of life; **whoever** comes to me **shall** not **hunger**, and whoever **believes** in me shall **never thirst**." (ESV)

Solution on Page 340

Puzzles

Bread from Heaven

```
P Z C A W G A T E M O M K H
Q H G C Y P A Y T Q C S Z I
G C Z H T H I R S T R U L Y
Y W S E W M O S E S S J Z Q
W D L R O W A X S G E K Q B
P J M A T H R H I S N Z B Q
F J A G P O P I U Z E U E P
N H N N O E O S T Y V V H T
F C N P B V R U O T A S C V
S H A L L E E F D G E U J M
A B L K H R L D O M H N H K
I K W T B B Y I O R S G I F
D W A M O R F C E W M I O B
N F Y Q N E V E R V N V G D
L K S T Y A A L I F E E S N
C P W I L D E R N E S S G J
```

Solution on Page 340

MARK 10:21–25

And **Jesus**, **looking** at him, **loved** him, and **said** to him, "You **lack one thing**: go, **sell all** that you have and **give** to the **poor**, and you will have **treasure** in **heaven**; and **come**, **follow** me." Disheartened by the **saying**, he **went away sorrowful**, for he had **great** possessions. And Jesus looked **around** and said to his **disciples**, "How **difficult** it will be for **those** who have **wealth** to **enter** the **kingdom** of **God**!" And the disciples were **amazed** at his **words**. But Jesus said to them **again**, "**Children**, how difficult it is to enter the kingdom of God! It is **easier** for a **camel** to go **through** the **eye** of a **needle** than for a **rich person** to enter the kingdom of God." (ESV)

Sell Everything

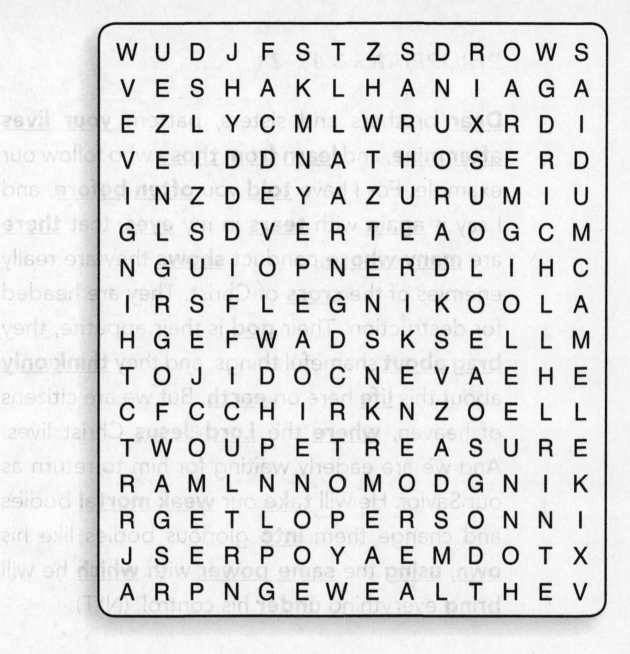

```
W U D J F S T Z S D R O W S
V E S H A K L H A N I A G A
E Z L Y C M L W R U X R D I
V E I D D N A T H O S E R D
I N Z D E Y A Z U R U M I U
G L S D V E R T E A O G C M
N G U I O P N E R D L I H C
I R S F L E G N I K O O L A
H G E F W A D S K S E L L M
T O J I D O C N E V A E H E
C F C C H I R K N Z O E L L
T W O U P E T R E A S U R E
R A M L N N O M O D G N I K
R G E T L O P E R S O N N I
J S E R P O Y A E M D O T X
A R P N G E W E A L T H E V
```

Solution on Page 341

PHILIPPIANS 3:17–21

Dear brothers and sisters, pattern **your lives after mine**, and **learn from those** who follow our example. For I have **told** you **often before**, and I say it **again** with **tears** in my **eyes**, that **there** are **many whose** conduct **shows** they are really enemies of the **cross** of Christ. They are headed for destruction. Their **god** is their appetite, they **brag about** shameful things, and they **think only** about this **life** here on **earth**. But we are citizens of heaven, **where** the **Lord Jesus** Christ lives. And we are eagerly waiting for him to return as our Savior. He will **take** our **weak mortal** bodies and change them **into** glorious bodies like his **own**, **using** the **same power** with **which** he will **bring** everything **under** his control. (NLT)

Solution on Page 341

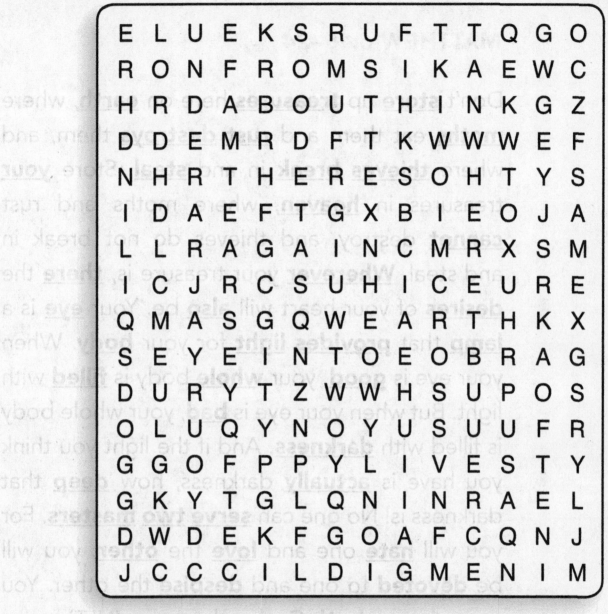

```
E L U E K S R U F T T Q G O
R O N F R O M S I K A E W C
H R D A B O U T H I N K G Z
D D E M R D F T K W W W E F
N H R T H E R E S O H T Y S
I D A E F T G X B I E O J A
L L R A G A I N C M R X S M
I C J R C S U H I C E U R E
Q M A S G Q W E A R T H K X
S E Y E I N T O E O B R A G
D U R Y T Z W W H S U P O S
O L U Q Y N O Y U S U U F R
G G O F P P Y L I V E S T Y
G K Y T G L Q N I N R A E L
D W D E K F G O A F C Q N J
J C C C I L D I G M E N I M
```

Solution on Page 341

MATTHEW 6:19–24

Don't **store** up **treasures** here on **earth**, where **moths** eat them and **rust destroys** them, and where **thieves break** in and **steal**. Store **your** treasures in **heaven**, where moths and rust **cannot** destroy, and thieves do not break in and steal. **Wherever** your treasure is, **there** the **desires** of your heart will **also** be. Your **eye** is a **lamp** that **provides light** for your **body**. When your eye is **good**, your **whole** body is **filled** with light. But when your eye is **bad**, your whole body is filled with **darkness**. And if the light you think you have is **actually** darkness, how **deep** that darkness is! No one can **serve two masters**. For you will **hate** one and **love** the **other**; you will be **devoted** to one and **despise** the other. You cannot serve **both** God and **money**. (NLT)

Solution on Page 341

Store Your Treasures in Heaven

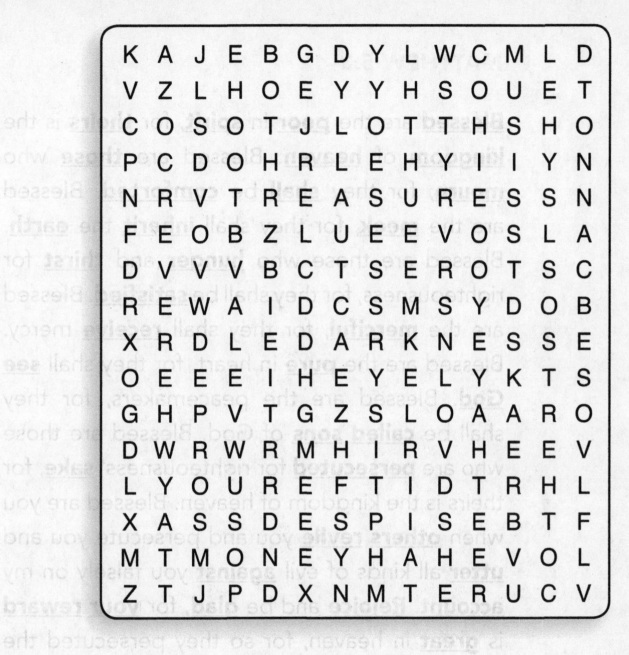

K A J E B G D Y L W C M L D
V Z L H O E Y Y H S O U E T
C O S O T J L O T T H S H O
P C D O H R L E H Y I I Y N
N R V T R E A S U R E S S N
F E O B Z L U E E V O S L A
D V V V B C T S E R O T S C
R E W A I D C S M S Y D O B
X R D L E D A R K N E S S E
O E E E I H E Y E L Y K T S
G H P V T G Z S L O A A R O
D W R W R M H I R V H E E V
L Y O U R E F T I D T R H L
X A S S D E S P I S E B T F
M T M O N E Y H A H E V O L
Z T J P D X N M T E R U C V

Solution on Page 341

MATTHEW 5:3–12

Blessed are the **poor** in **spirit**, for **theirs** is the **kingdom** of **heaven**. Blessed are **those** who **mourn**, for they **shall** be **comforted**. Blessed are the **meek**, for they shall **inherit** the **earth**. Blessed are those who **hunger** and **thirst** for righteousness, for they shall be **satisfied**. Blessed are the **merciful**, for they shall **receive** mercy. Blessed are the **pure** in heart, for they shall **see God**. Blessed are the peacemakers, for they shall be **called sons** of God. Blessed are those who are **persecuted** for righteousness' **sake**, for theirs is the kingdom of heaven. Blessed are you when **others revile** you and persecute you and **utter** all kinds of evil **against** you falsely on my **account**. **Rejoice** and be **glad**, for **your reward** is **great** in heaven, for so they persecuted the **prophets** who were **before** you. (ESV)

Solution on Page 341

Heavenly Reward

```
R C H U P N T S Q S I W C E
B E F T I R E H N I M T K E
T I R I P S O U S O M A V S
A K E O V O T P D K S G E O
E V J D F T N G H E D A R H
R U O Y E E N P E E I I U T
G A I R V I B E T M T N P S
E S C A K H F R S N O S O R
L V E C U G O S R E H T O I
I H U N O F J E I H S B R H
V O G D M U K C E T H L D T
E E M O U R N U H R A E R R
R E C E I V E T T V L S A A
R L U F I C R E M L L S W E
S U P U G L A D A Y R E E N
T R Q Y K H L C B C M D R S
```

Solution on Page 341

Answers

Chapter 1: Bible Topics

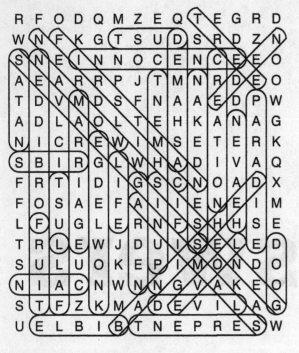

Adam and Eve

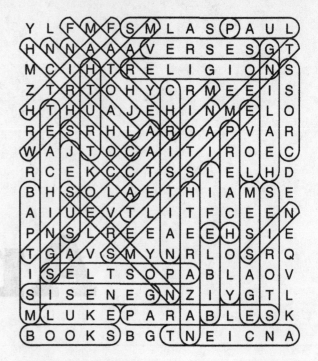

The Gospels

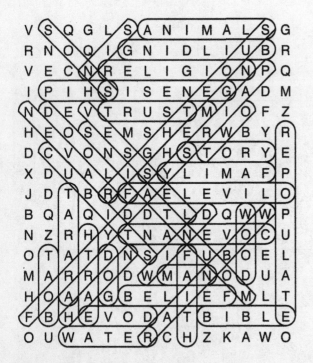

Noah's Ark

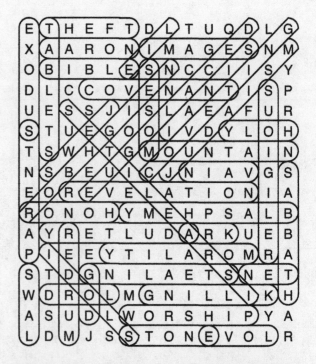

The Ten Commandments

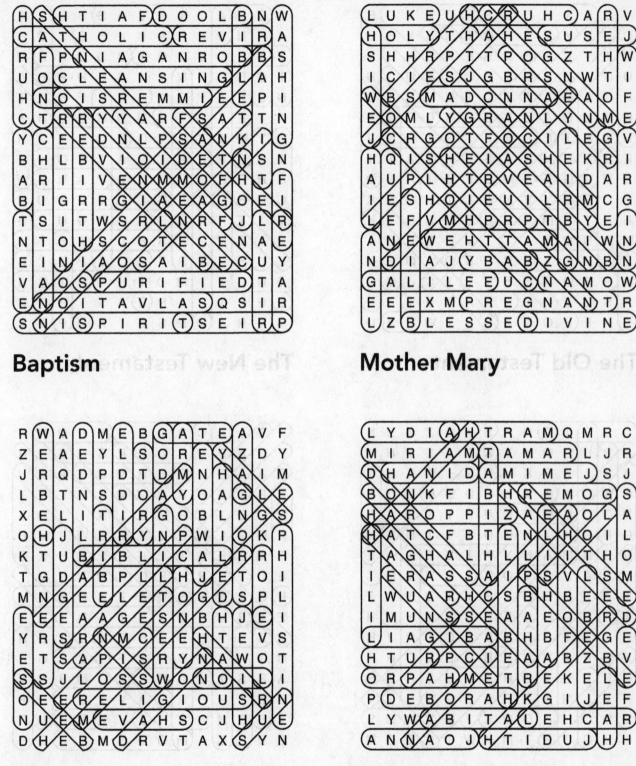

Baptism

Mother Mary

Samson

Women in the Bible

The Old Testament

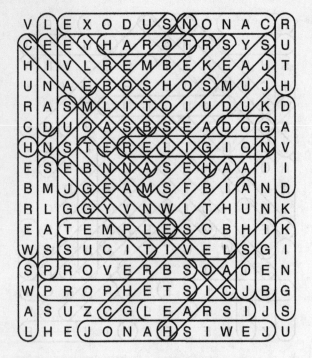

```
V L E X O D U S N O N A C R
C E E Y H A R O T R S Y S U
H I V L R E M B E K E A J T
U N A E B O S H O S M U J H
R A S M L I T O I U D U K D
C D U O A S B S E A D O G A
H N S T E R E L I G I O N V
E S E B N N A S E H A A I I
B M J G E A M S F B I A N D
R L G G V N W L T H U N K
E A T E M P L E S C B H I K
W S S U C I T I V E L S G I
S P R O V E R B S O A O E N
W P R O P H E T S I C J B G
A S U Z C G L E A R S I J S
L H E J O N A H S I W E J U
```

The New Testament

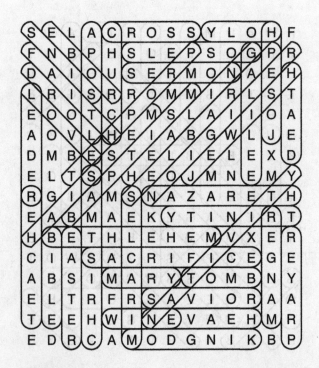

```
L S N A I T A L A G B S J A
A N H P A R A B L E S Z O P
T H E O L O G Y B O O K S M
I O B C S N A I S E H P E A
N J R A P O A G R E E K P T
T Y E L B I B U D R U O H T
D Y W Y Y T T G S U S E J H
I G S P S A L V A T I O N E
S R R S R L N L L P A U L W
C U E E B E R E L I G I O N
I T T K A V S H C R U H C D
P I T U P E S E L C A R I M
L L E L T R P G O S P E L S
E U L T I M O T H Y S T C A
S E L T S I P E A S T E R S
Y Y R A M E S S I A H P P V
```

Solomon

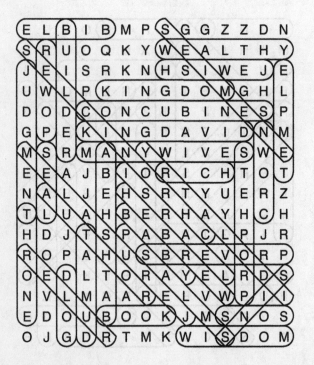

```
E L B I B M P S G G Z Z D N
S R U O Q K Y W E A L T H Y
J E I S R K N H S I W E J E
U W L P K I N G D O M G H L
D O D C O N C U B I N E S P
G P E K I N G D A V I D N M
M S R M A N Y W I V E S W E
E E A J B I O R I C H T O T
N A L J E H S R T Y U E R Z
T L U A H B E R H A Y H C H
H D J T S P A B A C L P J R
R O P A H U S B R E V O R P
O E D L T O R A Y E L R D S
N V L M A A R E L V W P I I
E D O U B O O K J M S N O S
O J G D R T M K W I S D O M
```

Jesus

```
S E L A C R O S S Y L O H F
F N B P H S L E P S O G P R
D A I O U S E R M O N A E H
L R I S R R O M M I R L S T
E O O T C P M S L A I I O A
A O V L H E I A B G W L J E
D M B E S T E L I E L E X D
E L T S P H E O J M N E M Y
R G I A M S N A Z A R E T H
E A B M A E K Y T I N I R T
H B E T H L E H E M V X E R
C I A S A C R I F I C E G E
A B S I M A R Y T O M B N Y
E L T R F R S A V I O R A R
T E E H W I N E V A E H M R
E D R C A M O D G N I K B P
```

306

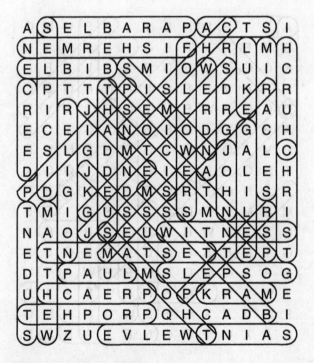

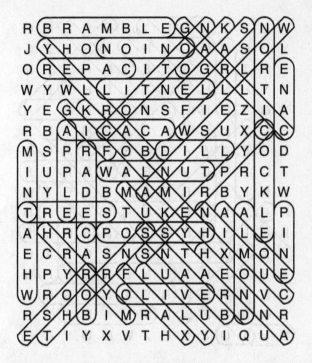

Biblical Studies

Plants in the Bible

The Apostles

Chapter 2: Love

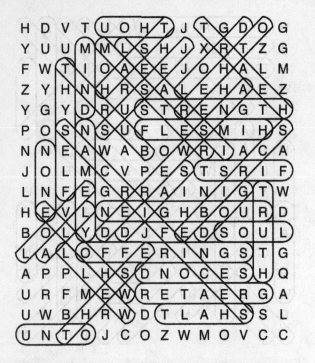

The First Commandment

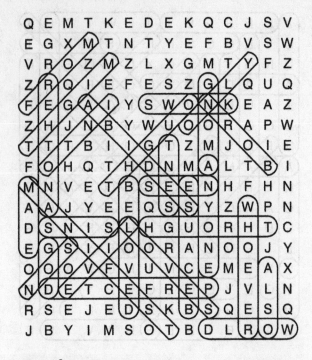

God Is Love

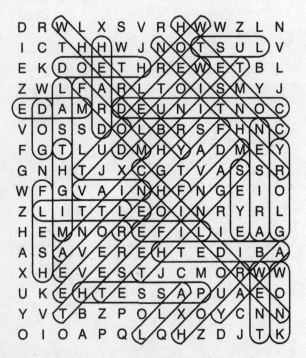

Do Not Love the World

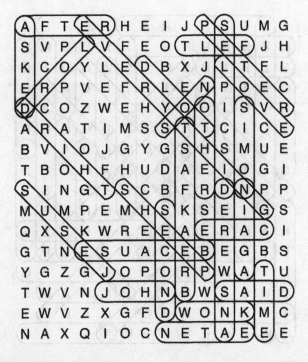

I Love You

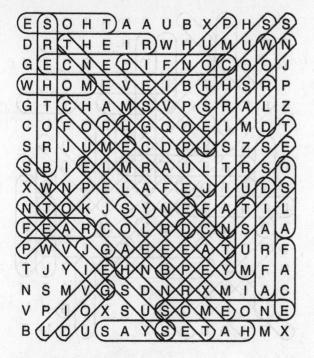

Perfect Love

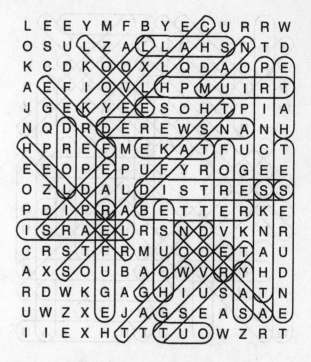

Love Endures Forever

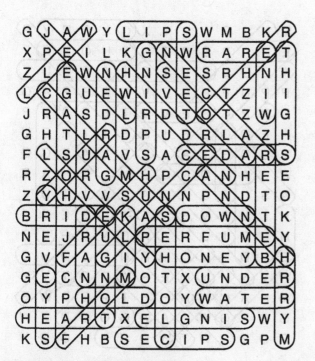

Better than Wine

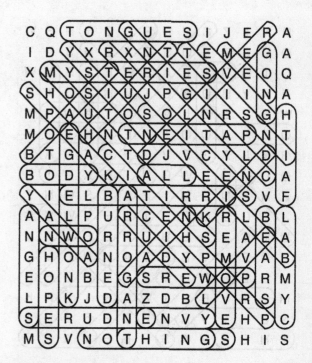

The Nature of Love

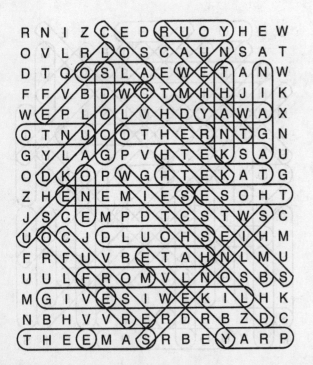

God Loves the World

Love as I Have Loved

Love Your Enemies

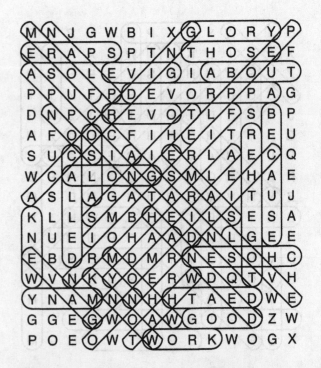

Those Who Love God

Chapter 3: Jesus

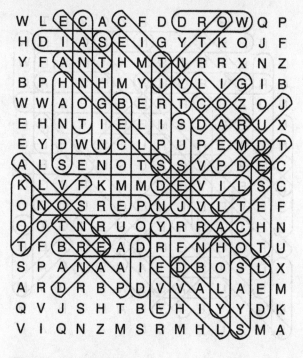

Temptation

The Betrayer

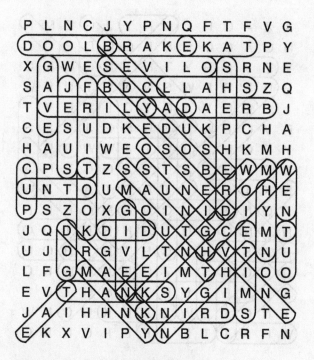

The Lord's Supper

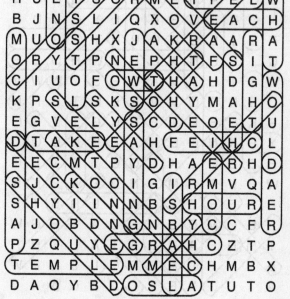

The Crucifixion

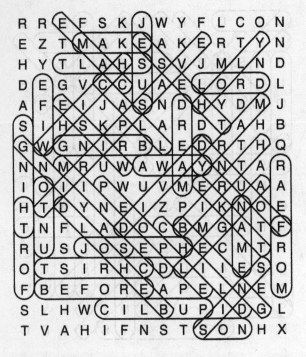

The Birth of Jesus

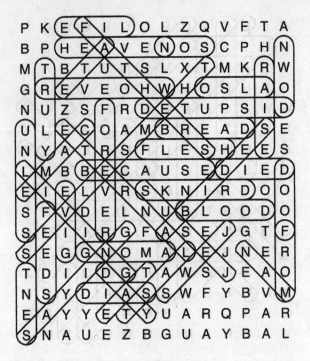

The Bread of Life

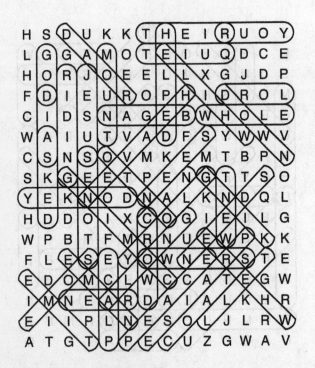

Donkey Ride

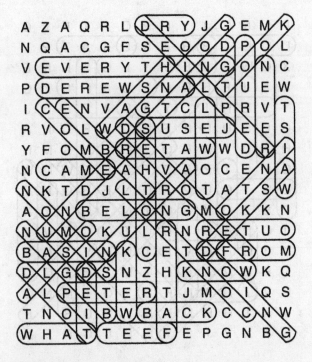

Washing Feet

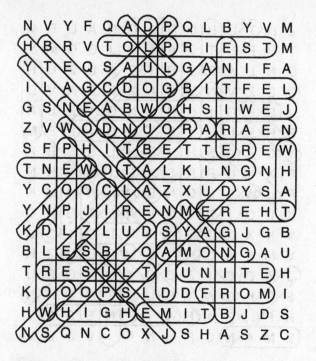

The Plot to Kill Jesus

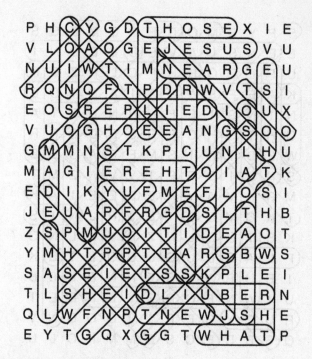

Moneychangers Thrown Out

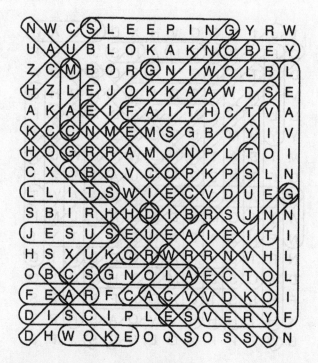

Calming the Sea

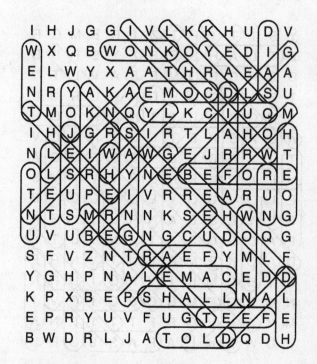

The Resurrection

Chapter 4: Inspirational

The Truth Will Set You Free

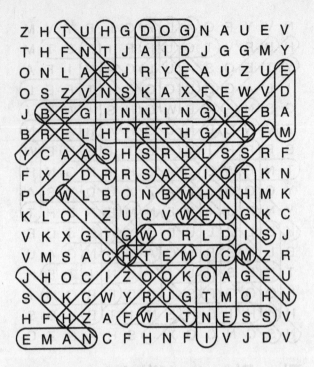

The Word Was God

Blessings

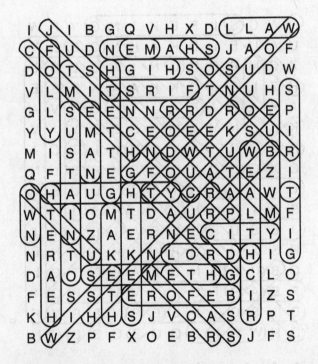

A Strong Tower

Hope

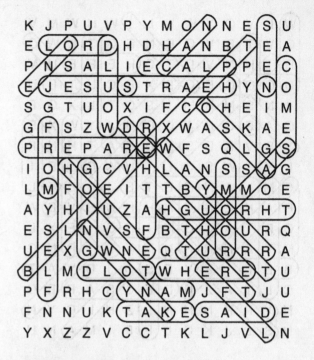

The Way, the Truth, and the Light

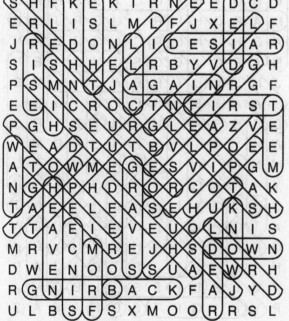

Do Not Grieve

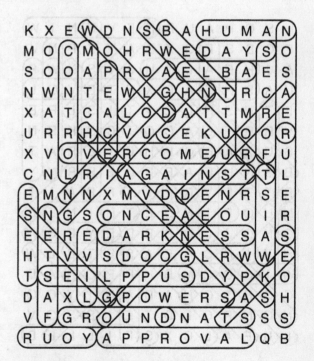

Put on the Armor

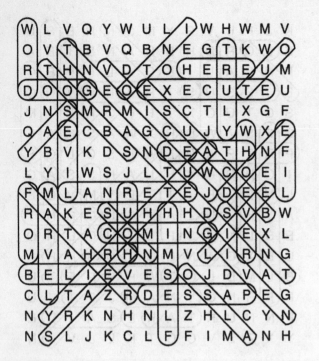

Eternal Life

All Is Vanity

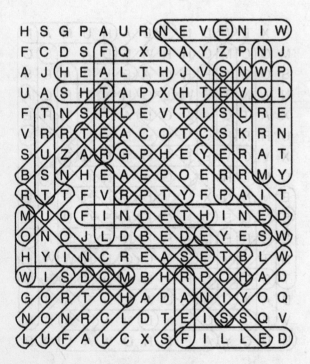

Trust in the Lord

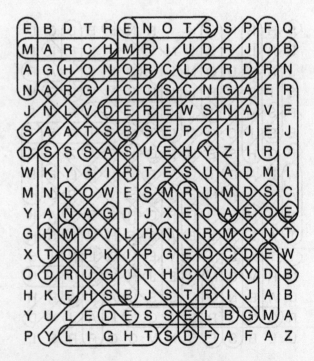

Rejoice and Be Glad

316

Chapter 5: Instructional

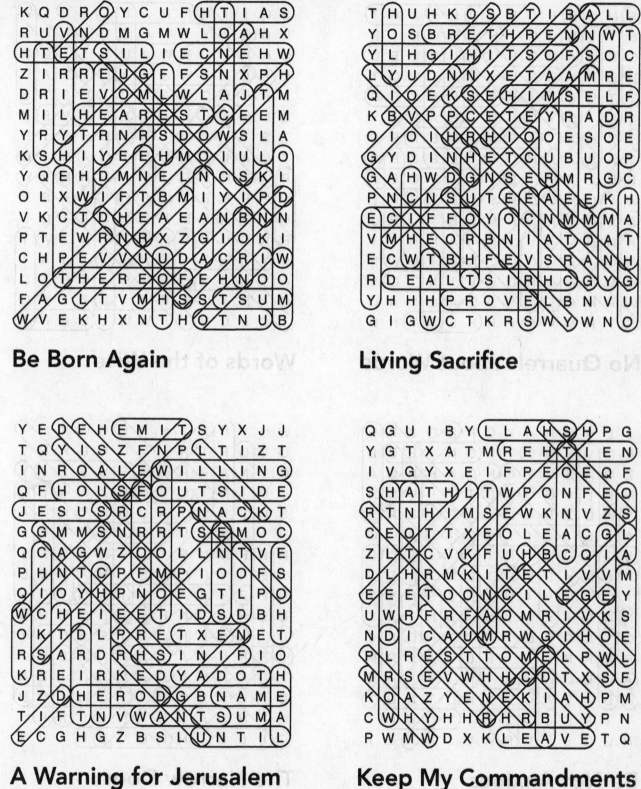

Be Born Again

Living Sacrifice

A Warning for Jerusalem

Keep My Commandments

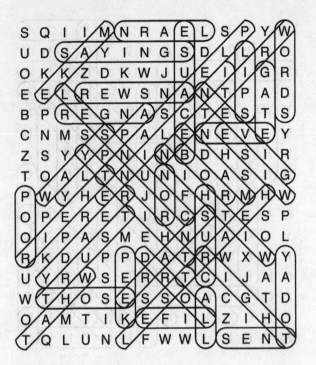

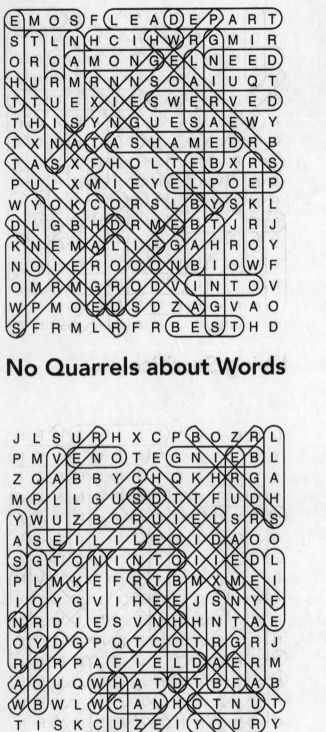

No Quarrels about Words

Words of the Wise

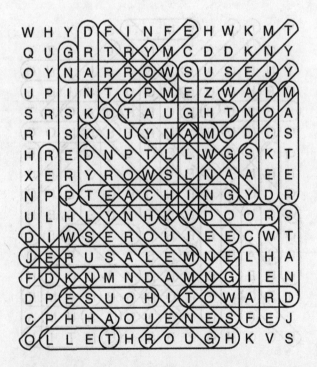

Be Not Anxious

The Narrow Door

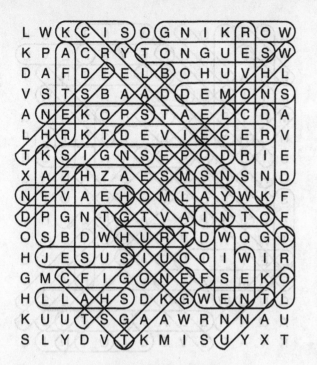

Go Into the World

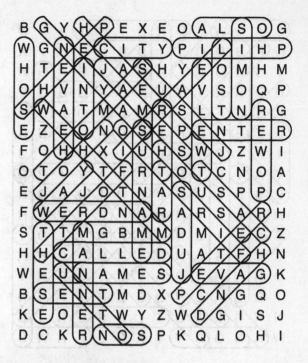

Instructions to the Apostles

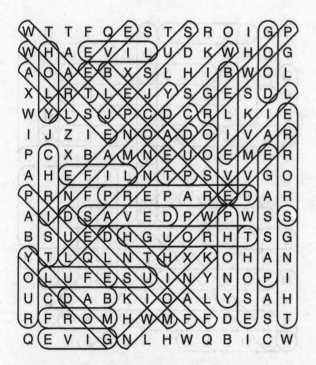

The Power of Scripture

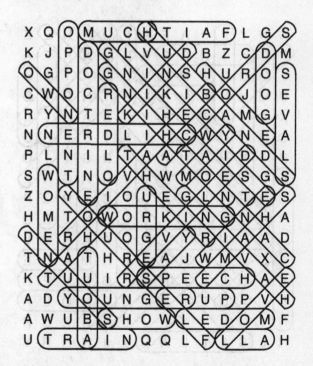

Teach Sound Doctrine

Chapter 6: Faith

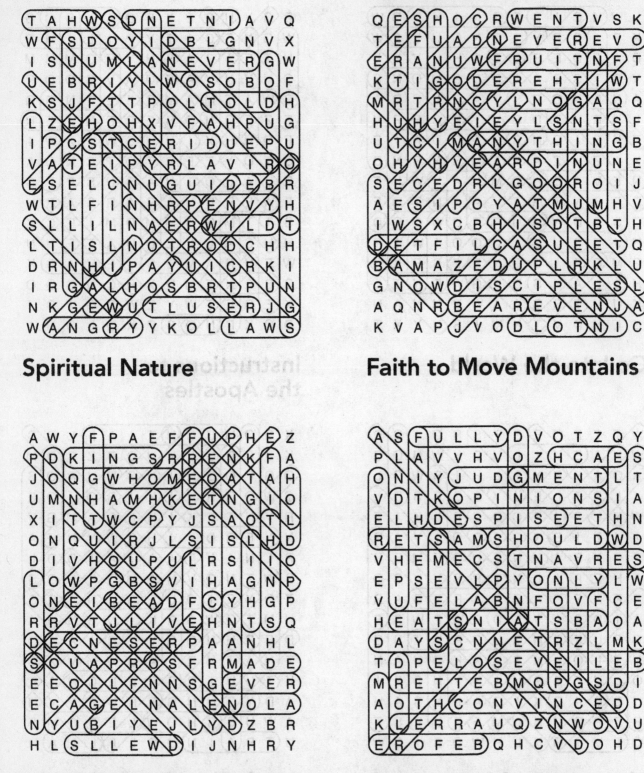

Spiritual Nature

Faith to Move Mountains

The Good Fight of Faith

Do Not Judge Faith

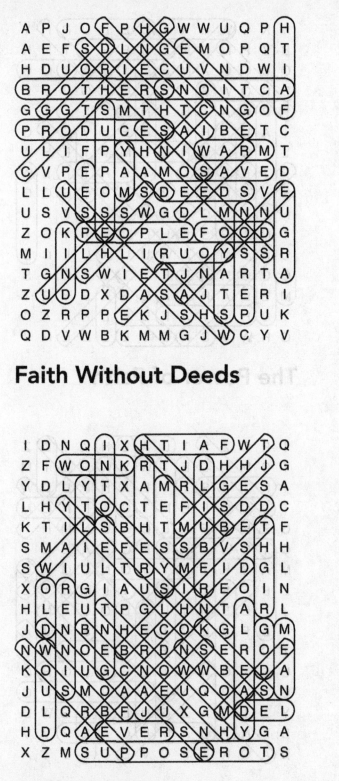

Faith Without Deeds

Live by Faith

Faith in Jesus

Faith Required

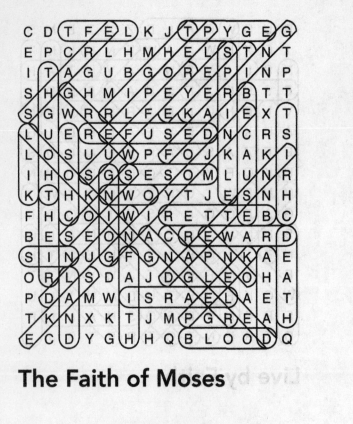

The Faith of Moses

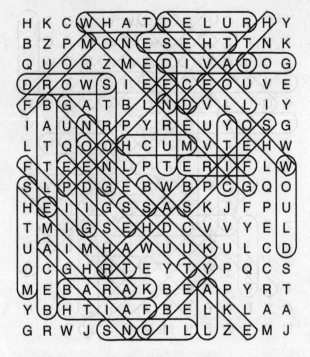

The Power of Faith

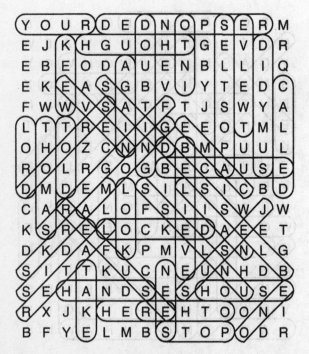

Doubting Thomas

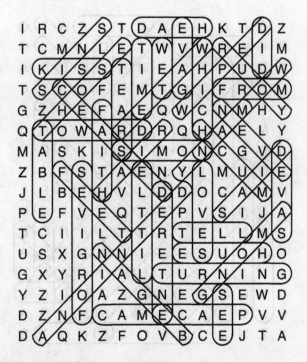

Saved by Faith

Assurance

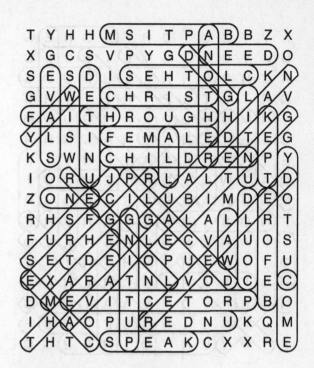

Children of God Through Faith

Chapter 7: Stories

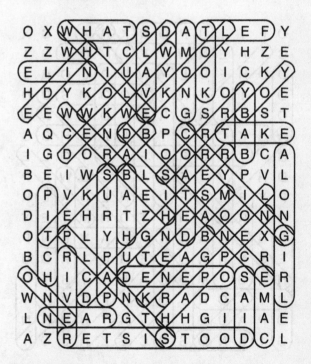

The Baby in the Basket

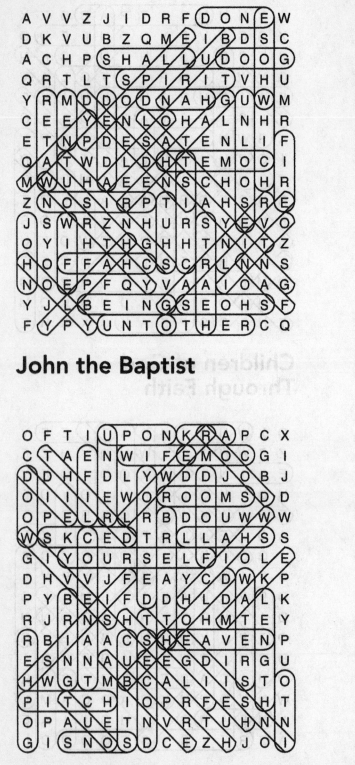

John the Baptist

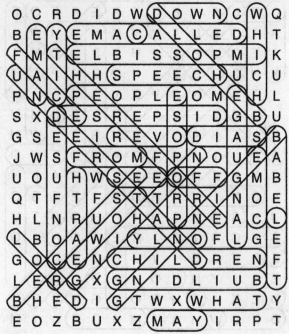
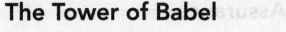

The Tower of Babel

Noah's Ark

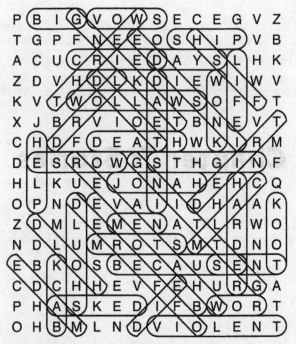

Jonah and the Whale

324

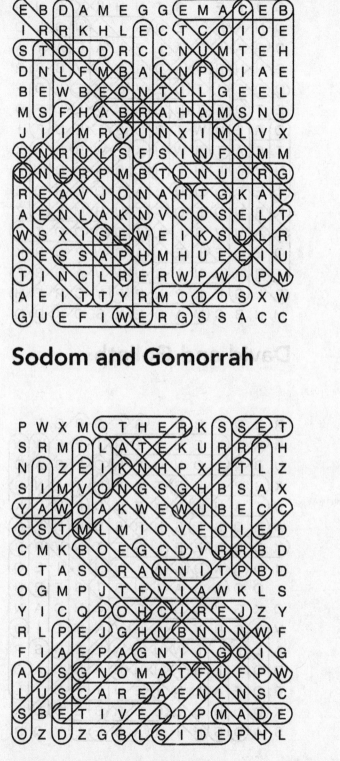

Sodom and Gomorrah

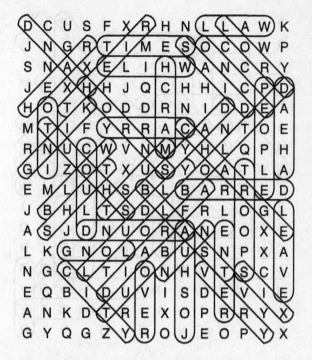

The Battle of Jericho

The Good Samaritan

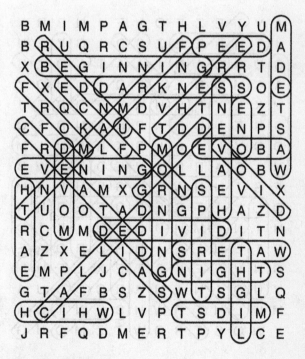

Creation

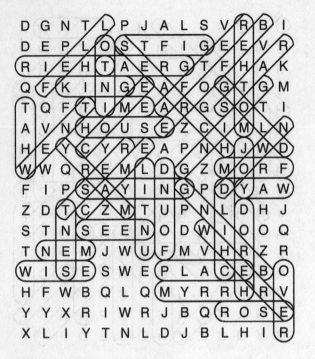

The Wise Men

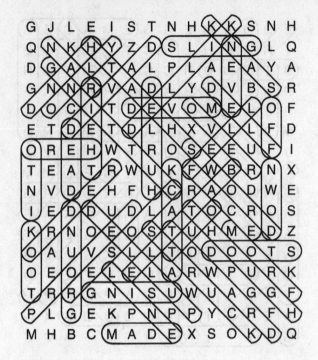

David and Goliath

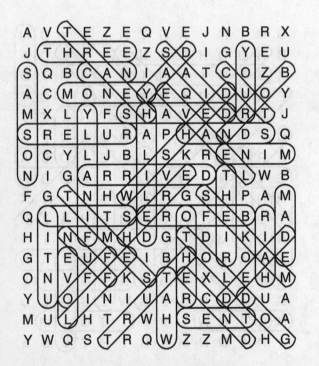

Samson and Delilah

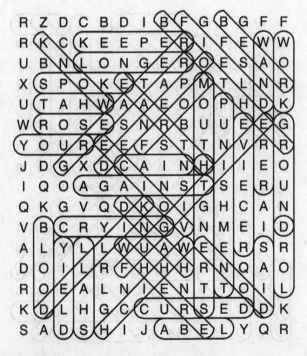

Cain and Abel

326

Chapter 8: Prayer

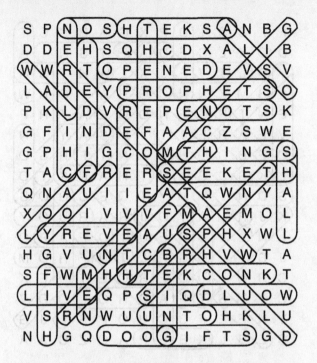

Ask and You Shall Receive

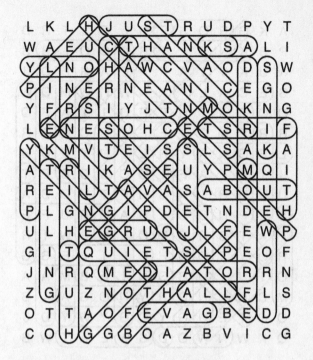

Pray for All People

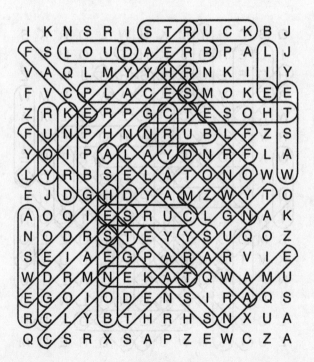

Prayer for the Afflicted

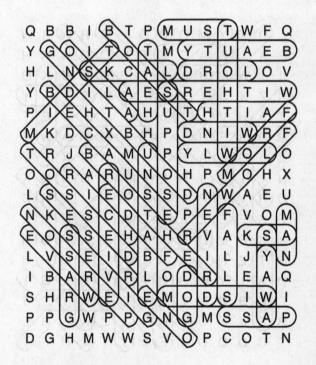

Ask for Wisdom

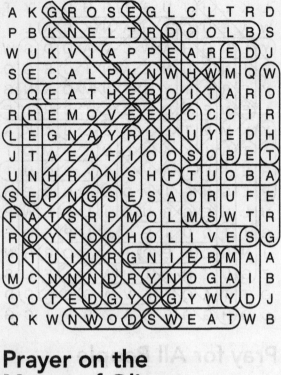

Prayer on the Mount of Olives

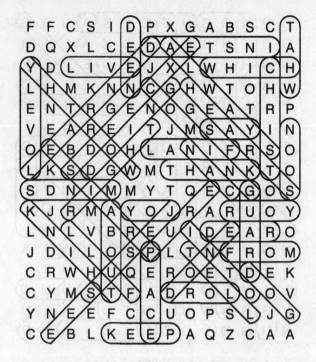

Pray about Everything

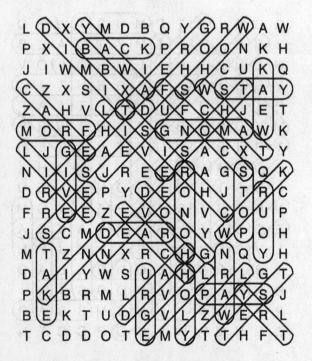

Never Stop Praying

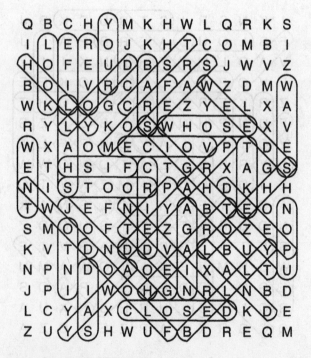

Jonah's Prayer

The Lord's Prayer

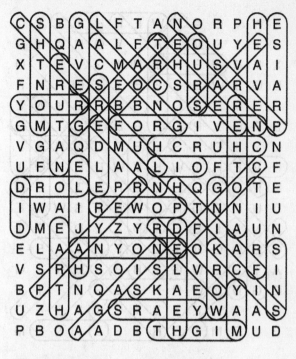

The Prayer of Faith

Believe in Prayer

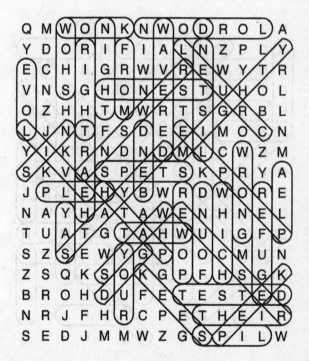

A Prayer of David

Chapter 9: Miracles

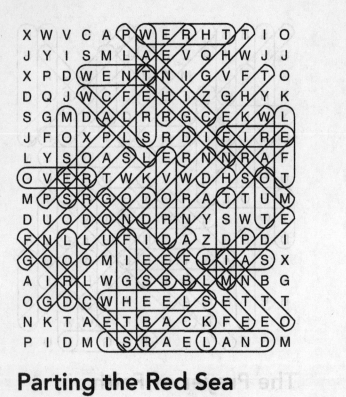

Parting the Red Sea

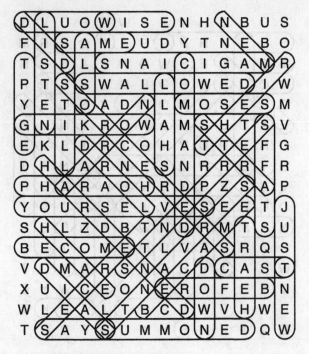

A Staff Becomes a Serpent

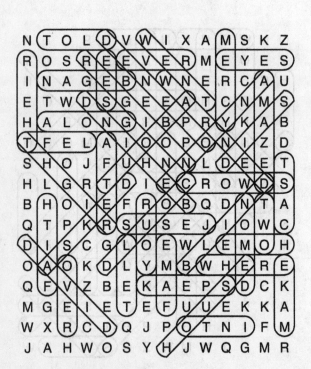

The Blind See

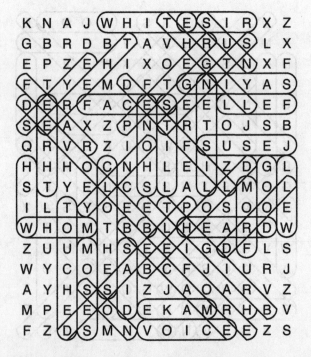

The Transfiguration

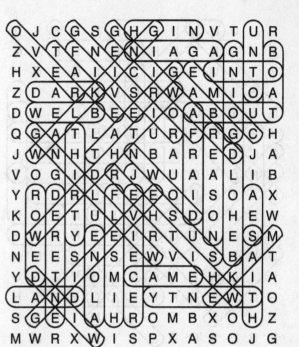
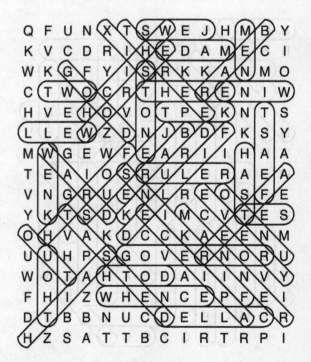

The Burning Bush

Walking on Water

Good Fishing

Water to Wine

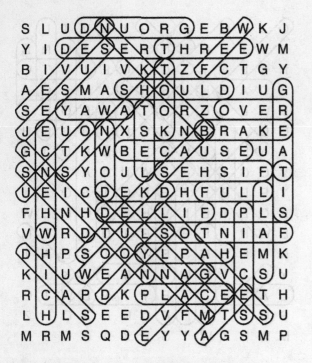

Feeding the Multitude

Healing the Sick

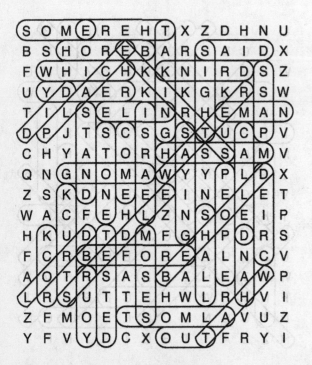

Water from a Rock

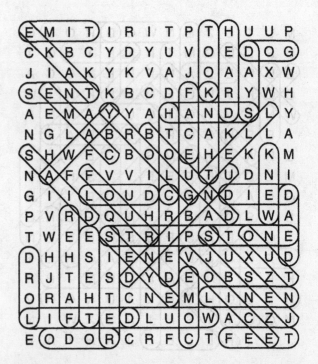

Raising Lazarus

332

Chapter 10: Holy, Holy, Holy

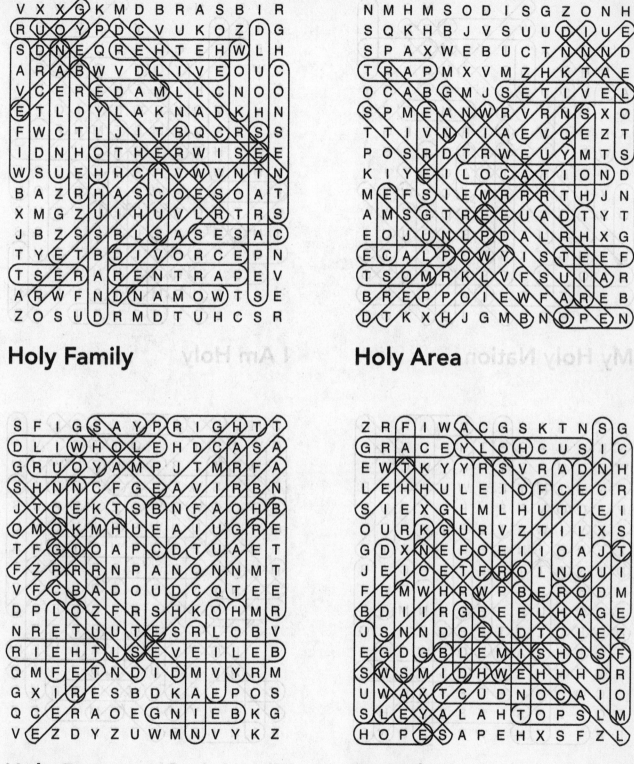

Holy Family

Holy Area

Holy Root

Be Holy

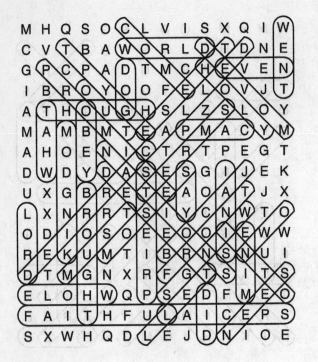

My Holy Nation

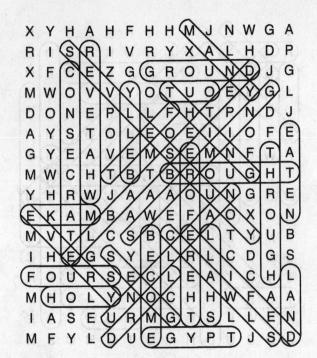

I Am Holy

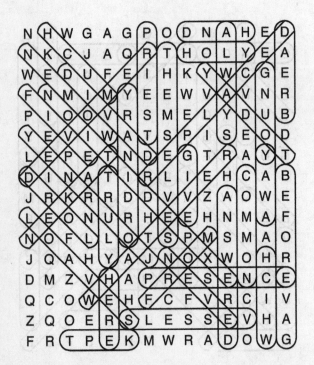

Holy Bread

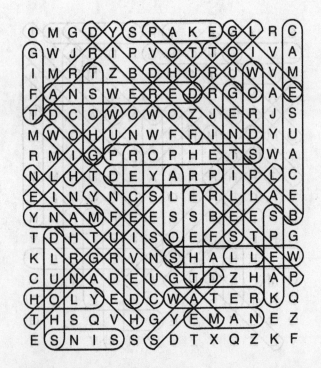

The Holy Ghost

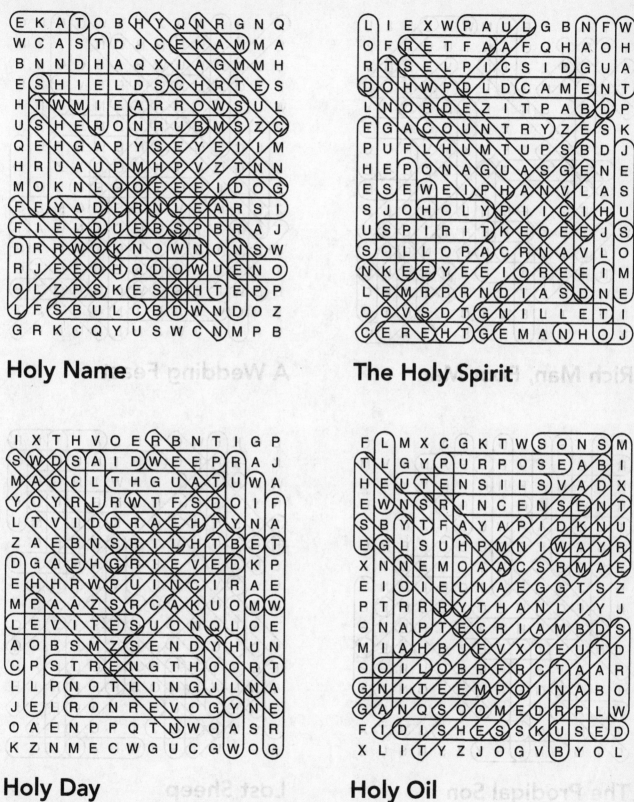

Holy Name

The Holy Spirit

Holy Day

Holy Oil

Chapter 11: Parables

Rich Man, Poor Man

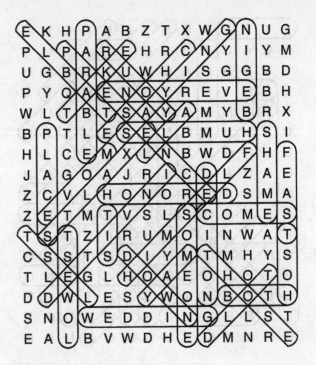

A Wedding Feast

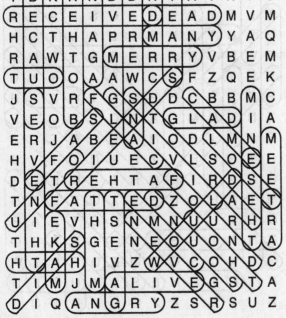

The Prodigal Son

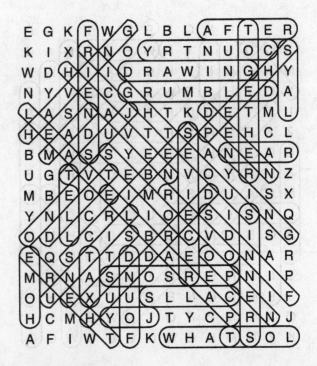

Lost Sheep

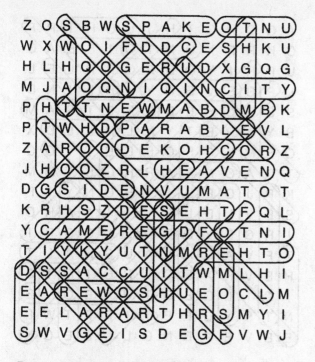

Scattering Seed

Two Sons

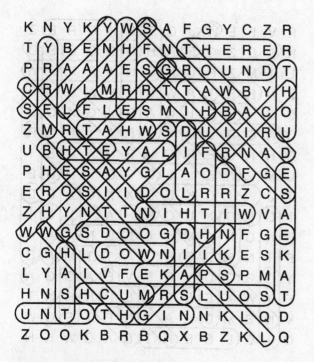

The Rich Fool

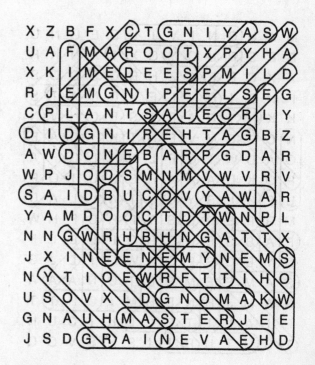

Weeds

```
Vineyard Workers

X O C A I Q M Q H H O U R D
Y P N A L Z G B C O D E E H
F K S L M G T R U E K R G F
P A A D Y E N O M R I I A Z
A E G L L D L U O H S E W
A A S A M U S W V Q A H V V
O W C U U I S O C D R M T K W
W H O S A N S W E R E D I T
N E F L U N C S C T T G T N C
E R I A F N U E T S U J H D V
U V E P A I D B E L P O E P
O E J M V E K A T E T S T U
Y N N E E R G A A O S R E N L
Q X D G N I H C R O C S A S
H H A B M W Z I P P N S W O
M K Y H V A F U L L T Q V H
```

Vineyard Workers

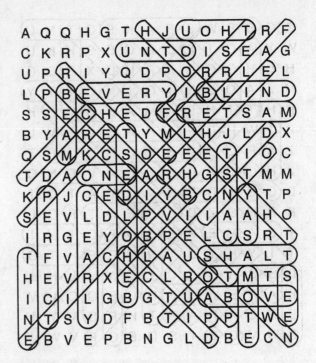

The Blind Leading the Blind

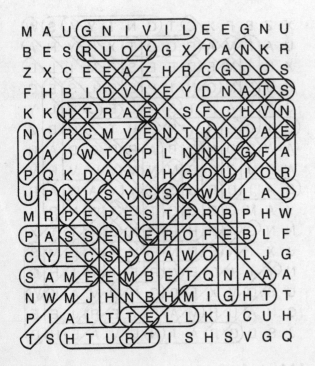

The Fig Tree

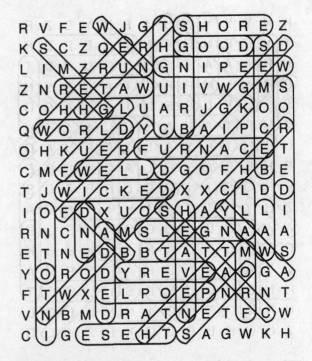

Fishing Net

Chapter 12: Heaven

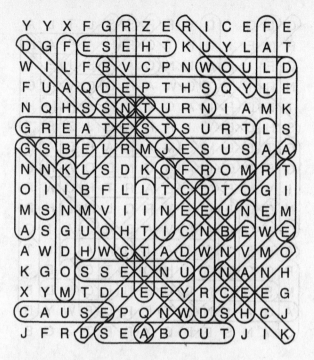

Greatest in Heaven

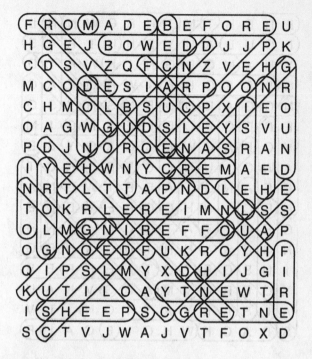

Fire from Heaven

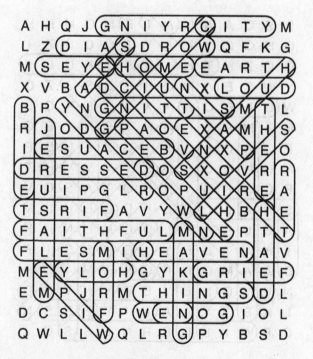

A New Heaven

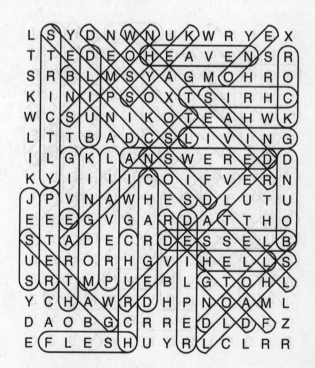

The Keys of Heaven

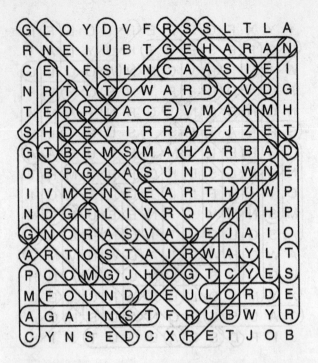

A War in Heaven

Stairway to Heaven

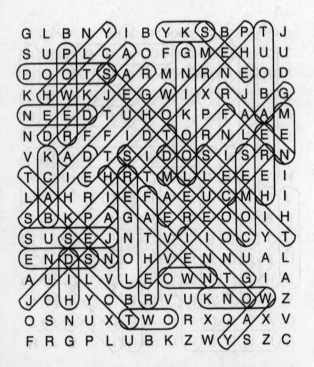

Jesus Ascends to Heaven

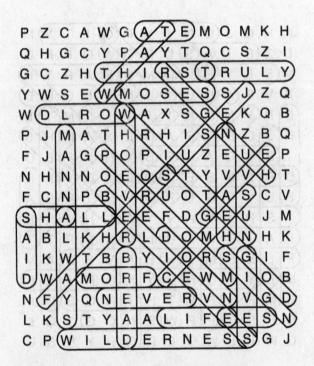

Bread from Heaven

340

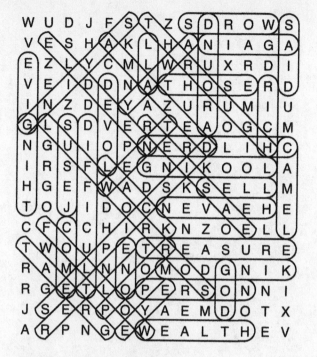

Sell Everything

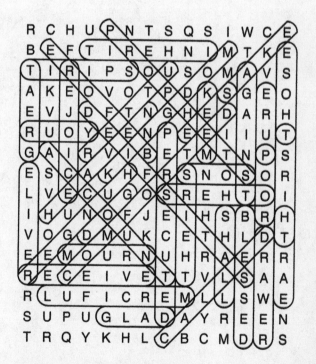

Citizens of Heaven

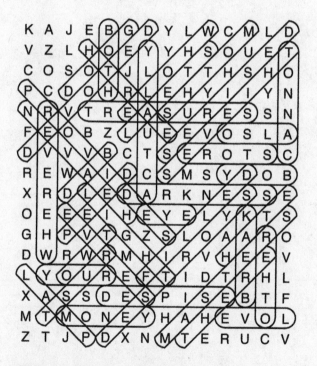

Store Your Treasures in Heaven

Heavenly Reward